W9-CLG-056

OUTLAW FOR GOD

The Story of Esther Bacon

OUTLAW FOR GOD
The Story of Esther Bacon

By J. Birney Dibble, M.D.

Founded 1910
THE CHRISTOPHER PUBLISHING HOUSE
HANOVER, MASSACHUSETTS 02339

Dedication

To
Bishop Roland Payne, Margaret Miller, Roslyn Sadler,
and all the others who loved Esther.

"Truth forever on the scaffold,
    Wrong forever on the throne,-
Yet that scaffold sways the future,
    and, behind the dim unknown,
Standeth God within the shadow,
    Keeping watch above his own."

James Russell Lowell
The Present Crisis

"Yes, she was an outlaw — an
outlaw for God."

Bishop Roland Payne
*First native-born bishop
of the Liberian Lutheran Church*

The Published Books of J. Birney Dibble, M.D.

Non-fiction

THE PLAINS BROOD ALONE. Zondervan.
IN THIS LAND OF EVE. Abingdon.

Fiction

BRAIN CHILD. Dorchester.
PAN. Dorchester.

Contents

Foreword

This book was written to describe the miracle worked by a missionary nurse, Esther Bacon, in medical care and in the indigenous church in Liberia. Long before she died she had become a legend in Liberia. Her life was an inspiration to all who knew her: tribal Africans, missionaries, Peace Corps Volunteers, government officials, church officials, truck drivers, family, and not least, the chronicler of her story.

But Esther Bacon was neither a myth nor a legend. She was a real person — a saint perhaps — in blue slacks on a brown horse carrying a kerosene lantern through a green tunnel of jungle to save the lives of a mother and her unborn child. She was a martyr in a blood-stained white uniform with her slip showing. She was an outlaw who would break any and every rule in the book if it would save a life.

When I moved to Zorzor in 1986, I soon noted that people were still talking about Esther Bacon, fourteen years after she died. The School of Nursing was named for her. A school in Monrovia, Liberia's capital city, was named for her. "Bayka babies" were everywhere. One of her adopted Liberian daughters worked in the hospital. Finally I told Dr. Mark Monson, the doctor in charge, that I just had to learn more about this incredible woman. He told me that her story had never been written. I was astonished.

He challenged me to write it and I have.

Esther Bacon, at the age of 25, came out of the obscurity of western Iowa and sailed through wartime seas to the even more obscure country of Liberia. There she worked for 31 years as a nurse in the upcountry village of Zorzor.

Many Americans have heard of her, especially fellow missionaries and mission-oriented church people. But because her story has not been fully told, many more do not know her or her work.

What had she done to warrant such renown in Liberia?

Why is she not better known in America?

Both questions are easy to answer.

The first question. When Esther began her work in the Zorzor hospital, pregnant women were so dependent on their witch-doctors and tribal midwives that they were afraid to go to the mission hospital. Furthermore, only those patients whom the witch-doctors had given up on came to the hospital. Thirty years later, in the year before Esther died, she and her staff delivered 1,300 women in the Zorzor hospital. And the four other wards of the greatly expanded hospital were jammed with patients with all sorts of surgical and medical illnesses.

The way Esther set about to deal with the problem, the way she worked her way into the tribal society, the way she handled a problem never before solved, the way she turned Kpelle-Loma-land upside down and made herself a legend in Liberia, is what this book is all about.

The second question. Esther is not better known because not enough has been written about her. Here is a woman who through hard work, love and compassion for her adopted people, love of her Lord, and incisive dedication, changed the lives of thousands and thousands of people. Generations of Liberians have grown up safely and healthily because they or their parents or their grandparents learned from Esther Bacon how to stay alive in a hostile environment. She herself wrote little for publication, and those were mostly short pieces in women's magazines with limited readership.

Dr. Monson warned me that there would be some people who would think her story should not be written: that Esther would not have approved of her story being told, that she never wanted earthly recognition for her work. That she would not want publicity for her selflessness and her gift of all she had of talent, time and money. That she would be uncomfortable if she knew she was the subject of a book.

I remembered that admonition as I wrote. So the purpose of this book is not to glorify or beatify Esther Bacon, although some will see that effect. The purpose is to show what happened in Liberia during the thirty-one years Esther Bacon lived there.

That story *must* be told.

Preface

In many ways Esther Bacon, the heroine of this moving story, bridged two eras in the world mission of the church. She went to Liberia when much still depended upon the vision and faith, the initiative and skill of missionaries. In 1941, few Liberians qualified as professional health workers — physicians, nurses, midwives, public health officers, health educators — precious few who were prepared to live and work in the remote, still undeveloped interior. Yet "up-country" from the coastal settlements and capital city of Monrovia is where Esther chose to serve. When she died three decades later, in 1972, Liberia had a new generation of dedicated, highly trained health workers and the facilities and programs to enhance their service to their people. For many of these young Liberians, Esther Bacon was the one who pointed the way.

Bridging two eras may simply require endurance and a certain longevity. Esther exhibited both, in spite of her untimely death from Lassa Fever. But to shape attitudes and methods of health care for future generations requires being a pioneer, an adventurer, and in some ways, a rebel. Esther was all of these. She anticipated the current emphases on primary health care and attention to the health of the whole person — body, mind, and spirit. Because she cared, she demanded much of herself and of others. Her single-minded devotion to those in need was surpassed only by her devotion to her Lord.

Now, at a time when the people of Liberia are living in the aftermath of civil strife, when the health, welfare, and even the survival of many is endangered, I commend this book to you. This biography captures an era, a place, and a person that are no longer with us. If not for the author's persistence and skill, Esther Bacon's story would still be local legend. Yet her legacy is larger than the place and years of her service. Her life and her work deserve to be known — the legacy of a truly great missionary who left behind a future of lives saved and lives changed.

Mark Thomsen, Ph.D., Executive Director
Division for Global Mission
Evangelical Lutheran Church in America

August 1991

Prologue

(October, 1942)

Late one afternoon in October, 1942, almost a year after her arrival in Zorzor, Liberia, Esther Bacon completed her work at the hospital and returned to her house for a cup of tea before going back down to the wards to make evening rounds. She sat quietly for a moment after drinking her tea, head nodding in a light doze.

She was awakened by fingers scritching down the screen of her front door. A deep male voice called "Bok-bok," the traditional Loma greeting. On the path at her door was a short, stocky Loma man, ebony black, his face and neck beaded with sweat. His long, grey robe of country cloth was soaked through and clung to his back and chest. He was just getting his breath back when Esther pushed open the screen.

She knew him. She had met him some weeks before in Kiliwu, a forest village an hour's walk from Zorzor. He had listened politely to her description of what she could do for his wife, who was then in the third trimester of pregnancy. He had not said "no," for it would have been a breach of etiquette to rebuff a stranger in his own home. But he had not said "yes" either and Esther had strongly suspected that once again the seed sown had fallen on stony ground. But she had said, in parting, "Well, anyway, Flumo, if your wife has trouble, you know where to find me."

He had nodded and said goodbye.

Now he was here, waiting on the hard dirt path for her to come out. She invited him in, but he shook his head and waited. She went out.

In broken Liberian English and scattered Loma words and phrases, he told a familiar story. "The child has been born and is dead. Dabio, my wife, is dying. The zoes say they can do nothing more and that the ancestors are calling her to them."

"How are they so sure the ancestors are calling her?"

*"I don't know. But they **are** there, of course. I could feel them, even hear them, in the gusts of wind that scattered the embers from the fire so violently that my wife had to be carried inside."*

*"She was **outside**?"*

"Of course. She was obviously unclean, bewitched we thought, under the influence of the evil spirit in the house, or she would have delivered long ago."

*"And the ancestors are in the **wind**?" she asked, a hint of disbelief in her voice. Taken aback, his eyes said, "You didn't know that?"*

Esther's heart sank. She had to be more careful. Flumo was certainly here to ask her to go with him. She must not show any signs of ridicule.

She brushed her hair behind her ears and softly answered his unspoken question, "No, Flumo, I didn't know that. It's not one of our beliefs. But I don't doubt the wisdom of your zoes."

The lines around his eyes flattened out as he said simply, "Will you come?"

"Of course I'll come." Her heart sang. Finally, finally, someone had called her, after almost a year of frustration.

*Flumo was not one of the influential men of his village, but he was a **man** and he had come to **her**. Lord, she prayed, stay with Flumo's wife and guard her till I can get there. Then, Lord, guide my hand, Oh **God**, this is so important — so **crucial**...*

She snatched up her lantern from the kitchen window ledge and swirled the kerosene around to make sure there was plenty. It would be dark by the time she came home and she would need the lantern. Briefly she considered calling out one of the schoolboys to go with them. No, that would take more time and time was critical. Flumo or one of the other village men would come back with her.

Esther Bacon would always be remembered by Africans and missionaries alike as the lady with the lantern. Now the slim, pretty, 26-year-old nurse from Iowa's farm belt began her thirty-one-year journey into legend as she picked up her lantern and ran over to the hospital.

Acknowledgments

I express grateful thanks to all those who gave freely of their time to furnish me with information about Esther Bacon.

To Betty Stull Schaffer for her many, many hours of work, sharing her artistic talents by doing the charcoal sketches and line drawings in this book.

To the following for allowing personal interviews: Lucille Anderson, Martin Appelt, Ruth Bacon, Ken Carlson, Jean Carlson, Edith Curran, Dr. Samuel Dopoe, Louise Faust, Gladys Holm, Deanna Isaacson, Jeanette Isaacson Kpissay, Elsie Leafstedt, Dian Marquardt, Rev. William Marquardt, Carolyn Miller, Margaret Miller, Grace Moleyeaze, Pewu Moleyeaze, Irene Morris, Bishop Roland Payne, Ruth Schuldt, Dr. James Stull.

To Roslyn Sadler and Dr. Earl Reber for taping material and sending it to me.

To Dr. Paul Mertens for allowing me to use the lengthy tapes he made shortly after Esther's death.

To Margaret Miller, Roslyn Sadler, and Dr. Mark Monson, for their exhaustive review of the entire manuscript and for their corrections, additions, and suggestions.

To Dr. Mark Monson for challenging me to write this story.

To Grace Monson for her hospitality in Zorzor.

To Martin Appelt for his work in setting up our research in Sioux City and Sioux Falls.

To Louise Faust for turning over the material she collected when writing Esther's story for *World Encounter*. And also for her hospitality.

To Elisabeth Wittman, Marion Olson, and Russell S. Deloney, Sr., for their enthusiastic help in the Archives of the Evangelical Lutheran Church in America.

To Donna Mertens for her hospitality in Monrovia.

To Delores Schmid, Lilliana Bartolomei, Fran Brouse, Betty Stull, Robert Dettmer, Della Mathies, Eleanor Raynie, for their letters and telephone interviews.

To Rev. James Vankpana for his help in locating the sites of the mission buildings in Zorzor in the '30s and '40s.

To Betty McCrandel for her help in the bishop's offices in Monrovia.

To Lovice Mitchell for her help in proofreading the galley proofs.

"The portrait of Esther's life has been done with a depth of understanding and detail that is beautiful."

Roslyn Sadler, former missionary to Liberia, wife of linguist Dr. Wesley Sadler.

"At this time when the health, welfare, and even the survival of many Liberians is endangered, I commend this book to you. This biography captures an era, a place, and a person that are no longer with us. Her life and her work deserve to be known — the legacy of a truly great missionary."

Mark Thomsen, Ph.D., Executive Director
Division for Global Mission
Evangelical Lutheran Church in America

"In Outlaw For God the author beautifully captures Esther Bacon's love for Africa and the African people she adopted as her own. Dr. Dibble intrigues us with the story of her medical skills and her commitment. We who knew Esther were aware that she was unusual — even unique. Now, after reading this book, I fully understand how remarkable she really was. Thank you for your book, Dr. Dibble. It was an honor — and gave me great pleasure — to illustrate it."

Betty Stull Schaffer, former missionary to Liberia and
now an artist living in Massachusetts.

"It is a very moving manuscript and will be of great encouragement to women who want to do something with their lives."

Elizabeth Handford, editor of The Joyful Woman.

"The author has succeeded in conveying the qualities and spirit of Esther Bacon, a remarkable person."

Gerald E. Currens, former missionary to Liberia,
currently Director for Planning and Overseas Operations
for the Evangelical Lutheran Church in America.

"The writing is excellent and the story fascinating."

Karen C. Simons, editor of New Hope.

"Esther Bacon was always a winner, and posthumously she has done it again! Somehow she has filibustered to get a physician to write her story. In this case, the scientist in the physician serves the biographer well."

Margaret Miller, former missionary to Liberia.

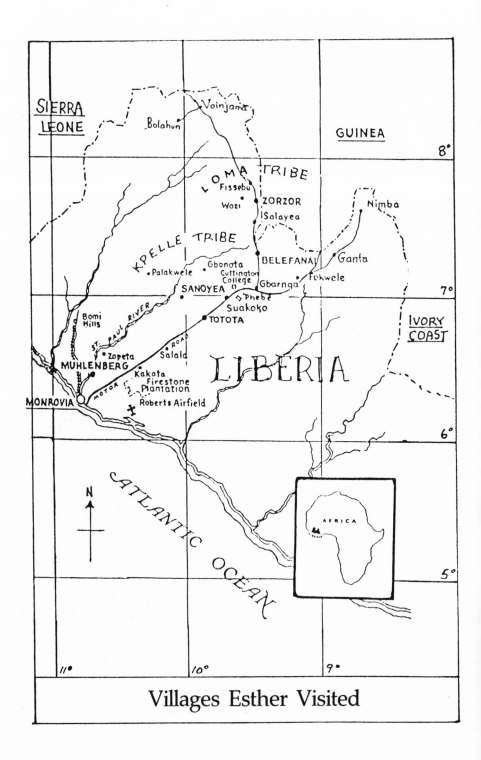

Villages Esther Visited

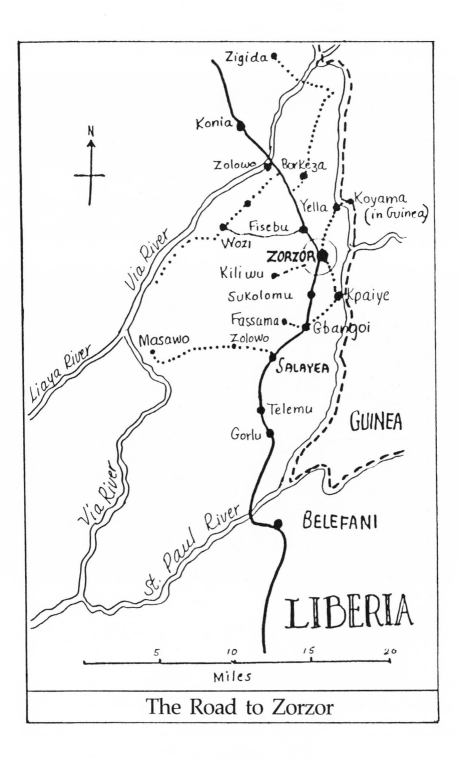

The Road to Zorzor

High Forest

to Esther's SPRING

ESTHER'S HOUSE (had been the doctor's house)

Uphill

HOSPITAL BUILDINGS

Stream

"Marsh"

← Causeway

↑ Downhill

CARPENTER SHOP

GUEST HOUSE

SADLER'S ZINC HOUSE

BOYS' SCHOOL COMPOUND

TEACHER'S HOUSE

CLASSROOMS

G. BUSCHMAN'S HOUSE

Downhill

BRICK KILNS

BLACKSMITH SHOP

Uphill ↑

GRAVEYARD

HEADMASTER'S HOUSE

ZORZOR MISSION

1941 when Esther arrived

"Marsh"

SOCCER FIELD ↗

SITE OF FIRST HOSPITAL which burned

TOWN OF → ZORZOR TOWN

← SITE OF NEW HOSPITAL (CONSTRUCTION not yet begun) Path to Monrovia

Drawn by Betty Stull Schaffer In consultation with Roslyn Sadler 1991 (NOT DRAWN TO SCALE)

- - - - footpaths

CHURCH BUILDING IN TOWN

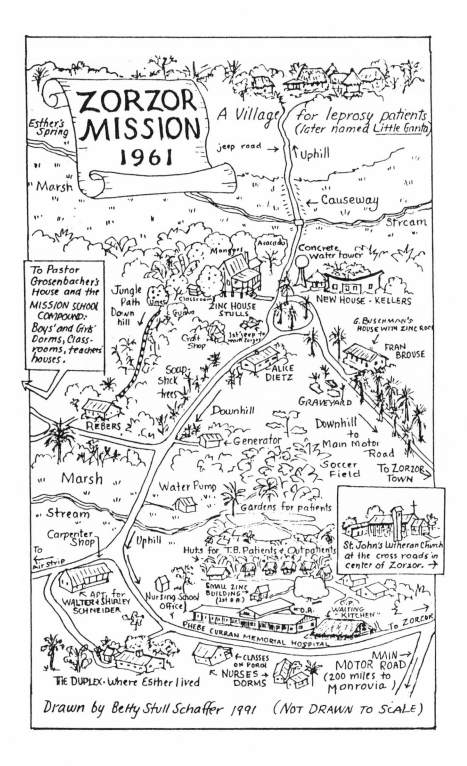

Notes on Spelling, Pronunciation, and Word Usage

Spelling.

Variations in spelling arise because the names are transliterations from Loma, Kpelle or some other tribal language. To be consistent, therefore, I have followed the spelling Esther Bacon used in her letters and other writings.

Harrisburg vs. Muhlenburg. Present-day missionaries in Liberia use "Muhlenburg" when referring to the old Main Station. Esther Bacon almost always used "Harrisburg," which was the village where the old Phebe Hospital was located.

Pronunciation. Liberian English, when written, looks exactly like American English. But when spoken there is a tendency to drop the final consonant from most words and syllables, using the syllable pattern of Loma/Kpelle. To illustrate: when the Liberian asks, "Will you please come with me?" it comes out like this, "Wi' yuh plea' cuh wi' me?" When "l," "r," and other consonants occur in a medial position, they are modified according to the phonemic patterns of Loma and Kpelle.

Other examples:

The town Zorzor, where most of the action in this book takes place, is pronounced "Zaw-zaw'." The name itself means "to do (or make) chatter,'' because it was — and still is — a market town where women gather!

The town Gbarnga is pronounced ''Bahng'-ah.'' Gorlu is ''Gaw-loo.''

Esther Bacon's name in Liberia, ''Bayka,'' is not a nickname at all. It derives from dropping the ''n'' from Bacon.

''Buzi.'' The reader will be confused by Esther's use of the word ''Buzi'' when referring to the language of the Loma people. Margaret Miller, linguist and longtime resident of Wozi in Loma country, explains: '' 'Buzi' originated from an important chief in Loma country, Chief Buseh, around the turn of the century, who sent his tribesmen to the coast as workers. When asked to identify themselves, they said, 'We are Buseh's people,' dropping the final possessive 's'. This was heard by English speakers as 'Buzi people' and became synonymous with 'Loma.' ''

Names. Many of the Liberians introduced in this book have names which sound non-African. For example, Roland Payne, Frances Leonard, Edith Curran, Irene Morris, Ruth Bacon (and many others) are all native-born black Africans. In most cases they or their parents took Western names when they converted to Christianity. Some, like Ruth Bacon, were orphans and took the name of the person who raised them. Others had descended from slaves who had taken the names of their owners.

The reader should therefore assume that anyone described as a Liberian nurse, pastor, etc., is a native-born black African.

Chapter One

(November-December, 1941)

(1)

The blacked-out freighter "Acadia" rolled slowly to port in the long trough, climbed the hill of the next comber, balanced momentarily, then slid down and rolled to starboard. The rising-balancing-sinking sensation reminded Esther of cresting an Iowa hill at fifty miles an hour. She had been slightly seasick at first but now after three weeks the motion soothed her impatience as a rocking cradle quiets a cranky baby.

Esther Bacon was on her way to Liberia. The year was 1941, the month November. Americans had not yet watched their fleet disappear at Pearl Harbor, but the North Atlantic was jammed with Allied cargo ships and tankers, prey to German U-boats. So Esther's ship, in convoy with other freighters and accompanied by three warships, had run almost straight south from New York through the Caribbean to Trinidad, then to Belem at the mouth of the Amazon, and across the Atlantic to the Union of South Africa.

Now in the moonlight night it plowed north along the west coast of the Union toward the Congo and the Cameroons. Then it would turn west past Nigeria, the Gold Coast and the Ivory Coast.

Except for the blackout, the ship reminded Esther of a hotel. She shared a stateroom with Miss Davis, a Methodist missionary returning to Sierra

1

Leone. The "grand" accommodations impressed her: small bath with hot and cold running water, her own lounge chair out on deck, and in the dining room a daily menu printed out on heavy paper listing a wide variety of foods.

In the warm tropical seas she spent most of the daytime hours out on deck. She read and napped in her deck chair, played quoits and shuffleboard for exercise. She chatted with new acquaintances, some of whom would become lifelong friends in Liberia. After dinner she retired to her cabin, but often slipped out on deck to lean against the rail and savor the warm dark night and the golden trail of the moon on the ocean.

In a letter to Mrs. Carl Ruhrer in Sioux City, Iowa, she wrote that there "was the expanse of ocean and sky in endless loveliness. Dame Rumor always busy with explanation of the route, the convoy blackouts, next time and place of port; the rocking of the boat to help one's appetite, fresh sea breezes, flying fish over white foam, a tropical moon."

Esther Bacon was twenty-five years old. She was of medium height (5′ 7″), slender, and moved with an athletic quickness. In the sun her golden hair shown with reddish highlights. Blue eyes sparkled with intelligence and warmth. Though quiet and unassuming, her humor was whimsical, even droll at times, and her grin was infectious. People liked her.

She was fulfilling a lifelong dream, the only future she had ever wanted. During high school, nurses' training, and four years as a working nurse, her heart was already in some foreign land. China, she thought at first. But no, the Lord had opened the door to Liberia instead.

Liberia. It had been a cipher to her when she was asked to go there by the United Lutheran Board of Foreign Missions.

And she certainly had never head of Zorzor, a thatched roof village deep in the rain-forests of the mountainous interior, two hundred miles from the ocean, accessible only by paths, porters, and a positive attitude.

But she had done her homework in the library of Trinity Lutheran Church and in the public library in downtown Sioux City. And there were two Liberian missionaries aboard the "Acadia," eager to share their experiences with her. Mrs. Miriam Miller had served in Liberia for eighteen years, Mrs. Gertrude Buschman for twenty-six.

Miriam had met and married James Miller in Liberia. In 1937 he became seriously ill, died en route home and was buried at sea. Now Miriam was back to replace Elsie Otto as the mission business manager in Monrovia.

Roslyn Sadler* describes her as "a glowing Christian and a joy to be with." In 1937 she had given a talk in Wesley Sadler's church; afterwards Wes said, "God tapped me on the shoulder that night and told me to go to Liberia as a missionary."

Gertrude Buschman was going back to Zorzor where she was stationed as a "Bible woman," one of those hardy pioneers of evangelism who worked mostly with the women, instructing both prospective converts and baptized Christians in the Bible. "Buschy" had come to Liberia in 1915 as a single teacher but in 1920 married Rev. Charles Buschman on the field. Rev. Buschman had died of black water fever, a virulent form of malaria in which there is such massive destruction of red blood cells that the urine turns almost black from the breakdown products.

So both Miriam and "Buschy" had lost husbands to the work of the Lord and had remained faithful, a fact not missed by Esther Bacon. If she wondered if she would find a husband on the field as her two new friends had done, it is not recorded!

Esther was not surprised to learn that West Africa — from the Belgian Congo on the east to Senegal on the west — was still considered to be "the white man's graveyard." To reinforce that impression, Gertrude Buschman told her the story of Reverend David Alexander Day:

In 1875 he had gone to Muhlenburg, Liberia, twenty-five miles up the St. Paul River from the ocean, to continue a work started in 1860 by Rev. Morris Officer. Two of his children died there in infancy. One of his children lived with a grandmother in the States until she was eight, then went to Liberia and died a year later. Mrs. Day became ill in Liberia and died in the United States. Rev. Day married again. After eleven years he wrote to a friend, "I think we have pretty well solved the problem of African fever." But twelve years later, fever felled him and friends persuaded him to go home. He died on the ship just a day out of New York.

It wasn't like that now, Esther thought, bracing herself on the rail as the ship plunged onward.

"It would have made no difference to her," says Bishop Roland Payne, first native-born bishop of the Liberian Lutheran Church, "if things hadn't changed. Esther Bacon was not afraid of anything. She was not afraid of snakes or leopards, nor of travel in the rainy season when the creeks were flooding or when she was in the jungle with a storm coming, when lightning would be striking and the wind coming or trees falling near her.

---

*See SOME OF THE PEOPLE IN ESTHER'S LIFE at back of book.

That did not bother her at all. Esther had the feeling God was really with her. Once she heard there was a woman in labor, she did everything to get there.''

She was right, of course, about the hazards being diminished. Most of the dread tropical diseases were preventable, if not abolished. She would take quinine daily to prevent malaria; boil her drinking water to avoid typhoid fever and other bacterial dysenteries; treat her vegetables with potassium permanganate or iodine to avoid amebiasis, ascaris, and other intestinal parasites; stay out of stagnant backwaters to avoid shistosomiasis; wear shoes to prevent hookworm. She was strong of mind, body, and spirit and she would be all right.

Neither she nor anyone else had heard of Lassa fever.

(2)

The ''Acadia'' steamed west to Freetown to deliver the Sierra Leone passengers, then doubled back to Monrovia. On Liberia's Thanksgiving Day, November 6th, 1941, she dropped anchor outside the sand bar. It would be another year before the United States sent men and equipment to dredge the river mouth at Firestone, near Robertsfield, to improve access to Liberia's rubber, desperately needed in the Allied war effort. The docks at Monrovia would not be built until after the war.

As Esther waited on the deck for transport ashore, she was outwardly calm except for blue eyes dancing with pleasure. Inwardly she was impatient to get ashore, to get upcountry, to get to work.

From the high deck she could see the city of Monrovia stretched out along the beach and starting to climb the hills and ridges beyond. Later she came to know it very well.

The main part of the city consisted of two wide, grassy streets intersecting each other, the houses along them built of wood. In the rest of the town the houses were mostly mud and wattle with thatched roofs. Here and there stone houses were going up. Several brick churches, one of them eighty years old, dominated their neighborhoods. President Barclay's three-story Executive Mansion stood opposite the State Department and the still-unfinished stone house of the deposed ex-president King. Shops and warehouses cluttered the streets along the waterside. To reach the Post Office one climbed a rickety, steep set of steps to a balcony. The monolithic Masonic Temple dominated the highest hill. No streets were paved and there was no electricity.

Now cargo lighters and passenger dories crowded around the ship. One by one the fifty missionaries and two hundred other passengers were swung out over the side in a canvas mammy chair slung from a cargo boom and lowered into dories.

Fifty passengers were young Firestone engineers and administrators, cool and spruce in Palm Beach suits and Panama hats, looking around them with ingenuous curiosity. They would quickly disappear northward into the Firestone compound a few hours away where their houses contained showers and electricity, where they swam in a big pool in the heat of the day and played tennis in the evening.

One hundred and fifty passengers were the vanguard of a veritable army soon to come: civil engineers, architects, technicians, skilled workers, and U.S. Army construction engineers, sent to build an airport, roads, and plan the harbor.

Nine muscular, bare-chested Liberians rowed Esther's boat ashore. On the dock she was met by Mr. Parker, a missionary teacher at the Muhlenburg Boys' School. He had been taking turns with others, commuting to Monrovia from the Main Station for two weeks, to be sure someone was there to meet the boat. They waited patiently in the hot, humid afternoon for their trunks to be off-loaded, then were driven in a pickup truck the thirty miles to Harrisburg. In the transfer, Esther lost her zipper bag which contained her film, bobby pins, hairbrush and some books. She never found it.

The road was merely a rough track scraped through the cut-over jungle, skirting salt-water inlets from the sea and slime-covered swamps where crocodiles and watersnakes lived.

On the Harrisburg side of the St. Paul River stood Phebe Hospital, with Dr. Flexman in charge, and the E. V. Day Girls' School, where young Norma Bloomquist and Ethel Emerick taught. Across the river was the Muhlenburg Boys' School, with the Parkers in charge.

Esther felt at home immediately. She stayed in the nurses' dormitory, Mango Haven, with Pauline Ziegler, whom she had known in the States. Pauline, Esther's age, had been there just a few months, but long enough to be well indoctrinated in the ways of the tropics. Their common room looked out across green lawns bordered with colorful flowers onto the beautiful St. Paul River, swiftly flowing now during the rains and flanked by tropical rain forest.

Esther crossed the river one evening to have supper with the Parkers and their "sweet" daughters, Judy and Vangie. "I crossed at sunset time," she wrote, "and sky, clouds, and water were indescribably colorful, truly a picture. Palm trees and hills accent the shore line. To the right the water comes bubbling over the rocks like a little falls, and several trees bedecked on every branch with white birds look like snowballs."

Esther stayed at Phebe for five weeks, learning how to survive in an environment hostile to the unwary. Dr. Flexman ordered her to take quinine faithfully and to wear her cork sun helmet whenever outside from 8 A.M. to 5 P.M. She learned to tap her shoes upside down each morning to get rid of insects, especially scorpions; to never put her hand into bushes or thick flowers without beating the ground first with a stick to scare away snakes; to never walk in the dark without a light, not for fear of the people or large animals, but because of the snakes, especially pit vipers, who loved to lie in the warm soil which held heat longer than grass and bushes. These and dozens of other lessons she quickly absorbed by watching and listening.

She joined the hospital staff for morning devotions, ward rounds, out-patient clinics, and evening vespers. Just before she left for Zorzor, she sat in on the week-long Annual Conference attended by all the Lutheran missionaries in Liberia.

The Phebe people fell in love with Esther and didn't want her to go north. They needed her youthful enthusiasm right there. But it was not to be. The Lutheran Hospital at Zorzor needed Esther more than Phebe did, especially now that the only doctor up there was even then on his way down to Phebe.

In late November, Dr. George "Skipper" Moore and his wife Smitz came down from Zorzor with 110 porters carrying them and their gear. Accompanying them were Rev. Wesley and Roslyn Sadler, the pastor and his wife from the Zorzor church. Roslyn was twenty-three, Esther twenty-five. An immediate rapport developed between them. That rapport would develop into mutual love and admiration. And moreover, Esther would save the lives of Roslyn's husband and one of their children.

Dr. Moore was on his way to the States to join the Navy and, due to circumstances beyond his control, would never come back to Liberia. Esther was unhappy because now there was no doctor at Zorzor, but she was glad to finally be able to talk to a medical person about the Zorzor hospital and its patients.

"So, Esther," Dr. Moore said, "you'll be doctor, nurse, and lab technician!"

Her laugh was warm and easy and accompanied by a quick, slightly lopsided smile that was one of her endearing charms. "A doctor I'm not. But I'll do what I can."

Dr. Moore gave Esther all the encouragement he could, but there was a problem he wanted her to know about. The Loma and Kpelle tribes around Zorzor were, of all the tribes in Liberia, the most heavily burdened with taboos, unscientific traditional beliefs, and dependence on their witch doctors (zoes — both male and female).

"Esther," Dr. Moore said, "let me tell you a little about what you're going to face up in Zorzor."

(3)

He told her quite a bit, that late afternoon, about the nature of the problem he'd dealt with for the past four years. Esther would face the same problem, the same challenge. She would learn considerably more as the months and years sped by: from missionaries at first, then gradually more and more from the Africans themselves when they realized how serious she was about understanding their culture and their values.

Esther and Dr. Moore sat on the veranda of the Flexmans' modest but comfortable home on the hospital compound, just across a dark green lawn from Mango Haven. Esther sat almost primly on a sturdy straight-back chair, but "Skipper" Moore slumped in a low, heavy, mahogany chair with a padded seat.

The mild daytime breeze had dropped off entirely but the heat and humidity had not. Though the high forest had been pushed back, it was not far away. People moved in and out of it, single file, for the paths were narrow even where the forest had been cleared. The men were lean and moved with a fluid grace in their long flowing robes of grey, blue, or white

homespun country cloth. The women moved more quickly, balancing their head-loads with grace and stateliness. Children ran alongside their mothers, laughing and screaming in play, seldom paying any attention to the missionaries on the porch.

Dr. Moore told Esther why the medical work at Zorzor was stagnant. The basic problem was that the men's Poro Society and the women's Sande Society dominated the tribal Liberians and controlled most aspects of their lives. This indoctrination began in childhood. The youngsters were taken from their homes and sent to schools deep in the bush, separated from their parents for three to four years. Here they learned the ways of survival, religious rites, and superstitions. They learned about sexual matters and parenthood.

The boys learned weaponry, slash-and-burn farming techniques, house-building. The girls learned how to dance and sing, to weave mats and bags, to make clay pots and jars, and how to cook. The girls said that this was where they ate a lot and got pretty.

"A finishing school," Esther said with a wistful smile.

When they finished this school, Dr. Moore went on, both boys and girls were circumsized. Only then were they allowed back into village life.

The instructors in these schools were called zoes, the local name for witch-doctors. Most of what a zo did — or claimed to do — was good. A zo was a person with power: herbal doctors, medicine men and women, master craftsmen (especially blacksmiths), and hereditary chiefs.

What kind of power? The power over life and death. The power to cure. The power to kill. The power to know things, such as who's guilty, where things are, what dreams mean. And above all, the power to communicate with the ancestral spirits.

Esther felt a sense of uneasiness. Men and women with such power over other human beings? "Dr. Moore, how do these people get such power?"

Some, he explained, were "born with the medicines," knew them in-nately from birth. Others joined one of the dozens of zo societies and took an apprenticeship. They went into the bush every day for years until the *leaves* finally got to know *them* and would work for them. The prospec-tive zo tested his power on his tribesmen. He went into the jungle, picked the leaves, made his tea or paste, and tried it out. If it worked, he was a zo. If it didn't, he wasn't.

Dr. Moore disappeared into the Flexmans' house for a moment and returned with a copy of Graham Greene's *Journey Without Maps*, Greene's account of his walk through Liberia in 1935, just six years earlier. He flipped it open and read, "It is a curiously Kafka-like situation: headmasters who wear masks and turn out to be the local blacksmith...there is an atmosphere of force and terror...occasionally beauty...meaning behind meaning, form behind form."

Being dependent on their zoes for everything, the tribes-people were afraid to antagonize them. So when they were forbidden to go to the Zor-zor Lutheran Hospital, they didn't go. In particular, the women didn't come in for delivery. Esther could hardly believe this. "None of them come in?" she asked Dr. Moore.

"Since 1928, when the first doctor went to Zorzor, up until 1937 when I arrived, there were exactly eleven hospital deliveries and nine of those were mission employees or wives of employees. In the past four years, though, I've seen it change slowly. Very slowly. They still won't let me — a man — come near them very often. But a few come for pre- and post-natal care and some come for the nurses to deliver." He smiled, and his handsome young face lit up. "I stand around where they can't see me and sometimes they let me come in if some sort of complication develops."

"The power of the zoes is still so strong? Doctor, this is 1941."

"Not up in Zorzor it isn't."

(4)

After Conference Esther divided the things in her trunks into sixty pound loads. Over fifty porters would carry personal gear and supplies for Salayea and Zorzor. Esther and her missionary companions would be carried in "hammocks" for much of the way. Though Pauline Ziegler would be staying at Phebe, she and Esther were given a "sample" ride a few days before Esther left, with much giggling from the other women and almost uncontrolled laughter from the porters.

Twelve carriers, hired by the missions and supplied by the District Commissioner or village chiefs, were assigned to each hammock. Four men carried for one hour and then rested for two.

The hammock was not what one sees on ships or in the backyards of America, nor was its purpose the same. "Palanquin" is more descriptive, the apparatus being a chair enclosed with roof and side-curtains that could be rolled down to protect the passenger from sun and rain.

For good reason there was an almost morbid fear of exhaustion, heat stroke, and sunstroke. Over-heated, over-tired bodies succumbed more readily to infection or parasitism. In 1941 only sulfanilimide powder was available for ulcers and other superficial bacterial infections, chloroquin was not yet available for malaria, and many other parasitic infestations were inadequately treated by modern standards.

Dr. George Harley, a Methodist missionary doctor in upcountry Ganta since 1926, had written with authority, "Nobody can walk long distances in this climate without danger." He ascribed the death of one of his colleagues to a "foolhardy" seven-day walk from Monrovia to Ganta.

So all missionaries at that time, men and women alike, were ordered not to walk more than twenty minutes out of each hour when on the path between nine in the morning and four in the afternoon.

While Esther packed for the trip upcountry, word came from Monrovia that Pearl Harbor had been attacked. Everyone's thoughts went immediately to loved ones who would enlist or be conscripted. And the old hands knew that there would be practical consequences for the missionaries in Liberia. Almost all their supplies came from the States — case lots of everything from soup to tins of margarine to soap to sugar. There were no stores in Monrovia that could handle the large orders the missionaries placed every six months.

An additional factor worried American Embassy officials and the heads of the Lutheran Mission. An hour's walk from Zorzor was the border between Liberia and French Equatorial Africa. France was still very much under the German boot. Now America was at war with Germany. Was it possible that the German armies invading North Africa might sweep down across the desert? Would the people at Zorzor be in any danger?

Rumors raged that all American women and children would be sent home. But cooler heads ruled that the proximity of French territory would pose no threat. The Zorzor contingent was allowed to proceed upcountry.

Esther was accompanied by missionaries Gertrude Buschman and Bertha Koenig, and by Frances Leonard, an attractive young Kpelle woman who had just finished six months' nurse's training. Wesley and Roslyn Sadler were also going back to Zorzor, but they would have to wait for the porters to return for them.

Bertha Koenig was a veteran missionary teacher. After graduating from Bethany College in Lindsborg, Kansas, she had worked as a "home missionary" at Allen Normal, "an institution for colored boys and girls," before going to Liberia. In her twenty-five years in Liberia she had taught at the E. V. Day Girls' School, Muhlenburg Boys' School, Kpolopele, and Zorzor. She now lived in Kpaiye, a town eight miles southeast of Zorzor on the border of French Equatorial Africa, where for ten years she had supervised the girls' school and visited in the villages, "teaching God's word to the women."

A pickup truck carried the four women to the end of the road at Salala (see map, page xvii), sixty miles from Phebe, one-third of the distance to Zorzor. Their porters met them there after a 2½ day walk. The women slept overnight in hammocks slung in the roof of mud and thatch guest houses. Villagers brought rice, water, palm oil and a chicken to cook over a wood fire. Each missionary carried pots and silverware and other camping equipment.

Frances Leonard cheerfully guided Esther around Salala, a town small compared to Monrovia, but large for an interior town. The District Commissioner lived there. There were barracks for government soldiers. Trucks, a few private vehicles, and people crowded the road through town. Rectangular houses were roofed with zinc, a sign of progress and prosperity. Muslim Mandingo tribesmen in their long, blue-bordered white robes strolled in the markets. Men from other tribes, dressed in striped homespun robes, labored under sacks of rice from their farms or roamed the markets, eyes wide at the profusion of goods.

The markets enthralled Esther, too. She fingered the rough homespun cloth of locally grown cotton, rich lengths of white and blue Mandingo cloth, brightly patterned two-yard pieces from England which the native women used for "lappas," their traditional wrap-around skirts. She frankly admired the workmanship of locally crafted tools of all kinds: hoes, machetes (locally called cutlasses), knives, pickaxes and shovels. In one enclosed store, a Lebanese trader sold pots and pans. In another were stacks of shirts for the men who even then had begun to wear western-style trousers.

Esther's nostrils twitched involuntarily as Frances steered her through aisles of tiny rickety wooden stands selling peppers, okra, palm oil, beans, onions, rice, ground peas, coconuts, pawpaw, bananas, pineapple, tomatoes, lemons, limes, oranges, grapefruit. On palm leaves spread out in the sun, women sold the dried meat of duiker, rats, bats, deer, snake, bush cow and fish. Live chickens hung by their feet from the improvised stalls. In little bowls or dried gourds wiggled huge, live, bamboo grubs which when sliced on rice gave it a warm, sweet taste. There was salt, sugar, and flour.

In some of the bigger stores on the main street, owned and run by Lebanese traders, one could buy guns, mirrors, lanterns, buckets, fermented cane juice, and palm wine.

She found no coffee, tea, bacon, weiners, cereal, soup, peanut butter, butter, honey, bread, canned food, soft drinks, or many of the other foodstuffs she had been used to buying in Sioux City without even thinking about it. Had she been looking for it, she also would have found that she couldn't buy Western-made beer, wine or liquor.

But she was not concerned about what she *couldn't* buy. In the Colorado sod hut of her homesteader parents, the foods were basic and unadorned. In her Aunt Nora's house in Sioux City, where she had lived during grade school, high school and nurse's training, the food had been plentiful but simple. So she didn't worry, actually never gave it a thought, counting on God to provide for her needs.

(5)

So twelve porters carried Esther Bacon in a hammock for five days through a different world, into a different world. She chafed at the restriction on walking and often stretched the twenty minutes out until Gertrude Buschman had to say softly, "Now, Esther..." Esther envied Frances Leonard, who being native-born walked the entire distance. But it is very clear that for Esther Bacon this was an adventure. It was exhilarating. It was *fun*, not an ordeal. She loved every minute of it, even when she was confined to her hammock.

There was another factor that Esther hints about and which Graham Greene quite clearly enunciates in *Journey Without Maps*: "One heard the hammock string grinding on the pole and saw the shoulder muscles strain under the weight. It was too close to using men as animals for me to be happy.''

The first twenty miles of the drive from Harrisburg to Salala had been through flat country: lagoons and swamps interspersed with scattered rocky promontories and slightly higher ground where crops were raised. Then the truck had taken them for forty miles through rolling hills, some of them heavily forested and others denuded in patches by the slash-and-burn farming practices of the local tribesmen.

Now the walking trail continued first through the same rolling hills, but soon the strung-out party snaked up steep escarpments and swung like driver ants in a long undulating column around hills almost big enough to be called mountains. Then they entered the real mountainous rain-forest of the interior which stretched into French Equatorial Africa to the north, Sierra Leone to the west, and the Ivory Coast to the east. The carriers with their loads of goods and hammock-borne missionaries picked their way across rocky, tumbling streams, waded through muddy, sluggish rivers buzzing with insects, clouds of multi-colored butterflies, and noisy with calling birds, balanced precariously on liana ''monkey'' bridges* which swayed excitingly in the wind.

It was the dry season, so the porters said, but it rained every day. Even after the rain stopped, huge drops fell from the tall trees. The low growth along the path brushed them with soggy leaves.

Whereas Monrovia sat on a ridge of basaltic rock, the interior of Liberia was part of the same Precambrian Shield that covers so much of North America, an ancient crystalline rock formation three billion years old: granite, schist, and gneiss. The soil, where exposed by paths, tipped-over trees and the hoes of farmers, was red, an evenly disposed bed of laterites composed of rust-red aluminum and iron oxides. The thin soil was more suited to tree crops, like rubber, cocoa, coffee, and the raffia palm, than to food crops. But the people had to eat and they planted where they lived.

For hours at a time the tortuous path carried them through totally uninhabited forest, as Esther described it, ''through little bush and big bush along the path thickly walled with towering trees and brilliant flowers to catch your eye, and bird's song your ears.''

Her reaction to all this was just the opposite of Graham Greene's, who wrote, ''We passed on twelve-inch paths through an endless back garden of tangled weeds...there was no view, no change of scene, nothing to distract the eyes...the eyes had to be kept on the ground all the way,

---

*Constructed by tying lianas from a tree on one side to a tree on the other.

to avoid roots and boulders...the senses were dulled and registered only acute boredom."

Now they were really in triple canopy rain forest. The first story was ground-covering ferns, palmettoes, and bushes with thick, broad, waxy leaves. The second story was 50- to 100-foot palms, corkwood, mulberry, zebrawood, "walnut," and many others. The third story was 150- to 200-foot red ironwoods, camwoods, whismores and other termite-proof hardwoods ideal for construction, but safe from loggers, too, because there were no roads.

Arm-thick lianas looped from tree to tree and tree to ground. Wrist-thick vines climbed upwards, around and around the trunks of 200-foot trees. Black ants' nests the size of bushel baskets clung to the trunks like obscene, brownish-black tumors, connected to the ground by narrow trails grooved into the bark by the passage of millions of little feet.

In the virtually roadless Liberia of 1941, the high forest still was ideal habitat for a wide variety of wildlife. Though most of the animals were shy and seldom seen, there were monkeys and chimpanzees; several kinds of duiker: the royal antelope (miniature 10-12 pound hero of many folk stories), the zebra duiker (collie-sized with vertical stripes), and the Jentik's duiker (almost black and the size of a whitetail deer); rodents, pygmy hippopotamuses, anteaters, elephants, bush cows (short-horned buffalo), leopards; eight species of poisonous snakes including two kinds of cobra, the green mamba, three kinds of viper, and the night adder; crocodiles, scorpions, lizards, bats, and at least 200 species of birds.

Occasionally the party passed through villages, where children and dogs trooped around them, chickens and pigs and ducks scattered in front of them, women stopped their work to wave and smile. This was Kpelle country, the largest tribe in Liberia, perhaps 200,000 strong in 1941, occupying much of Central Liberia and extending up into French Equatorial Africa.

It was to these people, and the closely related Loma tribe to the northwest, that Esther would devote the next thirty-one years.

Often the trekkers stopped in a village to rest. Esther was amazed at how cool it was inside the round, one-room, mud houses, windowless to keep out the "terrors of the night." The walls were constructed of vertical poles cross-laced with bamboo and vines (wattle), then plastered with mud and a thin layer of cow dung and finally rubbed inside and out with white clay.

Some of the houses were further decorated with pictures and designs drawn with charcoal and red laterite soil. The conical roofs, built of perfectly symmetrical sapling frames covered with palm-frond thatch, were capped with a fired clay cooking pot to keep out the rain. The floors were dirt, packed hard as concrete, relayered occasionally with mud and dung to keep down the dust, and swept as clean as an operating suite. The sweet smell of fresh thatch reminded Esther of June haying time in Iowa.

(6)

The first night they stayed in Sanoyea, a Lutheran station where three missionaries were in residence. One was Miss Kirsten Marie Jensen, who will be met many times in this story. She was a Danish nurse who had immigrated to the United States after a year of college. In the States she had taken three years of nurses' training and then two years at the Lutheran Bible Institute in Minneapolis. She arrived in Sanoyea in August of 1928.

The other two missionaries were the Rev. Dr. Harry Heilman, President of the mission, and his wife Bessie. (Soon after Esther's visit, Dr. Heilman would have a heart attack and reluctantly retire from the field. He would, however, have the immense satisfaction of seeing a nephew, medical doctor Earl Reber, join Esther in Zorzor in 1946.)

Esther was especially intrigued by the children, who considered the missionaries objects of curiosity, were shy and a little frightened. But, Esther wrote, "they peeped with their lovely brown eyes and smiles through the cracks by the doors or ventured shyly in, ready to run 'one time' (right now) should we move, but, should they receive a pinch of salt, giving evidence of delight greater than any youngster at home receiving his favorite candy."

Late on the second day (the third from Harrisburg) they crossed the St. Paul River at Pieta in dugout canoes. At times it was low enough to wade across, but in flood effectively blocked all traffic north and south. Neither monkey bridges nor log bridges were suitable for a river like the St. Paul. Across the river, the party proceeded to Nutown, where they stayed overnight, deep in the high forest, still in Kpelle-land.

(7)

They slept the fourth night in Salayea, a small station in Loma country on the main path to Zorzor, where the Lutheran Training Institute would eventually be established for high school students.

Then on the fifth day they made the final push to Zorzor. They climbed and descended thousand-foot ridges, one after another, their porters leaning far forward in the struggle upward, and then tilting back with loose-jointed knees and flapping feet on the steep descent.

Bertha Koenig and three porters left them at Gbangoi ("Bahng-wee"), where a path branched off to Kpaiye. Esther promised to come down to see the station as soon as she herself got settled. There was a beautiful light in Bertha's eyes as she said, "I can hardly believe I'm almost home."

Will I, Esther wondered, ever think of Zorzor as *home*?

From ten miles out of Zorzor, the path led them through mixed farms and high forest. Esther was fascinated and excited by this close look at her new "home." She noted that most of the rice was grown on the hillsides, not in flooded paddies as she had supposed. Frances Leonard explained that the Loma and Kpelle people were "forest people" and hated to work in the muck. And their inherent animism propelled them to "fight the forest trees, to show them that the people were stronger."

Many of the fields they passed had been harvested already but some were heavy with rice almost ready for the harvest. A few fronds of corn stuck out here and there. The rains which had plagued the trekkers almost all the way from Monrovia had not continued here in the mountainous north. The muggy heat of the lowlands had also abated, though to a midwesterner it was still hot.

They crested the last ridge on the afternoon of December 15th. There, on a low, flat-topped hill, across a swampy valley, lay Zorzor like a toy village. Two wide, meandering paths criss-crossed in the center, dividing the village into four quarters of about fifty houses each, all round and thatched and made of mud and wattle and daubed with white clay. In the courtyards between the houses, children played and women pounded grain with long poles in tall wooden tubs. Old men sat under trees or on benches in the shade of the houses.

A short distance from the center of town, crowded in on all sides by houses, stood the church, a large, white, thatched, mud and wattle structure with a wooden bell tower jutting upwards from the peak of its roof.

Esther, enchanted by the view, later would write, "Picturesque paths lead to surrounding towns also touched by the work here. Against the horizon on every side are green tree-covered mountains overhung with bright clouded sky colored in a thousand varieties at sunsets and dawns and sometimes varied with dark clouds of rainstorms. Here, one can surely lift up one's eyes unto the hills and receive fresh courage and strength for each day."

Bushy gently laid a hand on Esther's arm and pointed off to their left to a high ridge separated from Zorzor by a finger swamp.

"You can't see it yet, Esther, but on that ridge is the main mission compound — the Boys' School, the Sadlers' house, and my humble abode.
And beyond that hill is another swamp and another hill and that's where
you'll find your hospital."

Her smile warmed Esther's heart, and then she said, "Welcome to
Zorzor, Esther."

*Esther Bacon on graduation from the Lutheran Hospital School of Nursing,
Sioux City, Iowa, 1937.*

(It is necessary to interrupt this narrative at some point in order to fill in the twenty-five years of Esther's life which preceded her passage to Liberia. The reader impatient to follow Esther to Zorzor may skip this chapter temporarily and come back to it at another time.)

Chapter Two

(Growing Up)

(1)

Esther Eleanor Bacon was born in a sod hut on a forty-acre homestead near Burlington, Colorado, on March 19th, 1916.

In that same year the United States, still neutral in The Great War, invaded Mexico with General Black Jack Pershing in pursuit of Pancho Villa. Oil had not yet been discovered in Arabia but the Arab Revolt against the Ottoman Turks had begun. Out of the U.S. mint came a new dime, quarter and fifty-cent piece. Making their debut in 1916 were Lucky Strike cigarettes, Jeanette Rankin as the first woman congresswoman, the I.Q. test, heparin as an anticoagulant, the first radio news broadcast, the first Rose Bowl game, the first use of hybrid seed corn (in Illinois), and the first home refrigerator. Lord Dunsany's "A Night at the Inn" premiered on Broadway, and Douglas Fairbanks starred in "The Mystery of the Leaping Fish."

Esther's mother, Anna, was a Leander. She had three sisters, Eleanor (Nora), Lizzie, and Amanda, and two brothers, Alfred and Frank.

In 1909, seven years before Esther was born, Anna was a cleaning woman and Nora a legal secretary in Sioux City, Iowa. Amanda was married to Ernest Lundberg and lived on a farm near Alcester, South Dakota, about fifty miles northwest of Sioux City. Lizzie was still at home on the family farm. Alfred and Frank were homesteading in Colorado.

In 1909 Anna had a nervous breakdown "from working too hard" and moved out to the Lundberg farm where Amanda could take care of her. That she was actually suicidal is doubtful, but Elsie (Lundberg) Leafstedt, Amanda's daughter, remembers that her mother once did catch Anna "in the nick of time" taking the lid off the wood stove to burn her hair. Elsie also recalls that it was the strong-willed Nora who "decided it would be good to do something different so they talked it over and decided to go to Colorado." Alfred and Frank would help them get settled.

So Anna and Nora moved to Colorado where each homesteaded a forty-acre tract near Burlington in Kit Carson County on the Kansas border. With help from their brothers, Nora and Anna built two free-standing sod huts fifteen feet long and ten feet wide and roofed them with timbers covered with sod. They put in only one small paneless window in the front of the huts, not because of the "terrors of the night," but because they were too expensive and difficult to install.

Three years later, in 1912, when Anna was thirty-six, she married Alva Bacon, a tall, rangy man of thirty-five, who had homesteaded an adjoining claim in 1906. He was an avid horseman and had lost an eye in a riding accident in California in his youth. Nora then abandoned her "40" to the Bacons, got a secretarial job in Denver, then moved on to California where she was living in 1916 when Esther was born back in the Colorado sod hut.

Communication between Alva and Anna was poor. Anna never found out, for example, why Alva always slept with a gun under his pillow. She wondered all her life if he had been in trouble somewhere. When she had her "nervous spells," he was at a loss and sometimes beat her to bring her out of them.

Life may have been hard for the adults, but for Esther it was fun. She had dolls, a white cat with one black ear, and a pumpkin cart pulled by a pony. From the very beginning she was a cute little tyke; pictures show her poke-bonneted little head peering mischievously around the corner of the house and playing in the dirt with her dolls. Her dolls were always sick or bandaged up with a broken arm or leg. Elsie Leafstedt, who now lives in Sioux Falls, South Dakota, remembers that "she was always busy nursing her dolls and cats and dogs or any animals as squirrels or rabbits or pigs if she could catch them." She also had a pet turkey which she led around on a string. There is no record of whether she was able to eat the turkey when the time came!

While the adventuresome Nora and Anna were off winning the wild west, back home in Iowa sister Lizzie had married Charles Carlson and

soon had three children, Eleanor, Ruth, and Ken.* They lived in Howard-
en, Iowa, seven miles east of Alcester across the Big Sioux River.

In 1921, when Esther was five, Anna's "nervous spells" became more
serious and Alva became worried about her. He wrote Ernest Lundberg,
Amanda's husband, that he was not able to care for Anna and Esther
in the way they needed. Apparently he actually feared for their lives.
Eleanor Carlson (now Raynie) remembers that "their life together had
trials and hardships that could not be worked out without professional
help and that wasn't easy to get in those years."

Ernest Lundberg and Alfred Leander brought Anna and five-year-old
Esther back to Alcester. For several months it was unsafe to leave Anna
alone for any length of time. Elsie Leafstedt recalls that "sometimes she
would holler and she would just scream."

When Nora heard about the problem, she quit her job in California and
moved back to Sioux City to be available to take care of Anna and Esther
when Anna was well enough to leave the Lundberg farm. She arranged
for Anna's legal separation from Alva through the law office to which
she had returned as a secretary. Eleanor Raynie says that "Aunt Nora
was young and pretty then and had a few chances to marry but chose
a career first. She was always there to help members of the family that
needed her."

Gradually Anna improved out on the farm. When she was capable of
taking care of herself and Esther without worry about suicide, she and
Esther moved in with Nora in Sioux City. Nora became the sole support
of the little family. Esther started school and Anna took care of the
apartment.

Nora now had a second floor apartment at 1119 Jennings, a house owned
by David and Ann Rogers who lived downstairs. The Rogers' niece,
Delores (now Schmid), remembers Esther as a very frail child. Delores
was amazed when later Esther was able to overcome this disability and
accomplish what she did.

Esther spent vacations and many weekends in the Carlsons' house in
Hawarden and on the Lundbergs' farm near Alcester. The Milwaukee
Road had good passenger service in the '20s and '30s and it was a lark
to pack up a little bag, walk down to the station and ride the forty miles
north to Hawarden.

In Hawarden she played with her Carlson cousins, Eleanor, Ruth and
Ken. Eleanor was five years older, Ruth the same age, and Ken four years
younger. Ruth and Esther were so much like sisters that people called

---

*Much of the information in this chapter was obtained from Ken Carlson and his wife Jean.

them "the twins." Esther was the ringleader in their pranks, which were frequent. The Carlson children were quiet compared to Esther, who was full of energy and not the least bit shy. She got the Carlson children into mischief they normally wouldn't have thought up. One time she found a nest of rotten eggs that a hen had sat on and abandoned. She wanted to play catch with them to see how far back they could get before breaking them.

She was a great tease. She teased everyone — to the point of being a nuisance. Elsie Leafstedt remembers when her brother hurt his leg and had to sit with it elevated. Esther kept trying to touch the sore spot, persisting in tormenting the boy until she was told to stop. She said, "Why *shan't* I touch it? Why *shan't* I do that?"

Eleanor Raynie thinks the teasing was a longing for attention. For one period of time she interrupted the adults' conversation by pinching them and grinning. This stopped only when they decided to pinch her back. Sometimes she got her own way by teasing her mother until her mother became exhausted and gave in. When it didn't work, Esther walked away, pouting, and saying, "Well, I lost that one."

She loved to take dares. One time she pestered the Carlson children to dare her to put a fishworn in her mouth. When nobody would, she did it anyway. She climbed on roofs and in the haymow and up trees, one time climbing a tree that chickens roosted in and filling her ears and hair with chicken mites.

One time she climbed the fifty-five-foot windcharger and, Eleanor remembers, "pretended it was fun. Her aunts gathered around the bottom and held their breath. They felt she would fall any minute. Aunt Nora said, 'Esther, I'll bet you can't come down as fast as you went up.' She did because she thought it was a dare."

Ken Carlson says, "I don't think Esther ever had any bad thoughts against her mother due to her illness. Esther seemed to have that inner special ability to understand her sickness and accept it, even at a very early age. She always looked at the good side of things and made the best of any bad situation. I don't ever remember Esther complaining that her mother's handicap ever interfered with what she did. She listened to her mother's instructions, but could always add a little EXTRA FUN on the side while doing as her mother asked. This did get on her mother's nerves."

Nor does Elsie Leafstedt recall that Anna's illness affected Esther a great deal. "Nothing bothered her. She loved her mother very much and it never seemed to bother her when Aunt Anna had these seizures or mental breakdowns. She was always happy and full of fun. I never heard her say anything about leaving her father and coming to South Dakota with her mother."

Life was fun, an adventure. If it wasn't, she changed it to make it fun. She made a game of everything, even eating. She quickly tasted everything on her plate and then put aside what she liked best. That was her "goody bite" and it was eaten last.

Although Esther had ridden her pony a little in Colorado, it was on the Lundberg's farm that she really learned to ride, an accomplishment that would have a surprising and important bearing on her work in Africa. The Lundbergs had six work horses, one pony, and two colts. The work horses were just work horses without a lot of breeding. But they were gentle and easily ridden without a saddle. Esther loved to challenge anyone to a race.

All of the facets of Esther's character that are remembered by friends and relatives — the teasing, taking dares, loving fun, seeking adventure, studying the Bible, riding horses, living a good life — were childhood manifestations of the adult Esther would become. She would always be a tease — always love fun — always take dares — and she would always live a good life.

(2)

Aunt Nora was a charter member of the Christian Missionary Alliance Church in Sioux City. It was certainly her influence, more than anyone else's, that shaped Esther's life during her formative years. Ken Carlson says of Nora, "She was a Christian woman. She did not pressure anyone to follow the Lord, but her everyday living left no doubt in anyone's mind about her Christianity. She kept very close contact with *many* missionaries through the years Esther was growing up." There was also a deep faith abiding in most of the members of the extended Leander family that made a deep impression on the sensitive young girl.

From early childhood, Esther read her Bible nightly even if she had been outside playing all day. When she was only five she entered a church school contest in which a Bible was the prize. She memorized the names of all the books of the Bible, the Ten Commandments, the 23rd Psalm, and many other passages. Elsie Leafstedt describes the day of the contest. "She was five years old and stood up on the platform all alone and spoke it all very clearly and was not at all bashful and won the Bible."

But for some reason she didn't find what she was looking for in Aunt Nora's church. During 1929 and early 1930, when she was thirteen years old, she "shopped around" in almost all the churches in Sioux City before settling on Trinity Lutheran, across the street from "The Castle" where she would attend high school, and only a few blocks from Nora's apartment.

After seeing Esther in his church several Sundays running, Rev. Albert Schwertz came to call on her to see if she wanted to join. Her mother was very skeptical about letting her go, but Rev. Schwertz said with a smile, "We'll take good care of her, you don't need to worry." She was baptized at Trinity April 11, 1930 and confirmed April 20, 1930. Her mother took her downtown and had her straight but golden blonde hair marcelled for the occasion.

An exceptionally bright child, she had no trouble with lessons in school. At Central High School, a monstrous purplish-brown, stone-block building that for good reason was dubbed "The Castle," she excelled in everything but music. Outside school, she was active in Girl Scouts, loved camping, swimming and hiking.

There never seems to have been a time when she considered anything but nursing as a career. But first she took a year of general courses at the Methodist Morningside College. Her reasoning is not recorded, but in the light of her later academic achievements it is quite clear that Esther was intent on getting a broad education. Then she went into the Lutheran Hospital School of Nursing. Both schools were in Sioux City, the latter under the aegis of the Missouri Synod of the Lutheran Church at that time (and until 1956).

After graduating in 1937 she was employed for a very short time in the hospital of the little town of Hudson, seven miles north of Hawarden on the South Dakota side of the Big Sioux River. That didn't work out so she went back to Sioux City and got a nursing job there.

She remained content with Trinity Lutheran and would consider it her church home for the rest of her life. She went to first service on Sunday, even if she had been up all night at the hospital, then went out into the neighborhood and corralled as many kids as she could and took them to Sunday School. Then she went to the second service. Rev. Schwertz was still pastor and strongly reinforced Esther's inclination toward foreign mission service.

She joined a young ladies' circle called Mabel Dysinger's. Lucille Anderson, a member of that circle, now "83 years old and still hanging in there," recalls when Esther publicly dedicated her life to mission work: "Came time for a convention down at Des Moines.* It was the young people's group so our circle decided that we would go down. We got down there in time for the six o'clock banquet and we sat together. We were having

---

*Seventh Congress, Women's Missionary Society, October, 1940.

a good time. And then came the time in the program when they called up the people who were going to dedicate their service. And here we sat like this at the table and all at once comes Esther Bacon and never a word had she hinted to us. We sat there and she went down there...and she had her dedication and in a way we sponsored her.''

(3)

Both Anna Bacon and her sister Lizzie suffered from lung conditions. Eleanor Carlson remembers both of them coughing for years. Though tests for TB were negative, the condition was called consumption. In April of 1939 Anna's lung problem progressed to pneumonia and she died on the 23rd. She was 63, Esther 23. Esther continued to live with her Aunt Nora until she left for Liberia. Nora would remain in Sioux City until 1960 when she would retire and move up to Hawarden to be closer to the rest of the family.

Now it was time for Esther to prove herself. Her mother was dead. Her father was self-sufficient and would be well taken care of as he aged. Aunt Nora didn't need her now and would have family to help when she did. Yes, it was time to go.

She decided to let the Lord determine where she was most needed. She made contact with the United Lutheran Board of Foreign Missions in Baltimore. The Board scheduled her for China and brought her to Baltimore for several months training in the mission and deaconess schools. China excited her. The thought of living there, serving her Lord there, thrilled her. She read everything on China that she could get her hands on: encyclopedias, books, magazines, mission materials.

But the Japanese invaded China in 1939 and travel there became impossible. Disappointed but not dismayed, she continued her work in Sioux City, knowing that if the Lord closed one door, it was because He intended to open another. She could not know the reason at the time, but from the vantage point of the historian it is quite clear: she was needed in Liberia for a very specific task.

On May 1, 1941, the Board of Foreign Missions ''called and appointed'' Esther as a missionary to India. She wasted no time in accepting. She really didn't care where she went as long as it was in foreign missions. Her visa came. She bought her tickets and began packing trunks and boxes. She was ordained a missionary in a very moving service at Trinity by Rev. Schwertz who said, ''Esther Bacon will be fulfilling a double purpose, as a Christian missionary and as a registered nurse.''

She went down to Missouri to say goodbye to her father, who was now sixty-four. Their contacts apparently had been quite limited after she left the homestead. She had visited him only once or twice. He had come to see them once, a year or two after Anna and Esther had moved to Sioux City, probably with the idea of taking Esther back with him. Eleanor Raynie comments on this, "Esther's contact with her father was mostly in his later years. She would visit him in his nursing home to see that he was getting proper care. Their reunions meant much to both of them. He respected her work and was proud of her. After she led him to Christ she could go back to Monrovia with a burden lifted from her heart and a 'Thank You' to her God and his. She loved both her parents and did what she could for them."

Just days before she was due to leave for India, her visa was withdrawn with no explanation. This time her disappointment was deeper for she had been so sure that her call was for India. But again she went back to her job in Sioux City, resolved to wait patiently for God's will to become known to her.

In early October of 1941 she received a call to come to Baltimore if she would consider going to Liberia. This was on a Wednesday. On Thursday, in Baltimore, she listened to Dr. Moll, the Board Secretary, saying, "Liberia needs nurses desperately, especially up-country where there aren't any roads and living is extremely primitive. Will you go?"

"Of course," she answered, blue eyes sparkling, golden hair shining in the sun streaming in the window of the mission offices. "But it had better be quick. If we get in this war, and we're going to, there won't be any way to get there."

It was quick. Dr. Moll and another board member, Dr. Gerberding, held a commissioning service for her, and she left for Liberia from New York the following Monday.

Chapter Three

(January-October, 1942)

(1)

The three women and their train of porters, now reduced to thirty, swung down the slope, angled to the east, and entered the edge of Zorzortown. The porters, always happy, chanting, singing and chattering, showed their pleasure at being near the end of their trek. The women were all walking now, so the hammock-carriers danced and sang ahead of the load-carriers. The load-carriers themselves danced a shuffling two-step as well as they could with sixty-pound bundles on their heads.

Townspeople came out to meet them, shouting greetings, chanting, singing, and dancing. The women crowded around Gertrude Buschman with cries of welcome. When Esther and Frances Leonard were introduced as new nurses for the hospital, the women squealed with pleasure and began a round of finger-snapping handshakes.

(This custom, still universally used in Liberia, is done by shaking hands in the usual way, but then instead of releasing the hands, the two people slowly draw their hands apart, letting the middle fingers cling fast until each one's finger slides off the other's and strikes against his own palm with an audible snap. A pleasurable way of prolonging the greeting, it had been described as long ago as the 1880s by Rev. David Day, and even then its origin had been lost.)

The three women and their adulatory followers passed finally through the town. The palm-lined path now angled northwest toward the ridge that Mrs. Buschman had pointed out. On the left was a soccer field and then a small cemetery cut out of the jungle. Climbing steadily again, Esther could see ahead of her that the entire top of the hill was neatly landscaped and quite attractive.

On the right now was the cluster of five Boys' School buildings, arranged in a rough semicircle, all built of mud, wattle, and thatch. They stopped in front of a long, low, rectangular house of similar construction. "My house!" Buschy said, and directed her porters to drop their loads and wait for her return. Frances stopped with her porters at the nurses' dormitory, also a mud-and-wattle, thatched house.

Esther and Buschy went on past the Sadlers' house, down the very steep hill, across a long narrow causeway bridging a swamp choked with vegetation, and up the next low hill. Now on her right Esther could see the seven small, dark-brown, thatched buildings of the Zorzor Lutheran Hospital. But Buschy led her on a well-beaten path off to the left to the doctor's house, which Esther would occupy until a doctor came. Buschy left her there with the invitation to come for supper that evening.

"You'll be ready?" Esther asked.

"My cook is probably catching a chicken right now!"

Esther's porters stacked their loads in the front room as Esther inspected the house. It was a white-washed, five-room bungalow built of mud-and-wattle with a thatched roof, packed mud floors, four fireplaces, and a large veranda. Large sections of all four outside walls were made of wire screening and netting which allowed any vagrant breeze to flow through. Slatted bamboo curtains could be rolled down to give privacy at night and protection from the rains.

Esther, having lived first in a one-room sod house, then Nora Leander's tiny apartment, wrote Nora: "It is a regular mansion of a mud house! There are about a dozen goats, a sheep, two hogs, around. I also have a monkey and a cat, the latter to chase the rats, and likes roaches and spiders, too. So far health has been excellent, and we feel God's blessings have truly been many."

In the small kitchen there were sturdy chairs and a much-scarred table that she covered with a red-and-white checkered oilcloth. In the small cupboard she lovingly stacked a set of dishes she had bought in New York at Macy's the day before she sailed and had had to stow in cardboard boxes in the hold of the "Acadia." Not one was broken.

In the bedroom was a double bed, a chest of drawers and a small night stand on which she put the kerosene "farm" lantern she had bought in a small shop in Harrisburg. The living room contained two chairs, a crude and ancient sofa, and a small mahogany table on which she placed her Bible, hymn book, and textbooks. She had brought a kerosene pressure lamp from the States, which she at first was afraid to light but soon mastered. This she placed on the small table near the chair where she would sit at night to read and study.

That first evening she walked back over the causeway and up the hill to Gertrude Buschman's mud and thatch house on the Boys' School compound. Buschy's cook had indeed fixed a delicious chicken supper with fresh okra and long beans.

Buschy could hardly contain her joy at being back. Like Bertha Koenig, she was home. Later in the evening her pleasure was vindicated. Esther describes the scene:

"Into Mrs. Buschman's front room came Sonie, Mama Yama, Old Lady Wubu, and Mama Loupu. Faces beaming with gladness, they knelt prostrate before her and thanked and praised God for her return. What a greeting of welcome to a seasoned missionary, and proof that seed sown was fruitful!

"Would that you, Lutheran Women in America, might personally share in seeing and knowing some of the Liberian women here at Zorzor! As you walked about the town with its white-washed mud huts with thatched roofs, you could go in here and there and, by the light of the fire in the middle of the floor where the women are cooking, see their faces: some sad, others radiant with inner joy and peace that Christ alone can bring to hearts everywhere."

Esther would come to know these women well because they were the pillars upon which the Zorzor church was built. Mama Loupu had been a zo, a leader among her people in the old way. After conversion she discarded her medicine pots and came all the way in the Christian faith. She preached a vivid, fluent, and forceful message, in the hospital, in the church and out in the surrounding towns.

Old Lady Wubu, a good friend of the head zo, and mother of the town chief, spent her days visiting those in need with greens, beans, or an egg. She had known suffering but her face showed a deep joy.

Mama Yama was another of those faithful illiterate women who served the church council at Zorzor. Her sight was failing when Loma literature became available but she had that other Light.

Sonie, a little younger, was active in the growing Lutheran Church. When Loma literature appeared, she was eager to learn to read.

(2)

After a few days of unpacking and settling in to her little mud house, Esther set to work in the hospital with an energy that amazed everyone.

From the very first, she set no schedule for herself. She went from task to task, doing first what she considered most important. This would usually be the care of the most seriously ill patients. Then she would move on to something (or someone) else. She kept on until she was satisfied that everything was under control or until she dropped from exhaustion.

In later years she would draw criticism from fellow nurses for being "disorganized," for working irregular hours rather than adhering to the time-honored shifts, and for a host of other idiosyncrasies. But in those early years, as the only missionary nurse in a doctor-less hospital, she was free to work as she pleased.

She worked under the most primitive of conditions. The hospital was a row of seven small mud-and-wattle buildings and was very dark inside.* It was, Esther was told, only four years old. The original hospital up on the hill beside the cemetery had been struck by lightning and burned down in 1934. Relocation had been done in 1936 and 1937 by Dr. Norman Sloan and the newly-arrived "Skipper" Moore. (See Chapter 10 for further details of the medical work in Zorzor prior to 1941.)

The largest building was a fourteen-bed ward. The beds were of simply framed wood, with no springs or mattresses. The patients brought their own woven grass mats and blankets. The ward had a thatched roof that leaked during the rains and made the packed-dirt floor muddy and slippery. The nurses and aides moved the patients about so they wouldn't get wet.

Another task performed hurriedly by nurses and patients when Esther arrived was to scurry around and move everything off the floor or to the sides of the room. For Esther, intent on her rounds and looking only at her patients, would step on things in her way.

Other buildings housed a small drug supply room, a laboratory with an ancient microscope where stool and urine specimens were examined, a room which held two or three tuberculosis patients, and finally a small room used for the occasional patient who needed isolation or other kind of more private care.

The operating room was in a separate building constructed by Dr.

---

*It stood where the leprosy village Little Ganta is now located, a ten-minute walk through a palm-oil plantation from the present Curran Lutheran Hospital. All that is left of the original hospital is a low shapeless mound of mud.

Norman Sloan as a girls' school storehouse when Bertha Koenig was missionary-in-charge. The walls and roof were constructed of galvanized iron (called "zinc" locally, hence the name "zinc house" for this building). When the Medical Department took over the compound, Dr. Sloan installed an insulated ceiling but it was still extremely hot inside. Cupboards made of discarded kerosene cases held supplies. The operating table was an army folding model, not adjustable. A white sheet suspended from the ceiling over the table caught whatever dirt and insects might drop.

Esther would let the zinc house fall into disuse because she preferred to do her minor surgery on the main ward and didn't do any major cases.

Patients with chronic problems such as tropical sores were treated behind the hospital in "mud kitchens" — small huts with just a roof supported by poles, with no sides or just one. Local tax laws excluded wall-less structures so this was a common form of temporary construction.

(3)

She found that "Skipper" Moore had not exaggerated the situation: the vast majority of the local tribesmen shunned the Lutheran Hospital at Zorzor. Since 1928, five doctors (Erwing Lape, Norman Sloan, Jacob Jensen, George Guelk, and finally Dr. Moore) and many nurses had served at Zorzor. And none had been able to break down the barriers.

The power of the zoes was overwhelming. They threatened to withhold all help from any villager who even tried western medicine in preference to tribal medicine.

This was no idle threat. The people knew that they needed almost daily advice from their zoes in deciding the propitious time to plant, to marry, to go on a journey, to make their tools. They needed their zoes to bring rain, stop floods, prevent personal and societal catastrophes, make peace with the ancestors when they were angered, and a host of other things. In short, they needed their zoes for everything of importance in their lives. They could not afford to antagonize them.

The villagers actually needed little encouragement to stay away. They themselves were suspicious of anything new. The blood tests given the few children who came were reported as attempts by the missionaries to bleed the children to death. This was at a time when the mortality rate was almost 80% for children under the age of two.

Furthermore it was obvious to every villager that it was taboo for a **man** to aid a woman in labor, or to carry a hammock with a pregnant woman in it, for this would anger the ancestral spirits. Even after Esther had been in Zorzor for several years, two of her waiting obstetrical patients picked up their belongings and went home when Dr. Everett Veatch from Bolahun walked into the hospital on a visit.

Smallpox vaccination was often refused, one of the reasons being that yaws sometimes appeared at the site of the scarification.

Dr. Norman Sloan in the mid-30s had initiated the treatment of yaws with bismuth subgallate. This had cracked open the door a bit because the zoes admitted that they had no cure comparable to Sloan's "magic needle."

By the time Esther arrived in 1941, it was apparent that a divided scheme for medical care had begun to develop in the minds of the tribal people. There were "hospital" sicknesses: hernia and some other surgical conditions, intestinal worms, and yaws, all best treated by Western medicine. Then there were "country" sicknesses: epilepsy, mental illness, jaundice, and fractures, best treated by native medicine. (Dr. Paul Mertens, writing in 1974, says, "This dichotomy exists to the present, with additional illnesses being gradually shifted into the category of 'hospital' medicine.")

And there were some patients who defied their zoes. Enough that Esther and her three African nurses, Misses Walker, Leonard, and Brown, were kept busy. Two weeks after she arrived, a native evangelist's wife had her baby in the hospital. Two motherless babies came for admission. The Saturday well-baby clinic, which had grown slowly under the loving care of Dr. Moore, turned up 44 babies on the Saturday after Christmas.

The hospital inpatient census averaged about twenty in those first months. Almost all were those considered hopelessly incurable by the zoes, and, by implication, their ancestral spirits.

So for that first year, Esther treated mainly those cases who had been given up for dead. Many did die because they had incurable diseases such as cancer, far-advanced lung abscesses, tuberculosis, liver abscesses, tetanus, snake-bite, and yellow fever.

But some came with neck abscesses that could be drained, pneumonia that could be treated with sulfanilimide, leprosy that sometimes responded to injections of chaulmoogra oil twice a week, malaria that could be cured with quinine, cholera that could be treated with massive IV fluid infusion, blood-poisoning that could be treated by incision of the infection and hot packs and sulfanilimide, shistosomiasis that could be treated with tartar emetic, and of course the ubiquitous and endemic yaws that could be cured with bismuth.

Esther was faced with the law of inertia which states that a body at rest tends to remain at rest. What she needed to invoke was the other law of inertia which states that a body in motion tends to remain in motion. Change. The zoes were trying to be secure by stopping change. Esther knew that the most secure man is the one who recognizes that the world **is** insecure due to change.

(4)

But change ***would*** *come. Already the Kpelle people to the south were in the midst of a social unheaval which would forever change the tribe. The Loma people were being touched, too, but not to such a great extent. Not yet, but it would come. The Loma people would blame the breakdown of custom and tradition on* ***wui faa****, literally translated "foreign matters." Central government, Western education and culture, and Christianity were prime examples of* ***wui faa****.*

Later, construction of a bridge across the St. Paul River would open the flood gates for ***wui faa****, but many things were already changing even now:*

Some tribal iron workers, many of them zoes, had abandoned their smelters and were traveling to White Plains on the St. Paul River thirty miles from Monrovia, or to Firestone, to buy their iron.

Many women demanded ***kwii*** *clothes,* ***kwii*** *in Kpelle meaning anything of a sophisticated or foreign nature, typified by education and wealth, therefore exemplified by — but not limited to — whites.*

Women demanded iron pots to supplant the fragile clay pots which took so much time and labor to make.

Men sold rice, palm kernels, coffee and kola nuts to the German store in White Plains, and to traders in Salala and Toteta, initiating the first real cash economy the people had known. Firestone employed non-skilled workers, providing a cash income to young men who never before had had money to spend.

Soldiers now came regularly to interior villages from Monrovia and Salala to collect taxes, to buy rice, or to conscript men for portering, road-building and other labor. They needed lodging and food. They demanded entertainment such as liquor, dancing, and women.

The government-appointed District Commissioner had taken over the most serious disputes and criminal cases.

Men no longer fought wars over a kidnapped woman or the boundaries of a farm. Most of the chiefs and older men were glad that the burning villages and dying young men were a thing of the past.

Slavery was officially abolished.

What had not yet even begun to change was the total dependence of pregnant women on the zoes and village midwives. The way Esther Bacon set about to deal with these ancient strictures is what this book is all about. Roslyn Sadler says that Esther did not start "upcountry with her chin jutting to tackle the zoes." But it was her handling of a problem never before solved that literally turned Kpelle-Loma-land upside down and made Esther Bacon a legend in her own time and for all time.

(5)

Very early in that first year Esther recognized a problem that she would battle for thirty years: motherless babies. Most were newborns whose mothers had died in childbirth. Others were one of a pair of twins left to die because of inadequate milk or a tribal taboo. Some were toddlers who had lost their mothers through disease or accident.

A common misconception is that the "extended family" system in Africa obviates the problem of motherless babies. Not in Liberia. Margaret Miller explains: "If you live in a subsistence economy, there's no margin for anything. So no matter how willing a person may be, there's no slack to take up an extra obligation. Somebody has to extend himself to do it."

That somebody was Esther Bacon. She took them all. She could not forget the many times in her own childhood when she had felt abandoned, her father gone and her mother nervously wringing her hands in despair. She could not let these babies die just because they had no mother.

So she tackled this problem as she had all the others in her life: a straight-forward frontal attack with no subterfuge or apologies, an attack fueled by compassion, pity, outrage — and most of all, by Christian love.

It was a pattern of selflessly motivated action that would awe presidents and pastors and tribal people, that would confound and astound other nurses and doctors who would have to admit that they could never be like Esther.

A typical example was what happened on her first Easter morning in Africa. She saw a few of the sickest patients at the hospital early, then had the entire station in for breakfast at 7:30. She used a sheet for a tablecloth and Sammy, her boys' school helper, gathered fresh flowers and put them in a tin can on the table. The breakfast was interrupted first by a note from Wes Sadler that some more schoolboys had chicken pox. Then a baby boy arrived on the back of a little girl, probably his sister, with a note saying that his mother had been dead for a week and there was no one to take care of him.

Esther took the starving infant in her arms immediately and fed it bananas and milk from her own plate. This made a total of six she had in the house. (Later she named him Zizzi, and would keep him in her home for years until a home was found.)

(She did get to Easter service that morning and described the service as "lovely." The previous week the church women had freshly rubbed the church with white chalk mud and the day before filled it with fresh flowers and ferns. The service was in Loma, led by David Harris, the native evangelist from Fisebu. Esther lamented that she still didn't "hear" it well, but said, "These people surely can sing praises to their Lord!" Earlier she had written to Nora, "One of the first songs I heard sung in

Buzi was 'Lord, Lord, Lord, You've surely been good to me.' It aptly expresses the truth.'')

She took these tiny orphans into her own home for days or weeks until they could be moved to the hospital. She asked Roslyn Sadler to work with the carpenters to build little screened cribs on stilt legs. The legs were put into tins of water or kerosene so that ants and other crawly creatures couldn't climb up. The little orphans were then taken care of much as they would be in the States: bottle feedings, clean sheets, frequent baths and change of diapers, sterile conditions for handling the umbilical cords, and so forth.

But no matter what she did, they died.

Slowly the cause and the solution grew apparent. The babies were being handled *too* aseptically and without enough TLC. Esther began to insist that someone from the family accompany the child to the hospital: grandmother, aunt, older sister. The caregiver was taught how to sterilize the nipple and bottle. She carried the child on her back and let it sleep with her. In fact, she would treat it as it would be treated in the village with the addition of Esther's advice, medicine, and love.

And those babies thrived. Many, when they reached toddler age and could eat solids, returned to their home villages under the care of the relative who had been "trained" by Esther.

But right from the beginning she had problems finding enough milk for her young charges. Powdered milk would not be available until after the war. Imported condensed milk was very expensive. Cows, a sign of wealth — a walking bank account — were rarely butchered until they died a natural death, and, most importantly for Esther, were never milked because that would be taking milk from their calves.

So Esther bought a cow with a nursing calf. The cow reasoned the way the Africans did: her calf should get all her milk. The cow began hiding her calf in the forest by covering it with grass. Esther wrote, "I wish someone would write and find out how Carnation makes contented cows! First time, bucket and I went over a couple of times, next time a few spoons of milk, but the bucket went over, next time Sammy got a good kick in the shoulder but we did get a few ounces of milk."

She admitted her failure and sent the cow back.

She tried to get village mothers with living babies to nurse the orphans, but the women were absolutely horrified. One mother summed up their fears, "If I do that, the spirit of the dead mother will cause my child to lose his appetite and die so that the motherless child will get all the milk."

Esther's response when she first heard of this: "You might just as well scrape a star and use its dust to light a house."

The next step was to offer to pay the mothers to allow their breasts to be mechanically pumped. At first even that was refused. Finally, however, a Christian mother relented and allowed her breasts to be pumped. All the women watched carefully for problems to ensue. None did. The surrogate mother and the motherless baby both did well. Another near-term mother allowed her breasts to be pumped. And then another.

Esther fortified the babies' diet with a daily teaspoon of palm wine because it was high in Vitamin B. When she didn't have milk, she improvised a substitute out of bananas, peanuts, and orange juice.

So now Esther had food for her babies. But how to keep the newborns warm? Roslyn Sadler helped her devise incubators out of two tubs of different sizes. They put water in the bigger one and floated the other in it. Then around it they stacked hot bricks heated in an open fire right on the ward.

Roslyn, still childless until the latter part of Esther's first term, was of inestimable help at the hospital, in the gardens, at church, everywhere where she could be of assistsance. Another of her very practical contributions, used by Esther for years, was a wooden goat-milking stand. With the stand, Esther found that goats were much more manageable than cows. And sometimes the goats' milk was the difference between life and death for Esther's babies.

(6)

Gradually Esther began to be recognized as someone who had more powerful magic for some illnesses than the tribal zoes. Babies were living who should have died. Adults who would have died in the villages were walking home from the Zorzor hospital. The children of Liberian Christians rarely died because those teachers, nurses, evangelists and pastors heeded the advice of Esther and the other nurses at the hospital.

The villagers saw all this and marvelled. The zoes saw all this and had to admit that the foreigner in white had some secrets they didn't know.

Esther thought she could sense a subtle change, and prayed that she was not deluded by wishful thinking. Then a little girl named Dedi proved that she was indeed making progress.

Dedi was isolated in a Sande Society bush school with all the young girls from Fisebu, a village five miles north of Zorzor. She and others became very ill with dysentery and many died.

No man or other non-member of the women's society may see the girls until the Bush school is completed. For this reason they are not often brought to the hospital for care in the event of illness. But since Dedi's case seemed hopeless, the zoes agreed to let her people bring her in.

Esther describes what happened: "Her face looked sad and serious. She was very weak, and turned on the bed only when her grandmother aided her. It was difficult for her to take needed food. After several weeks of treatment, her condition showed improvement.

"Sometimes a girl from the Zorzor Christian School would drop in to visit her. She was encouraged to believe that she could get well.

"While still very thin she was given a little muslin dress with print trim. It was the first dress that she had had, and a little large. She laughed when she was told that she was supposed to get fat and grow into it.

"Just before she left the hospital she visited the Girls' School and said that she would like very much to come back there. The last time she visited the hospital she had improved so much and looked so well that we hardly recognized her. We hope she may enter school."

This was an unprecedented break in the rhythms of the high forest. Never before had a child been taken out of the Sande bush school for any reason other than death. Many years later when Esther had fully established herself in Loma-land, she would actually be taken into a bush school to minister to a small child, the first white person ever to do so. She would never talk about what she saw and did there: she respected the proscription against revealing any secrets she wasn't supposed to know.

What made the zoes accept this young white nurse in a way they never had accepted anyone before?

After all, Esther Bacon was merely continuing the work of the doctors and nurses before her. But there was an indefinable something else. There was a charisma about her, a force emanating from her, a radiance of love and compassion, which though present in her predecessors had not been so glowingly evident.

Edith Curran puts her finger on another reason. She says, "The women at first were afraid to reveal their secrets to her. But she had learned all about the human feeling and sometimes she would see from the expression on their face what they were worried about. Most of their problems were worry and most of them were not happy because of the worry."

Roslyn Sadler echoes this, "It was Esther's sort of inbuilt understanding of people that began to make such a change."

Perhaps the key word is *love*. She loved her adopted people. They could feel it. In her quiet, undemanding way her obvious love fostered *trust*. In adults, of course, but even more so in children. Children, quick to sense the emotions of their elders, know when they are loved, and they knew that Esther Bacon loved them. Wes Sadler says of her way with children, "She had the ability to combine tenderness and utility when she was holding a small patient."

(7)

The hospital began to fill up with more and more cases that weren't considered hopeless by the zoes.

Still she wasn't satisfied. She knew that many of the newborns dying in the forest villages died of infection, especially tetanus, and did not need to die. During delivery, or soon after, their mothers died of blood loss, infection, retained placentas, dehydration, and contracted pelves. They also did not need to die.

What to do?

The solution was as simple as it was iconoclastic. One day she said to Frances Leonard, "If the mountain won't come to Mohammed, Mohammed must go to the mountain." Leaving Frances in charge at the hospital, Esther took an interpreter with her and began almost daily walks into the forest villages. She went to Zolowo, Yella, Salayea, Faala, Gbalein, Sukolomu, Konia, Mwe, Fisebu, Kiliwu and even across the border into French Equatorial Africa (now called Guinea). Irene Morris, a Liberian nurse-midwife who became co-chief of the obstetrics ward in 1972, says, "There weren't *any* towns she didn't go to."

In the villages she talked with the women. From personal experience and from listening to others, Esther knew that the women were even more resistant to change than the men, for they felt greater responsibility to their culture and heritage. In a short monograph by Wesley Sadler about Esther in those early days, he writes of this very problem: "The women are, in many respects, the custodians of the Loma and Kpelle way of life, a way which they consider satisfactory, even ideal, and which they are loathe to leave. The people are quick to give their smiles to the outsider, the foreigner from Europe or America, and they will share a pleasantry with the slightest encouragement. But their loyalty and their acceptance of the outsider must be won with values which they can appreciate and understand."

The forest people, especially the women, lived in complete isolation. There was no contact with the outside world. The paths leading away from their home village simply led to other rice farms or other villages just like their own. In many villages Esther was the first white woman they had ever seen.

They greeted her warmly, as Wes Sadler had predicted they would. They offered her food and drink and a cool place to sit. From the first she was at ease in the kind of situation that would be very uncomfortable for most people. Ingenuously she sat on a low stool or a mat on the low buttressing wall of the house. She held the babies, teased the children, scratched the dogs' ears, sipped the palm wine offered by the women.

With a farm girl's curiosity, though she'd not lived on a farm since she was six, she asked intelligent questions about the growing of crops and fruit. She asked them to show her how they preserved their foods and cooked their meat.

She watched the men making a new field by slashing down the forest trees and underbrush, then burning it off while chanting, "Faa, vaa na be!" "Wind, come for me." She heard the women singing, "A de mama!", loosely translated, "Right on, girls!", as they planted grain and vegetables.

She learned a bit of Loma psychology one day: "Sheep are smart, they don't move out of the way so you must go around them; goats are dumb, they get out of your way." She wasn't quite sure how that applied to humans, especially in a motorized society, but it was fun to ponder the conundrum.

She also heard the proverb, "A deceiver has white teeth," and wondered if that meant *she* shouldn't smile too much!

But she was particularly interested in the customs and practices having to do with the birth of a baby. They told her that when a baby is born, the midwife dances up to the father of a newborn child with her hands full of green leaves. If the child is a boy, the father gives her a white kola nut; if twin boys, two white kola nuts. On the fourth day after birth, the child is shown to all the other mothers. The father then brings a goat, or five chickens, or perhaps palm wine, to the midwife.

And Esther learned other things by observation. She saw that during the cold, dry season the people lived indoors until the cold eased. Then as the land warmed they began to beat their drums and dance and sing the old songs. It was time to rethatch their houses, repair the fences and looms and chicken coops, gather palm leaves to weave into mats, make soda and soap from the forest plants, comb the seeds from cotton and spin it into thread to be woven into cloth for new clothes, to repair their nets and traps, to make pots and other containers for cooking and storage. It was time for the blacksmiths to make cutlasses, hoes, axes, and knives.

She learned that the forest was the sustainer of life for these people. It furnished roots, vines, trees and shrubs. It was home to the animals that the people depended on for meat, hides, bones, sinews, and feathers. But also in the forest lived spirits which trap men: genii, dwarfs, stick people, evil ancestors who had not received proper burial, witches, and above all, the Big Forest Thing, known only to members of the Poro Society.

Many things were only hinted at. To flesh them out she had to go to other sources, such as written material and oldtime missionaries like Bertha Koenig and Gertrude Buschman. She learned that the Loma and Kpelle people (and indeed, many other West African tribes) believed that a man has three souls. There is the "conscious soul," which is the normal person as Westerners perceive him. There is the "dream soul," which is what is left when a person is insane or unconscious. And there is a "third soul" which departs the body with its last breath. Each soul is as real, and as important, as the others. As a person dies, the Africans watch each soul depart, knowing that any of them can come back, so therefore the body must not be disposed of too fast.

Esther learned that when a person dies, his spirit goes to the mountain where all his ancestors live. Every year the important men from each family group go to their own sacred mountain to make sacrifices and to request protection. A special sacrifice can be made to mountain spirits for many problems: illness, weakness, cuts, stillbirths, incest, abnormal behavior, poor taxes — and the spirit will come down to the town and kill or harm the responsible person. Sometimes the spirit will come without being called in order to revenge itself.

Esther read Bertha Koenig's story of the Juju man in *Lutheran Women's Work*. Bertha put into words what Esther was already beginning to understand, that "the African's mind does not seek an explanation for seemingly miraculous things, but *believes* in the supernatural. His mind is a weird and strange world, and his beliefs may well be likened to the jungles of his country." But Esther also believed as Bertha did, that "as the weird and mystic noises of the night forest vanish with the break of day, so will the gospel light transform the animistic nature of the African."

(8)

So as she sat with the women in the villages she listened, she watched, and she taught. She talked to them of cleanliness in deliveries in order to avoid postpartum infection and tetanus. She showed them how to sterilize large banana leaves by holding them over the fire before putting them under the laboring women. She showed them how to minimize the risk of tetanus by sterilizing their knives before cutting the umbilical cords, and by stopping the prevalent practice of just laying the knives on the floors which had been "waxed" with a mud and cow-dung mixture. In the very first house she went into, she saw a dirty knife lying on the floor and she told them right away that you don't do this. "She was teaching, always teaching," Louise Faust says, "and what she taught were the principles of asepsis, antisepsis, and public health."

And always, before she left, she urged the women to come to the hospital to deliver their babies in order to get the best possible care if they had complications. If they could not come to her she would come to them. "Just send someone for me," she said, "I'll come."

At first she seemed to be getting nowhere. Still the women did not come to the hospital to have their babies, nor did they call for her to come to them. Still they feared the power of the zoes. Still their husbands refused to let them go to Zorzor because of *their* fear of the zoes. They knew, despite what Esther Bacon said, that there is never a non-personal cause for illness. Illness is always due to the ill will of some person who pays a zo to make magic medicine to victimize another person. Furthermore there was great skepticism about the knowledge Esther could have about delivering babies when she herself had never delivered a child of her own.

But friends of Esther's in the villages told her that some of the midwives were starting to use the techniques that Esther had taught them. They saw that their children were not dying as they had before. The word spread.

Few came to the hospital to deliver, but Esther was not discouraged. She was confident that someday someone would come, or perhaps someday someone would send for her to come to a village. She knew she was on the right track.

She must keep up her own enthusiasm. That was no problem. She had plenty of that.

She must keep praying that the Lord would speak through her to the women of the villages. That was no problem, either: she had her faith, the same faith that all missionaries had and which Roslyn Sadler called a "life-on-the-frontier faith." Esther knew that eventually God would open the ears of these women and they would listen to her message.

In the darkness of the night, she sat in the soft glow of the kerosene lantern and read her Bible. Outside, the jungle was alive with sounds of nightbirds. The singing of frogs and crickets in the swamps was sometimes so loud that conversation with her occasional visitors had to be carried on with raised voices. She sometimes sang to herself from her hymnal. She copied out the key verses of one of her favorites and sang it over and over:

> Take my life and let it be consecrated
> Lord to thee
> Take my moments and my days
> Let them flow in ceasless (sic) praise.

> Take my hands and let them move
> at the impulse of thy love
> Take my feet and let them be
> Swift and beautiful for thee

Take my voice and let me sing
always only for my king
Take my lips and let them be
filled with messages from thee

(9)

Although the work at the hospital, in the villages, and with her orphans took up most of Esther's time, it was not her whole life. A hundred and one things needed doing every day just to live in a primitive, alien culture. For that she needed help.

In the States a machine did her laundry, a stove cooked her food, a furnace heated her house. In Africa, without help, just living would be a fulltime job. She was there to be a nurse, not a fulltime housekeeper. "Besides," Buschy told her, "your workers can use the money."

So she had a cook, Helen Howard, who "came with the house," for she had worked for Dr. and Mrs. Moore. Helen had two little girls, Etta and Rose, who often played in the kitchen where their mother could watch them.

Esther had three sources of food. She ordered case lots of canned goods through the Mission Board every four to six months. Helen Howard went weekly to the open market in Zorzor. And people came by the house with eggs, chickens, sweet potatoes, potato leaves, tiny onions, and occasionally other foodstuffs, and hunters brought meat at times. There was no refrigeration, so fresh produce was scarce.

Esther loved to cook. Fran Brouse, a missionary nurse who would live with Esther some years later, says, "She was a good cook and she cooked like she worked. The menu was non-stop. She made some of the unusuals for Africa, such as cream puffs and ice cream." The ice cream, of course, would be after refrigeration came to Zorzor.*

Esther loved to browse with Helen in the market, tasting everything, at first asking what this or that was, then finally deciding that the last thing she wanted to know was what she was eating. The market wasn't as big as the one at Salala, where the truck had dropped them, but it had the same foodstuffs: peanuts and vegetables and fruits, dried meats of forest animals, chickens hanging live from posts. Bananas were 10¢ for an entire stalk of 50-100, peanuts 60¢ a tub.

---

*Her skills apparently deteriorated in later years. Jeanette Kpissay, who would come to Zorzor in 1966, says, "She was an awful cook because she didn't have time to cook. Her idea of a good meal was breaded tomatoes...or rice and gravy." Deanna Isaacson, who came with Jeanette, agrees: "Sometimes she just ate tomatoes right out of the can, and that might be her whole meal!"

Two school boys, Sammy and Willie, came before and after school to fetch firewood from the forest, water from the well, and matches, salt, and a few other things from the verandas of Mandingo traders in the village. They swept down the mud floors, filled lanterns, brushed cobwebs out of the corners, dusted tables, carried out the garbage for the chickens and goats, and did any other odd jobs that Esther or Helen could find for them. Outside they swept down the paths with a handful of twigs tied together, then cut the grass with their cutlasses to discourage snakes from crawling out of the jungle into the yard or house.

The boys also helped her with raising chickens and tending a garden. She tried to grow cucumbers but not a seed sprouted. She tried raising tomatoes and they did very poorly. But she found a half dozen plants growing in the trash pile behind the hospital and had fresh tomatoes for several weeks. Aunt Nora sent her packages of seeds, all of which she tried, and succeeded with beans, greens, and potatoes.

Flumo Molee came from the village to do laundry once or twice a week in a big tub filled with hot water from the kitchen. Yarpazua "mothered" the goats and other livestock as Esther accumulated it.

Within two months of arriving in Zorzor, Esther had a houseful of animals. Her first cat died ("too many rats, I guess," Esther said) so she got another, which was a bit wild and hid under the bed until the lights went out. She had a toad in the bathroom and cockroaches that ate paper and rayon clothes. In the marsh that surrounded the compound on three sides were millions of tadpoles, all of which she claimed as pets. Roaming the mission compound were nineteen goats, a sheep, and three pigs, which she also claimed. One goat delivered triplets just outside the maternity department, which Esther duly noted as being very clever. Later when Roslyn Sadler obtained two horses, Esther rode them both.

One night she had a special pet. A motherless baby arrived with a pan of "nice juicy larvae that grow on palm wine trees to feed it. They say the baby likes them plenty. The larvae are about two inches long, very soft, and fat, and look something like grub worms. They cut off the worm's head, and the baby sucks out the stuffins! The boys around here tell me they are very sweet. Mothers often feed them to their babies when they cry in the night, it seems. I had fun playing with one last night and feeding it spaghetti — really it looks kind of good, maybe."

She learned that a particular delicacy were the termites that swarmed by the thousands after the first rain. The women and girls collected them, dumped them into a hot pot to parch, then placed them on a rice fanner (usually a tightly woven grass tray) to winnow off the wings, and ate them with great relish by the handsful like popcorn.

Esther was already beginning to use some characteristic Liberian words and phrases, as in "the baby likes them plenty," and "thank you plenty." "Plenty" is used by Liberians to replace much, lots of, many, and sometimes very. "Very" may also be replaced by "too," as in "She likes bananas too much," or "The bird was too pretty." In the palm grub story she may have been using "sweet" in the Liberian sense of "delicious."

At first she was distressed by the "mis-use" of English. Then, through the wise words of Wes Sadler, she realized that Liberian English was not "wrong," just different, like the difference between American and British English. But she still thought some of it was funny, as for example some of the nurses' notes:

> "Pt. is allergic to a type of bird called Porwu in Lorma. This bird live in a swamp with a thin legs."
>
> "His father has two permanent wives and four extra outside wives that produced the twenty-six children for him."
>
> "The home is turn loose and not well care of because the father is an excessive drunker."
>
> "Pt. took country meds, no better result from those Rx, so decided to come in Hosp. here."

(10)

Word came in early January that Dr. and Mrs. Moore and Dr. and Mrs. Flexman had all sailed for home on Dec. 24th. Now Pauline Ziegler at Phebe also would be working without a doctor. Nor were there signs of any doctors coming out, although Esther was hopeful that one would soon join her. She was to be disappointed, for the first physician, Dr. Earl Reber, would not arrive until late 1946 and would not see his first patients until January 1st, 1947.

The closest physician who would come to Zorzor was Dr. Everett Veatch, a former Methodist missionary, stationed at Bolahun, a hundred miles northwest of Zorzor, four days walk through the forest. Dr. Veatch was now a researcher for Firestone, based temporarily at the Episcopal Church's Order of the Holy Cross Hospital*, close to the border with Sierra Leone where there was an outbreak of sleeping sickness. Esther first met him when he came to Zorzor for a week in April of 1942 and examined a total of 530 people, which shocked the entire station and must have sent ripples into the villages as well.

---

*A monastic order of the American Episcopal Church. In 1941 it was staffed by a German doctor, English nuns, and American fathers.

(11)

Though Esther lived alone, it was not a lonely life. She wrote to Nora, "I hope you are not lonely. I haven't time to be, and the people here wouldn't let one be lonely if he tried!"

Guests frequently dropped in: the Sadlers, Buschy, Bertha Koenig from Kpaiye, her Liberian nurses Brown, Leonard, and Walker. Pauline Ziegler and four other nurses came to Zorzor on vacation for a month. They weren't supposed to do any work but they cheated a little and helped out when things were especially busy, such as the time eight men fell through a high bridge and were brought in with an assortment of lacerations, contusions and fractures.

On her 26th birthday she came home from the hospital to find the Sadlers, Buschy, and her three Liberian nurses, all waiting with supper ready. Buschy had brought some hard-to-find cheese and Roslyn had made a big cake.

Bertha Keonig sent notes up from Kpaiye asking Esther to come down. Finally, one weekend she walked down, a distance of eight miles, in about two hours. She had as her guide young Tokpah Roberts whose home village was Kpaiye and now worked in the Sadlers' house.*

Up and down the steep ridges, through dense forest and soggy swamps, Tokpah led her almost to the border of French territory. In the few places where the forest did not crowd in around her she could see the mountains of French Equatorial Africa ahead and to her left. Then they dropped down one last ridge, waded a clear trickling stream, and climbed a low hill to the mud-and-thatch village. Bertha's thatched, stake-and-mud house was just twenty-five feet from the small church on the edge of the village.

She found that "Ma" Koenig also took in motherless babies and had five in her home that weekend. With a laugh and a disparaging wave of her hand, Bertha said, "That doesn't begin to compare with the ten or more that Kirsten Jensen usually has in her house in Sanoyea."

In the course of the very pleasant and all too short weekend, Bertha told her about a special young girl with a problem that Esther might help with. The girl's name was Edith Curran.

"Her native name is Nawenan, or something like that, I could never get it spelt properly in English, means 'father-love' in Loma. But she took

*Author's note: Mr. Roberts still lives in Kpaiye where I interviewed him in 1989. He was eager to share his memories of those early years and was prompted by Mr. John Sumo who worked for Rev. Harvey Currens in the church house in Monrovia in the 40s.

old Mrs. Curran's* name when she went to school."

Edith had lost a leg at age five or six, in 1934, when a tree fell on her. She was taken to the Zorzor Lutheran Hospital where Drs. Sloan and Jensen amputated the leg to save her life, over the objections of the family. When she recovered, the family would not take her back because they claimed she would be unfit for village society and they didn't want to see her suffer.

So the church took her in and sent her to school, something she had longed for all her short life but had been denied by her father.

Now she was ready to go on for higher education. "Esther," Bertha said, "she wants to be a nurse. But everyone tells her 'you can't be a nurse because nursing requires fast moving and you've got to be on your feet all day.' She's still on crutches. There's been no way to get her a wooden leg. What do you think?"

"I've got to see her."

She did, a month later. Edith came to the clinic and Esther talked with her and examined her.

Edith says now with a great sigh and then a big smile, "And so Miss Bacon say, 'No problem. You can do anything any other two-legged person would do. You just got to be determined.' " She was determined, she did become a nurse and would work at the Zorzor hospital most of her professional life.

Esther's relationship with Wes and Roslyn Sadler continued to grow. They were about her age, a very handsome young couple, and lived just a few minutes away in the new house that Rev. George Flora had finished just before going home on furlough. It had one of the two corrugated ("zinc") roofs in the interior — the other was the operating room. Wes was very busy with the Zorzor church, visitations in the surrounding villages, the boys' school on the mission compound, the girls' school at Kpaiye, and with the study of the Loma language.

Wes shared with Esther a dislike of hammock-riding. To avoid them and still reach his villages, he had three alternatives: leave late in the afternoon and stay overnight in the village, leave early in the morning and come back late in the afternoon, or use a horse. He preferred the latter and since Roslyn had ridden since she was five and had riding clothes with her, he depended on her horse sense to find one.

---

*Sarah Curran, longtime missionary in Zorzor. Wife of Rev. J.D. Curran who drowned at Muhlenburg in 1930. She died in 1937 and is buried in the Zorzor cemetery where her gravestone can still be seen. She left $12,000 dollars with which to rebuild the hospital. When this was done in 1948, it was renamed Curran Memorial Hospital. A few years ago it was changed to Curran Lutheran Hospital.

The first horse shown to Roslyn was a skinny brown horse, probably two years old. His body growth had not yet caught up with his head. She turned him down. Then she was shown two other skinny horses with ticks all over them. She bought one, rented the other, rubbed them down, picked off the ticks, fattened them up, and named them Gracious and Hefty.

She and Wes started using them to go to the villages and until their first child was born 2½ years later they often rode together. Roslyn says, "This gave me a view of village life I loved and made it possible for me to move from 'the little America' of mission compound life to life *among* the people with Wes and our children, which was unheard of at the time and frowned on by some."

Wes and Roslyn had begun a serious study of Loma. They had come out to Africa with a feeling that they must know it. The longer they lived in Zorzor conversing through interpreters, the more awkward it seemed. Roslyn said, "It was like living with a glass wall between us and the people."

By 1948 Wes's study would reduce Loma to written form, which had never been done before. He would then produce a Loma grammar, First and Second Readers, a Book of Fables, the Story of Jesus, numerous pamphlets, translations of the Gospel of Mark, the Common Service Book and Hymnal.

This was just a beginning, but it would open the doors to all kinds of progress in native literacy, missionary language study, Bible and hymn translation. He even took the old Loma songs that were used in tribal dances and put Christian words to them. He was one of the new breed of missionaries who wanted to preserve everything good in the native culture and use it if he could.

Esther, too, was concerned by her inability to understand the language, and bothered by her dependence on interpreters. This was in 1941 before Wes Sadler had written his teaching grammar for Loma and Dr. William Welmers his Kpelle grammar. It was before linguist Dr. Frank Laubach stirred worldwide interest in literacy with his "Each one teach one" program.

There was no language school, no handy "Teach Yourself Kpelle and Loma" booklets. So it was a matter of "picking up the language," or not learning it at all. It would be another seventeen years, 1958, before Fran Brouse would become the first missionary nurse to take a full-fledged language study; this would be at the deep-forest village of Wozi, about twelve miles from Zorzor, under the tutelage of Margaret Miller, one of James's and Miriam's daughters.

For several years Esther chastised herself for not making a decent study of the language. She did eventually get the flow and the fluency, and learned to communicate with the people, but Margaret says she never really mastered the grammatical constructions that would have made a tremendous difference in "cleaning up" her Loma and Kpelle.

(12)

Both the Sadlers developed a deep love and respect for Esther Bacon. They watched her with frustration, wanting so badly to help this young and inexperienced missionary, but not knowing exactly how.

Wes Sadler, in recalling those years when he and Roslyn lived so close to Esther and her work, says, "She could respond to only one rule, the rule of her genius, a rare one, stalwart and beautiful: the genius of her love."

He illustrates this with a series of conversations he had with her over a period of three years.

"Get some sleep. You're out on your feet."
"Yes, I am. But I'll see this child first, the one they just brought in."

"You're crying. What's the matter?"
"I'm not, really. Just tears. The baby — you know, the one I brought in from the village — he just died."

"What's all the anger about?"
"That zo — that medicine man! I told him twice: 'Use a clean knife when you circumcise — burn it in a flame.' But he didn't. He has cut three more. They're infected, maybe crippled for life."

"We're waiting dinner for you."
"Yes, I know. I'm sorry. I'm coming, but not now. The woman's still in labor."

"Look at your uniform!"
"It **is** dirty, isn't it? I'll change it later. I slept on the floor by Folomo's bed last night in case the pain came back, and I'll be there again tonight."

"What's the lantern for?"
"She sent for me, the woman who was here last year. She lost her baby, remember? She's pregnant again and in premature labor — for two days. If I'm not back tomorrow, send me some drinking water, please."

"Can't you stay? You just got here. It's dark and raining."

"I know, but I must go back. The path will still be open. I can walk it in three hours. A runner just brought this letter to me. A man fell from his palm tree. He hit the spikes on the way down. He'll need extra care. But thanks for inviting me for the weekend."

"I keep telling you, you can't give all your clothes away."

"You're right. But I have all I need: this dress, these shoes. And I have a sheet for my bed."

"Who told all these men to come into this operating room?"

"I don't know. They won't go away. This man on the table is their friend. They just brought him in. It was a hunting accident. You can see the arrow imbedded in his arm. Someone told him that there's a woman at the hospital who can take it out without hurting him. I'm that woman, I guess. They want to see. I can do it. But I wish we had a doctor here."

(13)

But even in this committed life, there came times when she had to "get away from it all." She was a *very* private person. Her favorite means of escape was to walk into the forest, sometimes for an hour, sometimes for a day or two.

One weekend she walked the twelve miles to Wozi in four hours and described the hundreds of wild orchids along the path, as well as the forget-me-nots and ferns and other flora growing wild. Near the mission house in Wozi she found "orange trees, full of fragrant bloom, a bittersweet tree loaded with fruit," and, not far from the station, on the Via River, a tributary of the St. Paul, "water rushing over the rocks, old logs bedecked with new growths far more lovely than any florist's creation. Things here seem to agree with me, and my heart is happy."

There is no doubt that she was contented. Dreams which had filled her days and nights for twenty-five years had come true. She knew that she was one of the fortunate few who were doing what they wanted to do and at the same time doing what God wanted them to do. She felt blessed with a "peace that passeth all understanding."

Many of her letters in that first year reflect this:

"I love it here, better than any place I've been. Of course there are many things that make one's heart ache, but yet life here is so brimful of happy incidents, and it seems natural to be here. I like the climate, too."

"When there have been problems and patients, prayer has always helped us through. It is surprising what being in such situations as this does for us."

"No planes, cars, trains, etc., but we may see electricity in our day here. However, I love it the way it is, people around their fires, beauty of flowers, trees, mountains, sky, mud house, and all."

After hearing the first rumors about probable evacuation of all missionaries from Liberia: "So far, this still seems the most peaceful spot on earth. I feel a security and peace greater than I have ever felt before. So far, we do not see that God has just called and sent us here, then would recall when workers are needed. And He surely did place us here!"

"Enjoying the work plenty."

"There is no lovelier spot to be than Zorzor. You'd love the people here, too."

"The sun, rosy and round that came up over the misty blue mountains, was especially lovely this morning. The rays were like a cross, different than I had noticed before..."

While waiting for Sunday evening services to begin: "Again, it is evening. Silence pervades the countryside. The village church is peacefully surrounded by the sleeping cattle, goats, and sheep, when the church bell rings. Then one must not tarry if one wants a seat, for soon the women with babies on their backs will have their side filled. The children sit on the floor in front if there are not enough benches.* The singing and service is in Buzi. How all seem to enjoy it with serious joy!"

(14)

The Zorzor mission station had been founded in 1923, only eighteen years before Esther's arrival, and was therefore in its infancy. But there was already a solid core of believers and an organized ministry.

---

*Author's note: In all African churches I have attended, the men sit on one side with the grown boys, while the women sit on the other side with the babies and small children. The missionaries usually sit with the men because there is more room there! Apparently Esther sat on the women's side.

Not for a moment did Esther forget that she was not only a nurse but a Christian missionary. She had a responsibility to be a witness to her faith on the station and in the local church as well as in her work. Unless she was tied up in the hospital, she attended the regular church services on Thursday and Sunday evenings as well as the Sunday morning service. Although the services were in Loma, she enjoyed the ambience, the fellowship, the worship, and the singing.

She was disturbed by the fact that only small portions of the scriptures had been translated and written down.

Sometimes she was amazed at how much scripture the native Christians knew by heart. She wrote, "Many a Bible verse has new meaning in a more literal setting out here. I wish the people had the Bible in their own language, it should solve many of the problems of the Christians here."

Gertrude Buschman held a Bible study class in the village church on Tuesday. The Liberian Christian workers met for prayers every Wednesday evening. Esther usually skipped these because she didn't understand Loma and didn't want to disrupt their meetings by asking for translations.

She very much agreed with Wes Sadler that the national Christians should have liberty to introduce their own rhythms and music into the Christian service. A Kpelle service such as Esther would have participated in, and would have loved, is described by Dr. Mark Monson (currently senior physician at the Zorzor hospital): "A single drummer starts the rhythm, then the other drummers join in with the sasas, gourds with beads on a string woven around the outside like macrame. Then the chorus starts, hesitant at first but then swelling, followed by the female leader-voice calling the verse with the choir on the chorus. The drums echo through the church, people tap their feet, sway, and occasionally turn their heads to the choir."

So Esther was dismayed when the Africans' natural harmonies, hand-clapping, and ululations were suppressed by well-meaning pastors and native evangelists in favor of the ancient Lutheran "dirges," like one she heard one Sunday, written in the 1600s by one Seelenbrautigau Adam Druse, with "horribly depressing lines" like:

> "...if the way be cheerless!!!"
> and "...if the way be drear, if the foe be near..."
> and "...when we seek relief from long-felt grief..."

and ended with the most depressing line of all:

"Show us that bright shore where we weep no more."

The Africans she knew were not cheerless, their way not drear, their foe not near, and she knew none who were weeping enough to be ready for that bright shore. She certainly wasn't.

(15)

Although she herself did not yet participate in the evangelical work (and never would do much direct proselytizing), she was thrilled when she saw the fruits of others' work. One mother, whose first twelve babies had all died, came with her thirteenth. When it, too, died, Frances Leonard talked with her for hours with the result that the mother and her sisters all eventually made their declaration of faith in Christ. Soon after, the lady's mother came with her whole family for study with Gertrude Buschman.

Another woman who had tried to hinder others in their belief until she lost a close relative in the hospital, came to know Christ in her sorrow and then won six other members of her family. Esther wrote, "Her testimony of how there just isn't any end to God's word thrilled our hearts."

A former patient, Rachel, began coming over to Esther's house every evening for prayers and Bible study. Her illness, Esther said, had proved rich in spiritual experience and showed that sometimes suffering was a blessing in disguise. She quoted Romans 8:28 for the woman: "And we know that all things work together for good to them that love God."

So it was that Esther's first year at Zorzor passed, new experiences and new friends tumbling as in a kaleidoscope through her life. Sorrow and frustration crowded her in the hospital when she treated cases which could be helped only with morphine and with love. But great joy was hers also when a patient who would have died in his village walked home in good health.

Her socializing, teaching, and persuading visits to the villages had fulfilled the Preacher's injunction in Ecclesiastes, "Cast thy bread upon the water," and would reap the Preacher's promise, "for thou shalt find it after many days." She could sense the increasing acceptance by the women and even some of the men who stood stolidly by as she talked with the women and cuddled their babies. The older children now ran gleefully to meet her with cries of "Bayka, Bayka."

But the maternity ward remained empty for days and even weeks at a time. Mothers and babies died in the forest just as they had for millenia. Esther agonized and prayed. But she did not despair. She knew that

God's concern was even greater than hers and He was working on the problem. She prepared her mind and her spirit for the breakthrough that she knew was coming.

When it came, she was ready.

(16)

She was ready when Flumo came running to her house that late October afternoon (see Prologue) and told her that his wife Dabio was dying in the high forest. Esther ran quickly to the hospital to get the large leather bag filled with everything she might need for a delivery in the bush. Frances Leonard stood close by, eyes wide with delight, sharing Esther's exhilaration. Esther stood for a moment in contemplation. Did she have everything? Once there she couldn't call for another nurse to bring whatever she'd forgotten. She checked it over.

In the side pockets with snap-down covers: syringes of different sizes in sterile, stainless steel containers. Needles ranging from tiny #25s to life-saving #14s and #16s. Blood pressure cuff and stethoscope. Conical stainless steel fetuscope. Several pairs of standard-size rubber gloves. Rubber bulb syringe and a fetal endotracheal tube for clearing the baby's airway, though sadly she reflected that neither these nor the fetuscope would be needed tonight.

In a small tin box, her drugs: silver nitrate for the baby's eyes, alcohol-soaked cotton in a small steel jar, pitocin, scopolamine, adrenaline, ergot, morphine, IV saline and tubing.

In the main compartment: a large sterile pack which she didn't open, but could tick off in her mind: elbow-length rubber gloves, towels, bandages, uterine pack, perineal pads, cord ties, long ring-forceps, scissors, artery clamps, sutures, ties, and scalpel. She closed the bag and with a smile for Frances strode rapidly across the clearing and up the path to her house where Flumo squatted on his heels, waiting with the fatalism of the tribal African.

As is customary in Loma-land, Esther led the way.* Flumo shouldered her bag and began to tell Esther about the precautions he and his wife had taken to ensure a healthy baby.

He told her that his wife, Dabio, had eaten all the right meats so their child wouldn't resemble a bush pig or anteater. She had avoided eggs

---

*If the man led, the woman could be seized by enemies and he would never know it. If there is a child, he walks between, because if he led and were careless, he might step on a snake.

entirely so the child wouldn't be born dead. Even, one night, the whole village had eaten bush cow, but not his wife. Oh, **no**, she knew that was bad. She ate chicken so her delivery would not be difficult.

He paused for a moment, then spoke proudly. "And we knew she was carrying a boy because only a week ago she dreamed she'd had a baby girl. The spirits always speak indirectly, you know."

"Yes, I know," Esther said. She was familiar with many of these beliefs. She had to control her tongue. Couldn't he *see*, couldn't *anyone* see, that there was absolutely no basis for their beliefs? The child was already dead, so avoiding eggs had done no good. The woman was dying, so avoiding bush cow had done no good. Couldn't they *see* that?

She wanted to sit down with this man (and everybody in Loma-Kpelleland) and explain to them that these beliefs *were not* based on real knowledge and had no bearing on the pregnancy. But she was wise enough to know that she had to work around these beliefs rather than try to dislodge them. Let them keep their beliefs, at least if they did no actual harm. But, *Lord*, let them accept mine, too, she prayed. They had to see for themselves that healthy babies and healthy mothers did not come from avoiding taboos or performing secret rites, but from a combination of good prenatal care in all cases and skillful midwifery in complicated cases.

As they followed the tortuous forest paths, humid heat closed in around them. It was cooler perhaps than out in the sun, but 80 degree heat, 85 percent humidity, combined with total absence of a breeze, made it *hot*. Esther's white uniform, often spotted with blood or iodine or potassium permanganate and sometimes with worse things, now caught green slashes from the giant ferns, rusty brown stains from the fungoid masses on the boles of trees, wine-dark smudges from the berries crushed as she shouldered through tight turns in the path.

They climbed ridge after ridge, and in the valleys between they waded through shoe-sucking swamps and small rushing streams. Esther's white shoes were soaked in the first creek they waded and her bare feet (she seldom wore socks or stockings) squished in them with each step. Her golden hair, which had not seen a permanent wave for a year, hung lankly on her head. Perspiration dripped from the tip of her nose and ran in rivulets down her neck and between her shoulder blades.

She noticed none of this. She just listened to Flumo talking as he walked behind her, his deep voice deadened by the jungle but rumbling up to her. He was intent on letting her know everything about his wife's pregnancy and labor. Esther smiled grimly. In her training days, she had heard many a general practitioner detailing the history of a difficult case to the obstetrician-specialist. Now *she* was the specialist. Oh God . . . she felt so unprepared.

(17)

Flumo told her that the women zoes had assumed that Dabio had somehow gotten *gbangba sale,* a medicine which causes the victim to have bad luck. So they countered that with *gula ma sale,* another medicine, to protect her. That didn't work. So in the agony of labor she was forced to name all her previous lovers; these men were grilled by the zoes to see if any had bewitched the woman. The verdict was that none had.

They said to Flumo, "You must go to the village diviner." So Flumo, anxious to use any means open to him, and to receive the support of his peers, did not hesitate for a moment. He went to the sandplayer, or sandcutter, who would tell him if someone else, such as his first wife, had placed a spell on this wife.

Flumo took a white chicken and a white kola nut and gave it to the sandplayer. White, because white binds people together. He gave no thought whatsoever to the paradox of white also being the color of terrifying things like the forest *genii* and the water woman whose skin was white and whose long arms were pale and glistened in the moonlight. Black was beautiful when the old women made dye, but black was also the color of darkness and Flumo would not insult the diviner with anything black. Red, of course, was the color of fear: only the most powerful zoes could wear red, but important people could weave red threads into their country cloth.

So Flumo gave his white chicken and white kola nut to the sandplayer and stood obsequiously to one side. The sandplayer squatted on his haunches, ate the kola nut, and sacrificed the chicken. Staring into the forest, his eyes glassy hard, he sought out the person who had bewitched Flumo's wife. He called on his own ancestors, then on his animal double in the forest, which in his case was the pigmy hippopotamus who lives in the deep, sluggish jungle streams. Finally he called on Flumo's ancestors.

With these spirits guiding his hands he let sand fall through his fingers onto the ground. He studied the patterns in the sand.

Bewildered, he looked up at Flumo. "I do not see a bewitchment here."

Horrified, Flumo ran fast back to his house. If no one could find the bewitcher, he might be forced to carry Dabio into the forest to be eaten by wild animals. NO! He could not. No matter how displeased the ancestors would be.

He slowed to a walk outside his house and called to the zo. She came out and told him the baby had now been born — dead. The afterbirth would not come out, no matter how hard the midwives pulled on the umbilical cord.

Dabio bled and bled, and neither the zoes nor the midwives could do anything more. They simply said, "Flumo, she will die."

"You can do nothing more?"

"No. The ancestors are calling her to them."

He remembered Esther then and her parting words, "Come for me, Flumo, if you need me."

He said to the chief zo, "I will go for the white medicine lady in Zorzor. She can do no worse than you."

With a fire in her eyes but with a subtle nod of her head, the zo said, "Go."

(18)

So he had gone, and now he was bringing Esther back to his wife. After more than an hour of steady walking, they reached the village. In a small clearing amidst 200-foot trees, stood a dozen thatched, round mud houses. A score or more people watched silently in courtyards and doorways, frank awe on every face. This was an unprecedented event. Never before in the history of that village had a white medicine woman been called to work her magic.

Flumo guided Esther to the door of his house and then left her. It would mean even worse bad luck if he were to be too close to his wife and the zoes.

The house was like all the others: round, constructed of saplings and mud, and topped with conical thatch and a clay cook pot. The heavy wooden door, a single slab of thick wood, groaned as its carved pivots turned in their sockets as Esther entered, then clunked shut behind her. It was so dark that Esther could hardly see. The only light came from a smoky fire in the middle of the room. She made out the huddled figures of women squatting on the floor around a prostrate form. A bloody knife lay on the cow-dung floor.

Esther did not know these women, but at least one would be a zo, another the tribal midwife, and another Flumo's older wife or mother. These were the ones who had supervised Dabio's pregnancy from the very beginning, had supervised the delivery, had used their leaves and roots and bark, their incantations and scattered chicken bones, all the powers they possessed over the forces of evil. Had now failed. And had finally allowed Flumo to go for Esther, confident that she too would fail with this hopeless case.

Esther knew what the zoes' failure really meant. Since *every* bad happening is caused by another person who has gotten medicine from a zo, these zoes had failed to find that person.

But Flumo had been right about the problem: a retained placenta. And he was right about the bleeding. The floor was literally awash with clotted blood. Dabio lay naked on the bare, hard-packed dirt floor, deathly still. Kneeling in the bloody mud, Esther gently lifted the woman's arm and felt for a wrist pulse. Nothing. She put a finger on a carotid artery in the neck and detected a fluttering, feeble pulse.

Thank God!

She said, "Dabio!"

The girl's eyelids twitched but did not open. Esther lifted one eyelid gently and could see even in the half-dark that the conjunctiva was ghastly pale.

Quickly she opened her bag, hung the saline bottle from the rafter, ran the tubing full, and deftly inserted a needle into the crease of the woman's elbow. She screwed the C-clamp wide open.

Then she stood up and called for soap and water. Carefully she scrubbed her hands and pulled on the sterile, elbow-length, rubber gloves. With two of the women holding Dabio's knees apart and another holding her pelvis steady, Esther knelt down and with a prayer on her lips, inserted her hand and then her entire forearm up into the uterus. Dabio did not move or even moan. She was so close to exsanguination that she was almost insensitive to pain.

The uterus was soft, flabby, entirely filled with clotted and liquid blood, and Esther knew it could be fatally ruptured all too easily by a false move on her part. Carefully she searched with her fingers through the massive clots for the placenta. She found it high in the fundus, firmly attached except for the one area which had become detached and was the source of the bleeding. With the placenta in place the uterus could not contract to close the mouths of the open blood vessels.

Breathing another prayer, Esther began to separate the placenta with back-and-forth movements of her cupped fingers, a maneuver known as "blunt dissection." She knew that sometimes the placenta actually grows into the wall of the uterus and nothing short of a hysterectomy would save the woman's life.

But within a very few moments the placenta came away in her hand and she was able to pull it out. A massive expulsion of purple-red clots and then a gush of bright red blood followed the placenta and then stopped. Esther gave the placenta to one of the zoes and gently pushed the girl's knees out straight. She palpated her abdomen, found the uterus and massaged it gently but firmly with both hands. A little more bleeding occurred, but then it too stopped. She injected one cubic centimeter of pitocin into the IV tubing. Then she resumed massage of the uterus until she could feel it harden into a tight ball.

When she was sure the bleeding had stopped, she helped the women give Dabio a thorough washing with soap and warm water. They dried her off, moved her onto a clean straw mat, and wrapped her warmly in colorful lappas. She managed a small smile and Esther squeezed her hand.

Then Esther looked up at one of the women and said, "Get four strong men to come with a hammock. And a fifth man to hold up the bottle. We must carry this woman to the hospital where we can properly take care of her."

The astonished family quickly complied. Surely this white woman had strong medicine such as they had never seen before.

Esther hung a fresh bottle of saline, for the first one was already entirely infused. She tied a perineal pad between Dabio's legs and sat beside her until the men came. One of them was Flumo, and as he knelt beside his wife to help lift her onto the hammock, he said to Esther, "The ancestors have guided me to you." Esther sensed that there were other things that he wanted to tell her, or ask her, but could not find the right words at that moment.

As for her, at that same moment, she was content with his version of the situation. Later she would talk to him and impress him with the fact that she hadn't used witchcraft or sorcery, nor had she appealed to his ancestors, but had used the expertise she had gained in her training. She didn't know just how she would do it, but somehow she would. And perhaps, later still, she could substitute her Christ and her God for his ancestors, for she knew that it had been her God who had guided Flumo to her, not his ancestors.

Esther led the way back through the green tunnel of the now dark forest, her lantern glowing brightly and throwing weird, elongated shadows on the ferns and vines and thick-boled trees, but guiding the feet of the men carrying the hammock. Esther prayed that this case would open the eyes of others, would open the long-closed doors of the hospital's maternity ward to the women of Loma-Kpelle-land.

Chapter Four

(1942-1945)

(1)

If this were fiction on the silver screen, one would hear the trumpets, feel the reverberations of bass drums, sense the epiphany as the angels sing, all heralding the dramatic events of the night Esther saved the life of Dabio Zayzay in the forest village. There were none of these. Nor did pregnant women suddenly swamp the Zorzor Lutheran Hospital.

But it was a breakthrough, no question about it. A week later, Esther got another call to go to a village to help with a birth, then another and another. Slowly the number increased.

(2)

On the mission station itself, life went on pretty much as it had. Esther got a package from home: knives, forks, spoons, seeds, samples, peppermint stick candy, lights, notions, film. The silverware came just in time. The wooden handles of her silverware had started to rot off in the fungoid humidity. She was glad for the film because she still had never gotten any pictures of Zorzor back to Aunt Nora, who was increasingly anxious to get a look at Esther's new home.

By October of that first year, her garden, under the supervision of Farm-boy ("Yes, that's really his name!"), began producing tomatoes, beans, greens, potatoes, and edoes. She bought what she needed of pawpaws, bananas, peanuts, and pineapples which came by the house riding on the heads of little children and little old ladies. She raved to Nora about the pineapples because they were so sweet: "You don't know what pineapples are!"*

Esther went with the Sadlers to Harrisburg just before Christmas for the annual missionaries' conference. Their route took them back through Salayea, Nutown, Pieta, across the St. Paul River, Sanoyea, and finally to the beginning of the motor road at Salala. Road workers had improved the road to Harrisburg, but thick gumbo mud, deep pools of water, tire-blowing rocks and gullies still provided grist for the junkyards of Monrovia.

Esther could hardly believe that she had been in Liberia for a whole year. As she looked back on that year she was appalled at how little she had accomplished. But when she voiced her frustrations to Wes Sadler he said, "Be patient, Esther. You've made a start. That's all you could hope for in a year. The animism and the superstitions of the Loma people have been here for a *thousand* years!" And Roslyn reminded her of all the motherless children she had saved from certain death and wouldn't listen to Esther when she started to enumerate the ones she'd lost.

The Conference was good for Esther, too. It brought her into contact with life-long missionaries whose patience and contentment were sooth-ing. It made her all the more anxious to get back to Zorzor to see her babies and her friends.

Her babies quite obviously filled a need. There is nothing on record about her recognition of this. But her notes, letters and other writings for thirty years are filled with references to her children. Her anxiety about their health, her longing to return to them after just a day or two away, her bragging about their accomplishments, all this a clear indication that what she felt for these orphans was mother-love.

When she returned to Zorzor, the medical compound had been com-pletely renovated for the Christmas season: trees trimmed and the lower trunks whited, the bushes and grass cut, the houses and hospital rubbed inside and out with new white chalk clay.

During her absence the inpatient census had gone down to a dozen adults and a few children. But on the Saturday before Christmas, she had "dozens of" babies in the morning clinic and five OBs for prenatal clinic. She gave the mothers caramel frosted cookies, the babies orange juice, and each a bar of pink soap.

---

*Author's note: The descendants of those pineapples are still in Zorzor! Even Hawaiian pineapples are not as sweet.

Esther didn't think of these gifts as bribes to lure patients to the clinic. She wanted the mothers to have something to eat, for often they had walked many miles. She wanted the babies to have a dose of natural vitamins, if only a one-shot deal. She knew how scarce soap was in Liberia, and how difficult to make in Loma-land. So although soap and other items may have been used as lures by some missionaries, and may have acted as lures for Esther's patients, she vigorously denied that motivation.

(3)

Soon after Christmas, in January of 1943, an eleven-year-old boy walked into the hospital carrying his baby brother on his back. Both the boy and the baby were covered with smallpox pustules.

Esther and an aide washed down the boys, put them into an isolation "kitchen" behind the hospital, and then pieced together the boy's story. He came from a village about four hours walk away. His father and mother were dead and he could no longer stand to stay in the house with the bodies.

Fortunately Esther had one batch of still-potent vaccine. She gathered together a group of porters without telling them where they were going and started out.

When they arrived at the boy's village they found that all the smallpox cases had been moved to another farm town. Esther started for this town, but soon came to a thick vine stretched across the path. To Esther it was just a vine, but to her carriers it meant death. They fled back down the path toward Zorzor.

Esther knew why they were running, but she just climbed over the barrier and found a small boy to guide her to the village. Some people were dead, others dying, the rest terrified. She did what she could to make them comfortable and returned to their home village to vaccinate the uninfected people. They all refused. She went from village to village and no one would accept vaccination.

Almost sick with frustration, she finally found a lady with a vaccination scar on her arm. Esther took this lady from village to village, arguing incessantly that this woman was well because she had been vaccinated.

Her persistence paid off.

Eventually she convinced enough important people that she was right. Teams trained by Esther went out to vaccinate those who agreed. When all had been vaccinated, teams went out again to bring the patients back to Zorzor for care. Esther's priorities are interesting. Clearly she felt that vaccinating well people was more important than treating those already sick. Ideally both should have been done simultaneously but her staff was too small for that.

The epidemic was wiped out. Furthermore, the villagers were convinced now that vaccination prevented smallpox. Esther had established a new principle in Loma-land. This would not be the end of smallpox because memories are short and new people are being born. The wheel would have to be re-invented several times in subsequent years, but she had made a start.

(4)

And now she began to be frightfully busy. She drove herself with an almost obsessive fury to do everything that needed being done. Dr. Earl Reber, who would work with Esther at Zorzor for almost seventeen years, has said that he didn't think Esther was a "driven person." There are many who disagree. Dr. Veatch was one. He rode his horse down from Bolahun to Zorzor, and after watching Esther at work for a few days, confided to the Salders, "Somehow you've got to slow that young woman down. She can't go more than another six months at that pace."

There was no way they could do that. But Wes Sadler had an idea. "Esther," he said, "why don't *you* get a horse?"

She smiled, shook her head, and said, "What would I do with a horse? The paths aren't smooth enough. There's these roots and stones and how would I ever get a horse across a monkey bridge, the way it sways back and forth with just me on it."

"Esther," Wes said, "Ev Veatch rode all the way from Bolahun on a horse. Pewu Howard says his father and other Loma chiefs have ridden horses for decades. Ros and I ride to the villages all the time."

She was adamant and Wes let it drop. Even then no one argued with Esther Bacon when she had already made up her mind.

But fate, or the Lord, took a hand in the decision. One afternoon a call came to Esther from Kiliwu, only four miles away but on a narrow track through almost impenetrable forest, up and down steep, rocky ridges, some with 45 degree slopes. She couldn't do anything there for the woman she had come to see, so she transported her back to Zorzor by hammock. The woman died en route.

A runner from Yapoa awaited her at the hospital. She walked with him for five hours and arrived about midnight. This time she found a pregnant woman whose membranes had ruptured thirty hours before. The midwives and zoes had been working on her with hands purified with cow manure. She had a very high fever and Esther knew that by now the inside of her uterus harbored a zoo of pathogenic organisms. The baby lay transversely and couldn't be budged. Esther gave the lady morphine and brought her back to Zorzor by hammock, a walk of almost eight hours because of their slow pace. Esther delivered a dead baby at the hospital, but the woman survived.

By now it was nine o'clock in the morning. Before she had a chance to rest she was called back to Kiliwu where she delivered twins but lost the mother. She brought the babies back to Zorzor, made ward rounds, worked for several hours on death and birth reports for Monrovia, and then was again called back to Kiliwu. There she found a dead mother and a live baby.

Wes and Roslyn Sadler watched all this with a mixture of awe and consternation. Wes sought her out the next day and challenged her with the suggestion that three trips to Kiliwu and one to Yapoa in twenty-four hours were too much.

She said simply, "They need me. Don't you see, Wes, it's what I've been waiting for, working and praying for, for over a year?"

Wes Sadler may have been the first, but certainly not the last, to wonder if Esther were going about this the right way. But, he concluded, she's going to do this and no one will stop her, so the thing to do is help her. He said, "I'm going to buy you a horse."

When she didn't argue, he took this as tacit consent and went on into Zorzor to look up Lavaleh Gboloi ("Lah-vuh'-leh Bowl'-lay"), a member of his congregation. He was the horse-trader who had sold Gracious to Roslyn.

He showed Wes the same skinny brown horse that Roslyn had turned down a year before. Now the horse's body seemed to have grown to match his head, though he was still skinny, dirty, and covered with ticks. But he was young, strong and said to be gentle. Wes bought him and all the necessary tack for five pounds (about $20), rode him back to the hospital, and gave him to Esther.

She immediately named him Lizard. With half the mission staff and all the children staring and giggling, Esther climbed aboard and rode him across the causeway through the swamp, up the steep hill, past the flag pole in front of Sadler's house, and into Buschy's yard. Buschy wasn't home but Esther was immediately surrounded by schoolboys clamoring for a ride. "Not today, boys," she said, and set Lizard into a jarring trot back to her house. He scrambled down the hill at breakneck speed with Esther hanging onto his mane, trying to slow him down, which he did only when they had crossed the swamp and started up the hospital compound hill. No Arabian stallion, Lizard.

But he was transportation. Esther used him that very night to visit a village. After leaving the house in the village, she led him to the plank bridge before mounting. Then, Esther says, "One man asked to lead him and he went frisky! Tried to bite, kick, charge anyone trying to catch him. He also chased the cows around the huts and had a merry time!" Esther finally calmed him down and for a long while after that didn't let anyone else near the horse.

She was seldom alone on her increasingly frequent treks into the high forest. Usually there was at least one grown man, and often two or three, to carry the heavy leather bags of medical supplies, food, water, and sometimes in hammocks the nurses themselves. Esther rarely if ever allowed herself to be carried. Here in the forest she was boss, although she never was autocratic about it. It was just obvious to everyone that when Esther said something was right, it was right. And if she didn't want to be carried, no one argued. Especially when she could outwalk all the women and most of the men.

Often a Liberian nurse went along to aid Esther and to interpret for her. And many times a schoolboy accompanied her to lead the horse and carry a torch. Pewu Moleyeaze*, at this writing District Commissioner for Zorzor district, and an important man in Zorzor's church, remembers the excitement of those midnight excursions into the high forest. He kept a supply of bamboo torches in those early years when kerosene was scarce or when he went to a village to bring Esther home and she had run out of kerosene.

Laughter rumbles deep in Mr. Moleyeaze's chest now as he says, "I would carry the torch and then sometimes I would find her twenty yards in front of me, in the dark, because the light would shine ahead and she knew the paths very well!"

Feeding the horse was no problem because it ate cassava, rice, guinea corn, and grass. There was never a shortage of them all at the same time.

The horse was not an unmixed blessing. After describing the purchase of a new cow and its rampages through the rice fields, she wrote, "Horse makes humbug too sometimes — eating people's covercloths, tearing operating room linens from the line, stealing rice, eating baby clothes on the piazza!"

A novelty at first, it soon became routine to see Esther riding out into the jungle at all times of the day and night. She wore slacks or culottes, canvas shoes, no socks, and a loose blouse. She had loved the image of a missionary nurse in a white uniform moving in the villages, but hesitated not a second when it proved impractical.

Many of her rides were uneventful except for the obvious act of Christian mercy at the end of the trail. After her first extended venture, a three-

---

*Until the late 1960s, Mr. Moleyeaze was known as Pewu Howard, a *kwii* name he took as a student. Moleyeaze is his family name.

day trip to the villages and towns* with another nurse, she wrote, "The horse behaved quite well and it seemed good to sleep the nights through. One of the towns is very lovely - has many fruit trees, not crowded with huts too close together, and a most delightful rushing rocky waterside." Her stay there was made comfortable by very hospitable villagers. It's obvious that she enjoyed the people and the countryside, and that she also enjoyed the brief escape from the long night hours at the hospital.

But at other times the excitement was in getting there or getting back. Two months after obtaining Lizard she set out at sunset for Zolowo, ten miles south as the egret flies and almost twice that by jungle paths. She was detained for several hours in Zorzor to help deliver a baby, then went on to Zolowo, reaching there at dawn. She was too late. The baby was stillborn and the mother died of hemorrhage despite everything Esther could do.

After a few hours sleep in the cool house of the clan headman's wife, she was notified by runner about a sick man in Luyema and went to see him, passing north through Zorzor and then through Konia and Gabaye. It turned out to be an eight-hour ride from Zolowo to Luyema and back to Zorzor because they had to cross a big river twice, and the Wonegizi Mountains around Luyema were as high as 3,000 feet. Lizard swam the river both times because the monkey bridge was too narrow and too fragile to bear his weight. The banks were steep and muddy but the horse made it safely. Adding to the problems was a wild wind and rain storm that caught them halfway between towns.

Another time she came to a river in flood and Lizard refused to cross. She took off her shoes, tied them in a knot around the pommel, waded into the river and led the frightened horse across.

A common sight now at the hospital was Esther trudging up the hill into the hospital compound, leading the horse with a sick patient or post-partum mother aboard. One of Esther's porters or schoolboys would be carrying the gear and another perhaps a newborn baby. Before Roslyn and Esther came, no one had ever seen a woman ride, for horses were for chiefs and were too expensive for the average tribesman. Now the village women were riding horseback.

Once after an all-night vigil, she came back leading the horse with no one riding him. When Wes Sadler asked, "Esther, is something wrong?" she answered, "Oh, no, he's just tired."

A "town" is any community that holds its own Poro initiation and therefore has its own Big Thing — Great Secret Personage — since he holds the initiation. Some "farm villages" are larger than some "towns."

And once she wrote home to Nora: "You should have seen the thrilling dive I took over the horse's head when he came through one of the bridges the other day and stopped suddenly!" This was her third fall, one of which was occasioned by the saddle girth breaking. But she was glad to "have such a handy horse."

Her children pestered her to ride and she let the older ones do so. Big Zizzi loved to ride around in a circle, one of the boys leading the horse, and howled when made to come down.

At first she couldn't get the other nurses to ride, but when a new Liberian graduate nurse, David Lake, arrived in mid-August of 1943, he often did, and was bucked off on at least one occasion. Frances Leonard was the first female nurse to try riding the horse to one of the towns, but it tried to throw her so she merely got off and sent the horse back to Zorzor.

Lilliana ("Lana") Bartolomei, a missionary teacher who had trained at NYU's Biblical Seminary and who was then teaching at the Zorzor grade-school, also got up the courage and began riding Lizard under Esther's tutelage. She says, reflectively, "The only difference between Esther and me with the horse was when I went out on the horse, I came back on the horse. When Esther went out on the horse, she came back leading the horse with somebody else on the back, or carrying a motherless baby."

(5)

When Edith Curran returned to Zorzor from nursing school, she also rode Lizard. During her year at Phebe, she had gone with Pauline Ziegler to see a U.S. Army doctor by the name of Wagner at Robertsfield. Wagner took measurements of the below-knee stump, sent off to the States for a prosthesis, and in a few months gleefully presented it to Edith.

So now she could walk without crutches, but still had difficulty walking through the forest for many hours. So she gratefully rode Lizard when accompanying Esther into the bush.

She tells of her first trip. It was in August. Rain had been falling for days. A man came from Fisebu at 5 A.M. with a plea for Esther to come with him to see a young woman called Gaamai, a cardiac patient in labor. The first of twins had delivered, but the other had not.

As Esther made ready to go with them, a man came in from Kpaiye, eight miles in the other direction, with an urgent call. A woman had delivered twins successfully but the placenta had been retained for thirty hours or longer.

Esther decided to go see Gaamai first because her problem seemed the most urgent. She asked Edith if she would like to go along.

"Sure, Miss Bacon, but how will I get there? The rivers are all high and the paths are muddy."

"You'll ride the horse."

"I don't know *how* to ride horse."

"You are going to *learn* how to ride horse!"

She put Edith on Lizard and they started out. The horse balked at the first swollen, muddy stream they came to. Esther took the reins, waded into the creek and tried to pull Lizard in after her. Lizard spun around and kicked Esther out into the river where she went under and came up sputtering, "Edith, hold fast! Hold fast! Don't let go."

So Edith held fast to the mane with one hand and the bridal with the other until Esther could crawl out on the muddy bank and quiet the horse. Characteristically, all Esther said was, "Oh, now I've had my morning bath!"

They went on through the river to the village. Esther examined the woman, sedated her, started an IV, and gave her some kola nuts to chew on. They waited. Esther was afraid to extract the placenta in the village because of the woman's heart trouble. Finally she convinced the men that no harm would come to them or the woman if they carried her hammock. She sent her to Zorzor with a note telling the other nurses what to do.

Then she and her retinue went south to Kpaiye on a path that bypassed Zorzor, reaching there about 4 P.M. The people there greeted her with, "Oh, Bayka has come, Bayka has come." Again she found a case of one twin born and the other recalcitrant. She delivered the second twin, then peeled off a retained placenta.

It was now about 6 P.M. and still raining. They rested in a sweetly-smelling dry house and ate soft rice waiting for the rain to stop. When it showed no signs of letting up, Esther put the patient in a hammock, Edith on Lizard and went back to Zorzor. They arrived at 1 A.M., and found another messenger from Fisebu waiting to escort Esther to a patient up there.

Edith was exhausted and went right to bed. Lizard, lathered and hungry, had been plodding along for several miles. Esther unsaddled him and tied him to a small tree outside the hospital. Then she walked the two hours to Fisebu, normally an hour on dry roads in daylight. She found a young girl having her first baby but unable to deliver. Since she could do nothing for her up there, Esther brought the girl back to the hospital, arriving at dawn, and successfully delivered her in the hospital.

Not all of her ventures were so taxing, but she did begin to stay out for several days more and more often. At first she had to send runners back to Zorzor for supplies, food and boiled water. Then Wes and Roslyn Sadler solved that problem by urging her to tell them what village or farm she was going to first. If she didn't come home that night, they sent food and water out the next morning. Often the runner would have to go from village to village until he caught up with her.

Sometimes the Sadlers would have to send her sun helmet along also because Esther would have forgotten it, especially if she had left home during the night or in the early morning. She was not nearly as careful about this as they thought she should be. But, as Earl Reber says, "Esther was Esther." She did not consider her own comfort and safety when she got a call to help a woman in trouble.

(6)

Motherless babies continued to be one of Esther's main concerns. By March of 1943 she had seven living and bewailed the nearly two dozen she had lost. "I can't keep count anymore."

One dear three-year-old girl came in weighing 11½ pounds. Her chin, lower lip, and some teeth had sloughed out from a spreading infection, perhaps anthrax. This one, little Buacoo, she was able to save by hourly feedings of a high protein and high vitamin diet: bananas, powdered milk, peanuts, palm oil, all mixed together, ground fine and liquefied with boiled water and orange juice. The ulcer healed, leaving an unpleasant-looking scar, but she was alive.

By now Esther had found she couldn't take care of all the children herself so she took over one of the still-usable buildings of the old hospital.* She still kept the sickest ones in her own house until they no longer needed her personal care, then moved them to the "orphanage" where they were cared for by one or two women whose wages Esther paid out of her own pocket.

She seemed to feel a little guilt about not keeping all the babies right with her. She wrote Nora, "Most of the time I have a baby or two up here at the house, but I don't keep ten at a time like Miss J. (Ma Jensen at Sanoyea) — most I've had at one time is five, and then morning soon comes." Later, with a touch of humor that would never fail her, she wrote, "Little girl here is on the floor. One of the mental patients is trying to feed her and there seems to be a bit of uncertainty on the part of both as to how a little girl drinks from a cup."

She also spent a lot of time with the young women, both in her clinics and in the villages. She saw them as her entree' into village life. The words of Dr. Moore rang constantly in her ears, reminding her that the power of the zoes had to be broken by substitution, not demolition.

---

*She had begun to use the new hospital (located on its present site closer to Zorzor), which had been begun by Rev. George Flora and Dr. Moore, and in 1943 nearly completed.

But there were strange and harmful practices not directly controlled by the zoes. These Esther could meet head on.

She learned that most of the villagers did not want twins so one usually died. She showed how both *could* be fed and saved. There was much resistance at first, but more and more mothers with living twins began to be proud of them.

She learned that orange juice and other fruits and vegetables were not considered good for babies. She showed the women the results of *her* diet regimen: the kids in her orphanage. She told the women, "The only thing I'm doing different is feeding these children good food and boiled water."

TWINS

She learned that it was customary for men to eat first, women next, children last. It was not unusual to see little children fighting over the last scraps of food. Esther could hardly believe that the adults failed to see how this custom exacerbated the malnutrition problem. She lectured them long and hard, but confessed she was mostly unsuccessful. She said, "But I do convince *some*, yah?"

She saw mothers force-feeding water and food into little infants' mouths, often causing aspiration, choking and death, or at the very least, pneumonia. Sometimes exasperated beyond what she could tolerate, she took a handful of food and slammed it up against a mother's mouth and pinched her nostrils to show her just how difficult it was to breathe and swallow at the same time. She did this with a smile on her face and a twinkle in her eyes, but the mothers knew she was serious and with nervous giggles began using tiny spoons or a flat stick.

Esther was only minimally successful in abolishing this custom. As late as 1986 Dr. Mark Monson wrote from Zorzor: " 'Stuffing,' a social custom of feeding children, is a major cause of death in infants in Lofa County."

Since many severe diseases of the gastrointestinal tract were water-born (Salmonella enteritis, typhoid fever, cholera, to name but a few), Esther taught the mothers to boil small amounts of water and carry it with them. For the next three decades, everyone in Loma-Kpelle-land could identify "Bayka babies" because they were fat and sassy and their eyes were bright and their skin glossy — and their mothers carried small bottles of boiled water on their heads.

One time when Wes and Roslyn Sadler were visiting in a village, a young woman held up for them to see a fat little baby with orange juice smeared on its face. Proudly the mother showed them a bottle of boiled water and said, "This is a Bayka baby." The Sadlers didn't need to be told, for, as Wes wrote at the time, "Whenever I see a woman walking through the town or in the high forest, a healthy baby fastened to her back and a bottle of boiled water balanced on her head, I think of Esther. It is her sign, her symbol, and it means life."

Her well-baby clinic was thriving. Some mothers came with their three- and four-year-olds still nursing. They stood between their mothers' knees, both hands gripping the breast and pulling it straight out, little bells on their ankles jingling* as they impatiently stamped their feet. Esther thought it was cute. Soon she found that all these children were extremely anemic because the only food they got was mother's milk, deficient for that age group in protein, iron and vitamins.

Since the mothers nursed baby boys for four years and girls for three, and cultural taboos kept husbands away from nursing mothers, Esther had a hard time convincing them to stop. It was a bit easier to get them to supplement the diet and she usually had to settle for that. She tried to add eggs to the diet, but the mothers were horrified to think she would take the hen's babies to feed their own babies.

Though her pre- and post-natal clincs were growing rapidly, most of the women still preferred to have their babies in their hometowns. There they were in familiar surroundings, had the protection through the zoes of their ancestral spirits, and had the support of mothers, sisters, grand-mothers, and men-folks. Besides, wouldn't "Bayka" come to them if they had trouble?

A new dilemma had arisen. By going out to the women, Esther had made it easier for them to continue shunning the hospital. "But," she said, "until I started going to the villages, *none* of the women were getting proper help when they got into trouble."

Gertrude Buschman was all too aware of this continuing problem: she had been dealing with it for a quarter of a century. Now she had more solid ground upon which to make her appeal to the village women, most of whom she knew personally. She could now cite cases, using names that people knew. Roslyn Sadler is convinced that Buschy, well-loved and highly-trusted by the villagers, played an important role in bringing the women to love and trust Esther.

So Esther's main thrust at this time was in the field of maternal and child health care. But there were other cases: "For variety we have several not too bad mental cases, a few chronic cases without family, a number of ulcer cases, and a few acute emergency patients, such as a man with a thorn entirely through one toe which had to be opened." And an in-creasing number of adult patients came with intestinal parasites, malaria, viral diseases such as polio and measles and hepatitis, snake bites and other animal injuries.

---

*A sign that the child was not weaned and the mother and father not conjugal.

(7)

Late in Esther's second year a curious thing happened. One of the workers on the mission station came to her with a problem.

"Bayka," he asked, "will a doctor be coming soon?"

"There's no telling, Beyan. Why?"

"Dr. Moore did the circumcision on my first baby with a special clamp." He beamed. "Now I have another boy."

Esther smiled. "I know."

"I want him to have the same kind of operation."

This was going to be a problem. Although Esther was doing all sorts of minor emergency operations — such as incising abscesses, suturing lacerations, casting fractures and the like — she did no elective operations at all. Though there was nothing in writing, the unwritten code was quite clear, even in Africa: nurses did not do elective surgery.*

"Then you'll have to have your zo do it," she said. "Or take him to Monrovia."

"I don't want the zo to do it. And I can't afford a trip to Monrovia."

Esther could understand that. She had seen many infections and other complications from the big contaminated knives the zoes used. And the trip to Monrovia would take a month or more: a week's travel each way plus two weeks for the surgery and waiting for the child to heal.

"Come back tomorrow," she said.

She sent for the zo in Beyan's village. He came reluctantly, and was astounded at Esther's proposal. But he agreed to do as she wished, such was her reputation by then.

On the appointed day, in the operating room, Esther supervised the zo as he scrubbed his hands, put on rubber gloves, washed the operative site and painted it with zephiran. Then using the special circumcision clamp just the way Esther showed him, he did a perfect circumcision.

Everyone was happy. And the zo offered Esther all kinds of inducements to let him take one of the clamps with him to use in the bush. Esther was tempted, but in the end refused.

She had a much more unnerving time later that same year. Wes Sadler developed a tooth abscess in his lower jaw with so much pain that no amount of local or oral medicine relieved it. Roslyn had brought with her from the States a small dental kit given her by her dentist. It contained a pick, long-handled oral mirror, temporary filling powder, and a drug called "Eugenol" which she had used many times to help people suffering from toothache, once even the District Commissioner's wife.

---

*See comments by Dr. James Stull, Chapter 7, Section 29.

But none of this helped Wes. His jaw and tongue continued to swell. A fiery red inflammation appeared on his neck and spread down onto his chest.

The nearest doctor was Dr. Veatch in Bolahun, four days away by foot. Roslyn describes the scene: ''. . . and here was Esther with her first missionary patient. And I marveled at her ingenuity in the way she rigged up an irrigation system so that we could irrigate Wes's mouth and hold his head in such a way that hot salt water could be poured in without choking him. Wes was so ill he was delirious and his temperature was way up. All the water had to be boiled for this irrigation system and you can imagine me at two o'clock in the morning out in the kitchen stoking the wood stove to boil more water. And I was about four months pregnant with my first child and I didn't know if he was going to have a father when he arrived. But Esther and the Loma nurses all worked — as did Buschy. They all did.''

Esther sent for Dr. Veatch but he wrote back that he could do nothing that Esther wasn't already doing. By then the fever had broken, Wes was recovering, and the red was fading. It was Roslyn's first personal experience with Esther's healing powers. Her second, four years later, would be more personal and even more dramatic.

(8)

In those first years Esther developed a loose routine which she maintained for the rest of her life. For her, it was ideal. For others working with her it would sometimes create difficulties.

She usually got up about six o'clock, and by the light of the kerosene lantern dressed quickly in white uniform and, when visitors were expected, a white cap. By 6:15 she had checked over the babies in her own house and was on her way to the "orphanage." After checking the children and then playing with them for a few moments, she returned to the hospital drug room, worked there awhile and assigned some work to whoever was working in there.

Then she went home for a bath and breakfast.

The bathhouse behind her house was an enclosure of bamboo sticks stuck in the ground, had a log floor but no roof. She carried in with her clean clothes, a bucket of water, bar of soap, and a towel.

For breakfast she often just drank a cup of coffee and ate a banana, but sometimes there was gruel or an egg. Always during breakfast, notes came from hospital, school, friends, or patients and these needed to be answered so the runners could get back. Often a caller or two came while she breakfasted.

Then it was time for morning devotions with the Christian staff at the hospital. In the early years Esther usually led them, choosing a text from her own reading at home the previous evening. Earl Reber, who later participated in thousands of these sessions with Esther, says, "She lavished on her small circle of worshippers a talent for writing deeply spiritual devotions."

Following prayers the staff discussed administrative problems and aired grievances. The atmosphere was generally relaxed; internal friction was at a minimum. There was little conflict of interest, little jealousy of another's pay or hours or workload, little striving for recognition or status.

On most dispensary days, Buschy or one of the native evangelists came to lead services for waiting patients. In those years the evangelist was usually a bright young man who had served in a missionary home as a servant, and who had slowly grown in the Christian faith to the point where he wanted to share it. His effectiveness depended on how well he had grasped the significance of the Gospel, and how well he still identified with his own people. At the hospital, no one was forced to listen. Reaction was varied. A few patients listened with great interest. A few walked away, out of earshot. The majority listened with polite indifference.

After the morning's work on wards, clinics, or in the general outpatient dispensary, Esther sometimes went home for a bit of lunch. Often, however, she sailed from one project to another and forgot to eat or just grabbed a handful of peanuts or a banana.

The afternoons were taken up with outpatient clinics,* minor operations, ward procedures such as starting IVs, changing dressings, and all the other details of running an increasingly busy general hospital.

She spent a lot of time teaching the nurses and aides. The aides, being untrained and usually fresh from the villages, needed constant supervision and teaching. When Mr. Lake arrived, there were now five Liberian nurses, enough staff to put Miss Tisdell on permanent night duty, the first time this had ever been tried at Zorzor.

Esther had much needed help from her Liberian nurses. Edith Curran, Esther wrote, was "blossoming out into a dependable, efficient nurse who truly loves her people."

Mrs. Mary Keller, wife of the mission's Boys' School headmaster Henry Keller, and living on the compound near the soccer field, often helped in the hospital and in the clinics.

---

*In a tropical hospital these usually are: leprosy, tuberculosis, pre-natal, well-baby, dressings (for conditions requiring daily changes such as ulcers, osteomyelitis, drained abscesses, burns), "shots," (for conditions requiring periodic injections without hospitalization such as infections, shistosomiasis, yaws, severe anemias), and when a doctor is in residence, pre- and post-operative clinics.

Frances Leonard remained a steady, dependable worker, and often accompanied Esther into the villages to act as her interpreter. As late as mid-1943, Esther continued to complain about not being able to hear the language: "If only I could speak Buzi! And yet I hate to leave to learn, too." It was an accepted fact, then as now, that a full-time, year-long study period was necessary, uninterrupted by other duties, best accomplished by living with an English-speaking person proficient in the native language, and spending six hours a day with an informant who was a native speaker of the language being learned.

It was about this time, in mid-1943, that Esther felt she had developed a close enough rapport with the village midwives to begin a class at the hospital for anyone who desired to learn more about her own techniques. There was, of course, concerted resistance, not so much from the midwives as from the zoes. But she persisted, and she persuaded, and soon they began to come, with or without the blessing of their zoes. She told them, "We can learn from each other." And so they learned and began to develop a new pride in what they could accomplish back in their villages.

(9)

In July of 1943, Roslyn Sadler, seven months pregnant, came to Esther and said, "I want you to deliver my baby."

Esther shook her head. "No."

"Why not?"

"Two very good reasons. One, it's your first. Two, I'm not a trained midwife. If you have trouble — like needing a C-section — you should be in Monrovia."

"Dr. Schnitzer? The doctor from Europe?"

"Yes."

"You could do the job just as well!"

Esther smiled her lopsided grin. "Probably."

"Then you'll do it?"

"No."

She was adamant and Roslyn went to Monrovia in August to await the birth of her baby. While she was down there, Buschy took over some of Wes's duties so he could spend more time on the Loma language. She had always been highly supportive of the Sadlers' language study and now in this very practical way showed it. Wes thanked her in 1951 by dedicating to her his Loma language text, "Untangled Loma."

On the 28th of September Esther received word in Zorzor that Byron Kezele (pronounced "Kess'-i'lee") had been born in the Methodist Hospital. Both mother and baby were fine. They returned to Zorzor in November. The baby was baptized in Loma at the Christmas service by his father. Mama Loupu, Gertrude Buschman, and evangelist David Harris acted as godparents.

Esther described that Christmas for her Aunt Nora: "Another Christmas is past, or should I say begun? For Christmas surely doesn't end with Christmas day, especially not here. One can be continually reminded of the Babe who came, and the setting. The stars shine silently, steadily; cattle gather at night with the sheep and goats in the town. If one's sense of scent is keen, he catches stable odor, tho, from the cow dung used to rub the houses.

"The people bring gifts to us and one another all thru the year. A common form of greeting is 'What did you bring me?' And packages from home, Christmas greetings and letters arrive all through the year. But most of all because individuals receive the Christ and come to worship not just one day but all through the year.

"Christmas Eve, Christmas morning and evening there were special services. The village school 'kitchen'* which serves as church now was decorated with palm leaves and flowers and ferns. The place had been newly cleaned and rubbed. 'Joy to the world, the Lord is come' — was sung in Buzi.

"Christmas morn, Rev. Sadler baptized his baby and Zizzi Harris, baby of evangelist David Harris, using Buzi. Mama Poupu beamed as she held young Sadler.

"Christmas evening a special offering was brought. Some brought money, others foodstuffs, as rice, chicken, etc. Zorzor Christians have been giving toward building a church to replace the one that blew down last Easter time.

"Sunday morning following Christmas was to have been a Communion service, but it was postponed because Rev. Sadler went to one of the towns for funeral of a man who had just been baptised the day before Christmas."

(10)

Esther's own children were growing up.

Big Zizzi, straining to keep up with the big boys, loved to ride Lizard. He had started to learn his prayers, first in Loma, then the classic children's prayer, "Now I lay me down to sleep." But he always stopped at "If . . ." "Little fella," Esther wrote, "he knows all too well of death."

---

*An open-sided structure used as a classroom.

In place of, "If I should die before I wake," he began to substitute, "God bless Zizzi and Little Zizzi," and then named all the children living with him in Esther's house and in the orphanage.

Little Zizzi was beginning to walk. Edwin, Daniel, Major and all the rest were thriving under the regimen of good food and loving care.

Buacoo, renamed Lillie, was four years old in mid-1944 when Esther began making preparations to go home on her first furlough. Esther had hoped that Lillie would start school soon, but Lillie's parents came and took her home because they didn't want her to become a Christian and go to school.

Esther was not anxious to go home, partly because of her kids, partly because of the sun, the birds, the rain, the flowers, and the garden.

But she did, in June of 1944.

(11)

Her first term was completed. She had been at Zorzor for a little over 2½ years. Never at any time had she indicated by spoken or written word that she considered going home to stay. She was committed to a lifetime of service on the mission field. But if there had been a shadow of doubt, it would have been dispelled by what happened just before she left. Dr. Sadler describes it:

"When she was preparing to leave Zorzor for her first furlough in the States, Loma and Kpelle women came to visit her bringing gifts, expressing their regrets, and telling her, 'Li na e va.' Go and come. It was an impressive spectacle, done with simplicity and sincerity, and with love. Many of those present owed their lives and the lives of their children to the woman whom they had come to speed on her way."

Pan Am's amphibious China Clipper was now flying out of Fisherman's Lake near Cape Mount, forty miles northwest of Monrovia. Esther, fretting already about being away from her patients and her babies at Zorzor, was ferried with Gertrude Buschman, Roslyn and nine-month-old Kezele Sadler from Monrovia to the Clipper in a tiny float plane.

The Clipper crew gave them a tour of the plane that evening and then put them up in a hostel ashore for the night. The next morning Esther flew to Brazil and then New York with Buschy, Roslyn, and Kezele. Wes Sadler had stayed in Zorzor because his replacement, Rev. George Flora, had been delayed in the States by the illness of one of his children. Wes would remain in Zorzor for almost another year.

As Esther flew to New York, D-Day on the beaches of Normandy had already taken place. The Allies were well established and on the move in France and

Belgium. Within a month Hitler would barely escape assassination. In July, the western Pacific islands of Saipan, Tinian, and Guam — the Marianas stepping-stones to Japan — would be liberated.

So Esther came home to a country tired of war but growing increasingly optimistic about an end to it. Gasoline and sugar were still rationed. Servicemen jammed the trains. High school girls wore their cardigan sweaters backwards and made their brothers or mothers button them up the back; they wore bobby socks and tucked a penny into the slot in their loafers. Crew-cut boys wore jeans during the week; on Saturday night dates and for Sunday morning church they wore white T-shirts, dress pants, and sports jackets.

Judy Garland belted out "Meet Me In St. Looie-Looie," and Bing Crosby crooned "Would You Like to Swing on a Star?"

Known only to a very few Americans, an automatic general-purpose computer made its first labored calculations at Harvard. With the transistor and silicon chip years in the future, the radio-tube-operated monster filled an entire room, had 760,000 moving parts and 500 miles of wires. It took four seconds to perform simple multiplication and eleven seconds to perform simple division. Skeptics hooted but the scientists at Harvard smiled smugly.

Esther went almost directly to the little town of Hyden, near the somewhat larger town of Hazard in southeastern Kentucky. She was enrolled in the Frontier Nursing Service, one of the few American schools of nurse-midwifery. A high percentage of her fellow students were also headed for the Third World. Esther laughed with them as they agreed that "in America, *doctors* deliver babies."

But there was no doctor in Zorzor and she had no idea when one would come. Already she had had too many horrible experiences trying to do things she had not been trained to do. She remembered with sorrow the babies and mothers she had lost because she just hadn't known what to do to save them.

She wrote Aunt Nora from Hyden, "I am getting good experience in every way here — surely this is where I was meant to spend my furlough. And am getting so many things besides midwifery." She meant, of course, that God had led her to Hyden. Through the retrospectoscope of the years since then, it is obvious that she was right.

She visited with Gertrude Buschman and her daughter Betty in Louisville, then tried to convince Aunt Nora to come to Hyden for a few weeks. Nora knew that if she went to Hyden, Esther would not come home, so she held out for a different plan: Esther was to come home. Nora won this little battle. Esther went home for two weeks before returning to Liberia.

(12)

In mid-March of 1945 she started back. Not yet did one get on an airplane in New York and fly overnight to Monrovia. Her first stopover was The Towers Hotel in Miami, where she was delayed for ten days awaiting passage. She used part of the time to do some last-minute shopping: yeast for Bertha Koenig at Kpaiye, shoes for herself, and hatchable eggs. On her last day in Miami, late in the afternoon, she finally found a dozen fertilized white leghorn eggs. She carried them through customs and FBI checkpoints in a brown paper bag and broke only one. The FBI agent didn't think it at all funny when Esther dead-panned, "Don't you want to open the eggshells?"

The next leg of her journey was on the Pan American Clipper to Belem, Brazil, where she had another long delay. At the mission station there she met up with Miriam Miller and her two daughters, Pauline Ziegler, with whom she had stayed at Mango Haven when she first arrived in Liberia, and a dozen other missionaries who gathered each morning for prayers. Her eleven eggs were still intact.

She got into town almost daily and complained that "Pauline has me almost shopped broke." But she got a doll for Mrs. James Frazer's little girl at Hyden, and for herself a fountain pen, umbrella, watch, and rain coat. And in one of the bazaars she found just the right birthday present for her father, a billfold, which she sent to him in Burlington, Colorado.

Alva Bacon was now 68. He had left his homestead ten years before and since then had lived with his brothers William and Vern in Bethany, Missouri, and with his niece Mrs. Harold (Della Leander) Matthies in Burlington. He would continue this rotation until a stroke in 1955 when he would go to a nursing home in Brush for the final two years of his life.

For the impatient and energetic Esther, the days were almost too relaxed for she was anxious to get back to her work, her friends and her babies in Zorzor. There was always that special tug on her heart, drawing her inexorably back to Africa.

She was far from alone in this.

"Africa," says Hal Faust, "is the kind of place where once you go there, you *go* back!"

Smith Hempstone* has written, "Africa is an outsized continent filled to such an extent with joy and sadness, cruelty and kindness, manifold sins and great compassion, that it inspires in the stranger either a loathing or a curious passion and fascination. Nowhere are there greater opportunities for good or evil, or for the recognition of one's essential self...I

---

*Longtime U.S. ambassador to Kenya, East Africa

found the pull of Africa intolerable; and now I am back and I am content."

And Barbara Greene, a cousin of Graham Greene who accompanied him on his walk across Liberia, writes of "the overwhelming magic of Africa. Like a drug it gets into the brain and sends it to sleep, so that nothing remains alive but the senses. The warmth flows into ones limbs, the music of the harps into the soul, the timelessness into the spirit, and the rest is perfect well-being with a tremendous peace."

After almost a month in Brazil, Esther finally got passage across to Liberia. Monrovia had continued to undergo dramatic changes. United States troops, stationed in Liberia since 1942, used huge earth moving equipment to enlarge Robertsfield, construct piers and docks, build and pave roads, flatten shanty-towns and erect buildings of stone and concrete and brick.

The missionaries noted that the GIs working without shirts and sun helmets seemed to suffer no ill effects from the sun and humidity. Sun helmets became a thing of the past for most of them, especially the younger people like Esther and Roslyn Sadler, who were quick to "forget" their helmets.

Now Esther wasted no time in getting up to Zorzor. In the year she'd been gone, the road had been extended to Belefani, leaving only a three days' walk by path. Esther was quick to note that having a road was not an unmixed blessing. Cars and trucks took incredible punishment and broke down constantly. Accidents were common, due partly to inexperienced drivers, partly to the road surface, which was sometimes soft, sometimes rocky, often muddy or slick with clay, always serpentine and always up and down and around hills and mountains. Esther was happy not to have such nuisances at Zorzor.

Her return after a year was an emotional experience for her and everyone else. She no longer wondered if she would ever call Zorzor "home."

Here were her babies, clambering on her lap and vying for her kisses, studying with wide eyes the tears that flowed from her eyes: Big Zizzi, growing strong and proud; Little Zizzi, almost as big as Big Zizzi; Buacoo, her name changed back from Lillie, now in school after all and becoming a Christian; Kombeh, who had torn the head off Buacoo's doll to see what it was made of; Boama, who had been deserted at age four because she was convulsing and obviously bewitched, now five and ready to go home to her parents at Kpaiye; and all the others who came running to Bayka, not appreciating yet that they were alive because of her.

Here was her new hospital, now fully completed by builder Rev. Lewis and the Sadlers. There were the new beds, and the mats under them for the patients' relatives to sleep on. There were the three six-foot-high mud-and-stick fireplaces Roslyn Sadler had built in the main ward for the patients because they complained about the cold nights. Originally whitened with clay, they were blackened now, as were the rafters overhead because there were no chimneys and the smoke merely drifted upwards.

But most of all, here were her patients, her friends, her nurses, all waiting for Bayka.

She moved slowly through the ward, chatting with the nurses, greeting familiar faces in the beds. Kirsten Marie (Ma) Jensen had been in charge for the past year, and was looking forward to getting back "home" to her babies in Sanoyea. With her rolling r's and mispronounced th's, she passed on the news that the nurses' training school was to be moved from Phebe to Zorzor.

Esther was very pleased because she knew that Zorzor would now get at least one more missionary nurse. And, Ma Jensen added, "Zorzor will get the first doctor who comes out from America."

Esther walked out of the main ward and looked in the OB room. There was the delivery table that Roslyn Sadler and the carpenter had built a year before, using as a model a picture of a delivery table in an old OB textbook. They had come up with a very functional table, even painted it silver and found some little wheels for it. Esther would use it for many years.

She smiled to herself as she remembered how she had initiated it just before her furlough: three little girls born on Easter Sunday morning. Then with an involuntary shudder, she considered — not for the first time — how very little she had known about obstetrics during that first term. But she had done the best she could do with the knowledge and the skills she had, which were much more than those of the village midwives. So, long ago, like other isolated doctors and nurses, she had made the justified rationalization that if she hadn't done what she could do with what she knew, nothing would have been done to change the existing obstetrical conditions in the bush. Now she could hardly wait to put all her new skills to work.

Esther smiled contentedly and walked out for several hours along the paths and streets of the compound and Zorzor-town, snapping fingers in greeting with dozens of people en route. She visited in the houses and checked out the old hospital compound by the cemetery where most of the buildings had now fallen down.

And beyond, in the bewitched and fetid jungle, were the towns and villages, her special fief.

(13)

There were other changes. Lizard had learned to lie down in the river in order to get riders off his back. He had also put Roslyn Sadler's horse

Gracious into such a condition that would have utilized Esther's new skills if she were human. The leopard that seemed to consider Zorzor part of its territory had returned to take two goats. Workmen were fixing the new hospital shutters and — finally — installing screens.

Frances Leonard was now Mrs. Morris and was expecting her first child. Roslyn Sadler, the resident "dentist," was still in the States so Esther would have to do extractions and fillings. When the Sadlers returned from furlough, they would move to Fassama, ten miles south of Zorzor.

Rev. George Flora, his wife, and four children, now lived in the zinc-roofed parsonage which George and "Skipper" Moore had built during the Floras' three-year term at Zorzor from 1938 to 1941.

George Flora, thirty-four years old in 1945, came from Oshkosh, Nebraska, to Zorzor in 1938. He had taken his Bachelor of Divinity degree at Western Seminary in 1936 and served two parishes in Nebraska while awaiting his call to the mission field. George Flora was another missionary who, like Esther Bacon and the Sadlers, would not wait for change to come to him. He was a doer. And one of the things he did would irrevocably change the interior of Liberia.

In just a few years he would drive a jeep to Zorzor.

(14)

Since a doctor was expected "momentarily" and would live in the "doctor's house," Esther moved in with Sarah Curran in the former nurses' dorm, up on the main mission compound, across the path from the Sadlers' house. Living with Sarah were her sister and her three children. The small, thatched, mud and wattle house contained two bedrooms, living room and kitchen.

Not surprisingly, Esther spent most of her free time in her bedroom, propped up against the headboard of her bed, typing letters or reading. On her windowsill at night slept a rooster, her "organic alarm clock." An arm's length from her bed was a rathole in the dirt floor. She wrote, "Two or three of its occupants have been chasing each other around my room this evening — wouldn't be too hard to catch, but I don't feel like murder and besides they're comforting companions with their mischievous antics..."*

After five weeks back in Zorzor, Esther very reluctantly made the arduous trip down to Harrisburg for Annual Conference. She never welcomed

---

The British Government Blue book on Liberia, May, 1935, states: "The rat population may fairly be described as swarming."

these separations from her patients and her children. Always in her mind and in her actions was the compulsion to get back to Zorzor. This was, of course, especially true when she was the only fully-trained nurse-midwife and there was no doctor on the station. But it continued throughout her life, even after nurses, midwives and doctors came to Zorzor.

Buschy had now returned, crippled some with rheumatism, but anxious to get up-country. She was being held down-country by her doctor until he felt she could undertake the still-taxing trip. She would, in fact, continue to serve in Zorzor for six more years.

Norma Bloomquist, still teaching at the girls' school, bubbled with happiness as she showed off her new ring. She had had a whirlwind 21½-hour courtship in Belem with a serviceman she met in the USO. They would marry after the war and come to Liberia together. Esther was happy for her, but in relating this to Aunt Nora she quipped, "Buschy reached from the States in a week, with no such catastrophes."

Esther never had any serious romantic attachments. She must have had the opportunity, for she would have been very attractive to men: sparkling blue eyes, softly waved blonde hair, perfect complexion, trim figure, and a quiet wit that made her fun to be with.

Margaret Miller says of her, "She was a very pleasant person, that's why we wanted her to visit. We liked her. She was an easy person to talk to. Not a silent person. Not a person you had to draw out. But not a garrulous person either. She didn't talk nonsense."

Then, of Esther's lack of love affairs, Margaret says, "One time I was driving her to Wozi and I said, 'Esther, how come you didn't get married this time when you were home?' And she said, with sort of a sideways glance and a sparkle in her eyes, 'The Board didn't say we could bring out husbands.' "

And then Margaret added with real feeling, "Her whole life was just tremendous."

(15)

One of the first things Esther did when she returned to Zorzor from conference was to organize midwifery classes for her nurses. She knew she would have to teach them, at least until a doctor came out. She never considered this added work. It was *part* of her work. She expected to be called to the villages even more than she had during her first term. She had already noted with great satisfaction that there was a decided increase in the number of women coming to the hospital to have their babies. So it was important for the other nurses at the hospital to know everything she could teach them.

Though she had held classes for the village midwives, she hadn't felt competent to teach the nurses. Now she was. And she really liked delivering babies. Once when she apologized to Aunt Nora for not writing oftener, she added, "WHO wants to write letters, anyway? Somehow writing is such a dull occupation compared to catching babies...now please — this is not for publication, yah!"

Before taking the Frontier Nursing Service midwifery course, she had thought her "library" at Zorzor adequate. Now she looked it over with a considerably jaundiced eye and immediately sent home for three textbooks: *DeLee's Obstetrics for Nurses* ($3), *DeLee's Obstetrics for Doctors* ($10), and *Beck's Obstetrical Practice* ($7).

As she was writing to Aunt Nora to order the books, she was called to Kpaiye where a mother had delivered one twin but the other was caught in a transverse lie. Using a maneuver which she had learned at Hyden but had not yet used at Zorzor, she turned the baby and delivered it alive. (The maneuver is called a "podalic version" because the operator reaches into the uterus from below, grasps the baby's feet and pulls it out feet first. Esther would teach it to dozens of midwives and a succession of doctors from Earl Reber to Paul Mertens.)

She brought the mother and both little boys back to Zorzor on Lizard, saw them admitted to the maternity ward, and finished her letter to Nora, "Thanks to God, it was not too late." Two months later the mother made her declaration of faith in Christ and was baptized.

This was the *modus operandi* Esther would follow the rest of her life. She would not take credit for anything: it was always the Holy Spirit working through her and on the hearts of the people. She always said, "Thanks to God, it was not too late."

Whether or not she had the inclination, she did not have the time to do much direct proselytizing. But she did often pray with a patient, whether or not he or she were Christian.

Sometimes when a mother was ready to leave the hospital with a baby recovered from a serious illness or difficult birth, Esther would sit on her bed and say softly, "You should thank God for your baby. The life she has now, God gave her. We all thought she was going to die. Now God has kept her here with you rather than taking her to heaven with Him. Whenever you can, you should go to church and listen and thank God for leaving her here."

Her compassion, her love, and her kindness showed in everything she said and did. She could take in her arms children with the grossest deformities and cuddle them as if they were the cutest little babies she had ever seen. It was as if she were totally blinded to the grotesqueness of physical imperfections.

She had a supreme reverence for life. Margaret Miller says, "I've seen her fight for life. There was a kid I'm sure was dead. But Esther was giving it mouth to mouth respiration. I mean, I've seen her *fight* for life. Nothing else existed in the universe except the energy she was putting out to save that kid. Even when she had been here years and years she would still throw herself into the fight for life. One time when a child died she threw herself sobbing over the body and cried, 'This one should not have died.'

"She was never pretentious. You'd never hear her say anything in praise of herself. But there was no *false* modesty. Just matter of fact and on to the business at hand."

Bishop Roland Payne echoes these thoughts. "For her it was really a pleasure to be with a patient. Not only an OB but with other patients. I know she gave her life, gave her breath, to many people...she was so kind...she didn't care for material things at all. She gave all her energies to her work."

This reverence for life carried over to animals. When thatchers were putting a new roof on her house, a heavy rainfall came before they were finished and soaked the inside of the house. As she built a fire in the middle of the bedroom floor she suddenly realized that the rain had put out the fire in her kerosene incubator where five eggs were ready to hatch. One little chick had already started to peck through the shell and was near death. Leaving Sarah Curran to guard the fire in her bedroom, she carried the egg cupped in her hands to the hospital where by the fire in Mama Loupu's room it revived and finished its job of getting out of the shell.

When bats flew through the wards, the Loma people knocked them out of the air with anything handy. Esther picked them up by the back of the neck, carried them around a while and then released them outside.

Once, years later, some boys knocked a five-foot snake out of a tree just as Dr. Paul Mertens walked by. He recognized it as the banana tree snake, *Boiega blandini*, a rear-fanged, mildly poisonous snake. He recovered it and put it in a box in medical stores. Later, as he attempted to take it out, it coiled around him in such a way that he couldn't handle it. Esther happened by and nonchalantly uncoiled it for him, then began telling him about a black snake she had had in her house for years.

Another time, also in a later year, a leopard came in the night onto the veranda of her house and killed her two monkeys, Jocko and Josephine. Esther heard the noise and without thinking of her own safety dashed outside and scared off the leopard. But the monkeys were dead. Practical as always, she used the monkeys next day in her anatomy class.

(16)

When things were quiet at the hospital she took long walks. One walk she loved was along the edge of the swamp which extended far into the high forest from both sides of the causeway between the hospital hill and the school compound hill. She wrote, "So many lovely things there — the many ferns, bits of brightness on leaf and flower, vines, orange wild fruits, birds and frogs and crickets." As much as she loved her patients and her children and her work at the hospital, she cherished those moments alone in the unsettled places.

She may never have read Chekhov's "Ward Six," but she would have agreed with his assertion, "True happiness is impossible without solitude." And knowing this, she would have found it strange, as Thoreau did, "that so few ever come to the woods to see how the pine lives and grows and spires . . ." But she was not a "loner" in the sense of disliking contacts with other people.

She derived much pleasure from her treks to the villages, especially as the years went by and she developed deep friendships with the people. Bishop Payne says, "She had a personal love of the people. She used to go to the villages just to go into the houses and sit down with the people. Oh, she had lots of medical reasons, but they were her friends. If she had a day off and there were no serious cases around, she'd take a walk to Kiliwu or Fisebu or to Yella or to Zolowo. (All four to eight miles from Zorzor.) Just to see an old friend."

She enjoyed having guests in her home. Those who got to know her well recognized this. Others saw only the nurse driven to long hours of apparently selfless service. But she had a zest for the life around her on the mission station and in the high forest.

Once, in a letter to Aunt Nora, she playfully invited her to dinner: "You'll get rice and soup at my house, cooked by Doughie. If you visit Mrs. Buschman, and there is flour here which is neither too moldy nor too wormy (but we sift these out) you're very likely to get cake or pie or bread."

She loved to give parties for children. Christmas Eve afternoon in 1945, she gave a party under the big mango tree on Rev. Flora's lawn for her orphans, children of the hospital workers and villagers, and the Floras' four youngsters. Somehow she had found some little pails which she filled with popcorn and hard candy. She sat under the tree watching the little eyes bug as they took the paper covering off the tops of the pails. She wrote Nora, "Where toys as we know them hardly exist, these little gifts were much appreciated. Believe it!"

After Christmas morning service the next day she visited several houses in town and was given an egg by one lady and a chicken by another.

Later that afternoon there was a family dinner at Floras' where they ex-changed gifts. Esther's gift from the Floras was a hen and seven fluffy peeping chicks just hatched. Only two of Esther's eleven leghorn eggs, brought laboriously from Miami, had hatched and both of those chicks shortly succumbed to some mysterious chicken malady. So she was particularly grateful for this Christmas present.

(17)

A runner called her away from that dinner. Since it was daytime and the farm village only forty minutes away, Lana Bartolomei went with her. The situation in the village as described by the runner was a familiar one to Esther, though she would never really get used to it. Lana was aghast.

Esther recognized the name of the woman. Aside from her intrinsic value as a human being, she was of consid-erable practical and monetary value to her husband and family. Her husband had given a very large dowry for her,* part of it in labor which he had done for her family for years. Her own family depended on her for everything. She planted the cotton, harvested it, made thread from it and dyed it, readying it for her husband to weave into cloth. She collected wood, tended the fire, cooked the meals. She was, in short, a perfect African wife.

Spinning cotton thread

As Esther and her train came into the village, they found the husband sitting dejectedly against the wall of his house, head hung in despair, almost unthinking. It was he who had sent for Esther in a last-ditch at-tempt to save his wife. He got to his feet as Esther approached, "Bayka, Bayka, you've come!"

His wife had been in labor for over 48 hours and had been given up as hopeless. The zoes had ordered him to abandon her in the bush. Clearly she had done something evil which would overshadow the whole town, for it was obvious that the ancestral spirits were highly displeased. The poor husband had already taken her into the high forest and left her there to die.

Lana stared wide-eyed at the man, then turned to Esther. "He just left her in the jungle — to *die*?" She had not yet grasped the power of the societal and animistic conventions which made it clear to this good hus-band that he had had no choice.

---

*Loma custom directs the husband to "repay" his wife's family for having removed a valued family member "out of their hands" (*kulo te ya*).

But Esther understood. She said, "He did what he *had* to!"

He took Esther through the now darkening jungle to the isolated spot where his wife lay crouched in thick undergrowth, hoping to avoid nocturnal predators. Esther assessed the problem immediately.

The mother was actually in fair condition. She was dehydrated and fatigued, but alert and cooperative. As she had done so many times before, Esther hung a bottle of fluid from the branch of the kola tree overhead and started an IV in the woman's arm. She sent a runner to a nearby stream for water, scrubbed her hands, put on sterile rubber gloves, washed the woman, and examined her.

In vain Esther tried to deliver the baby's head. If it had been simply a matter of an unyielding outlet, she could have done an episiotomy. But in this case the bony pelvis was too small to allow the head to pass. Even as she worked, the baby's heart tones got slower and slower and finally could not be heard.

"The baby is dead," she said to the husband. Numbly he nodded in comprehension. This meant to him that his wife would also die. There was no alternative in his lexicon of life.

Esther had no such pessimism. She sent a runner to Zorzor to bring back Miss Smarte, a Liberian nurse, with some instruments she didn't routinely carry.

As they waited, Esther ordered fires to be built around the woman and hot rocks placed close enough to warm the air all around her. In the heat of the fire she sterilized huge banana leaves and put them under the woman.

Lana, expecting just to observe, was quickly put to work. She found herself doing things she had never envisioned in her wildest dreams about life in Africa. But when Esther in her humble and down-to-earth way asked her to do this or that she did it without question.

When all had been done that could be done, they sat down to wait. Miss Smarte came with the instruments.

Esther sent the husband back to the village. She did not want him there during the next hour. What she had to do was one of the most unpleasant tasks ever to be performed by anyone, anywhere. She had to use specialized craniotomy instruments to crush the baby's head so that she could deliver it. Though she knew that the baby was dead, though she knew the mother would soon die if the baby were not extracted, this hardly diminished the horror of the sight and sound of what she did.

But she did it, around midnight of Christmas Day, in the light of a kerosene lantern, in the jungle under a kola nut tree. Then she buried the baby and returned to the village where she and her party slept overnight. The next morning they carried the resurrected woman to Zorzor, where she stayed for only a few days before returning home with her grateful husband.

Chapter Five

(1946-1950)

(1)

In early 1946, near the end of his second year as president of Liberia, William Vacanarat Shadrach Tubman made his first official visit to Zorzor.

President Tubman was born in 1895 in Harper, far down the coast on the tip of Cape Palmas, and raised in poverty under the strict discipline of his stonemason father. He attended daily family prayer services, went to church and school regularly. He slept on the floor because his father thought beds too soft and degrading to character development.

At 19 he was already a Methodist lay preacher with a job as junior collector of customs. In his spare time he studied law and at age 23 passed the bar. He rose rapidly in politics, and at age 35 — in 1930 — was elected to the Liberian Senate. Witty, cigar-smoking, he labeled himself the "Convivial Cannibal from the Downcast Hinterlands," and set about to oppose the entrenched establishment as a member of the True Whig Party.

In 1944, as a darkhorse candidate, he was elected to the presidency, a post he would hold until his death in London in 1971 at the age of 76. The list of his contributions to both Liberian and continental African life is endless, but a few may be recorded to give a picture of the man: he introduced women's suffrage and property rights, authorized the direct participation in government by all tribes-people, established and expanded nationwide schools (especially in the interior), opened Liberia's natural resources to capital and specialized knowledge from abroad, abolished provinces and created counties, built roads into the interior, established teacher-training programs, encouraged foreign aid, encouraged mission programs especially in rural areas, placed specific and calculated emphasis on national unity, and initiated Liberia's role as arbiter and advocate of African peace.

In 1946, when he walked out from Zorzor-town to the Lutheran Hospital, he brought along his personal physician. They were greeted by Frances Leonard Morris and other members of the staff. The head of the hospital, Esther Bacon, was in the delivery room at that moment, up to her elbows in blood and trouble with an obstetrical patient. She immediately enlisted the doctor's help. President Tubman returned to town.

Before Esther and the doctor had controlled the patient's bleeding, a message came from President Tubman that he wanted the doctor in town. The doctor stepped back from the table and prepared to leave.

"Doctor!" Esther said. "You can't leave now."

Startled, the doctor replied, "When the president calls, I go."

With a glint in her eye which others present recognized as a warning signal, she handed the doctor an instrument and said, "Just keep working, doctor, I'll take care of President Tubman."

He stayed and together they saved the woman's life.

After surgery Esther sat down and wrote a long note to President Tubman, explaining the situation and apologizing for keeping the doctor tied up. Characteristically, the president chuckled when he read the note and said, "Her actions were entirely appropriate."

This was the president's first contact with Esther Bacon. His second came just a few days later.

Pastor George Flora was off on a bush trip, visiting villages in the high forest. Saturday night came and he had not returned. Who would preach at the Sunday morning service in the Zorzor church?

Esther, knowing that President Tubman was a lay preacher, sent him a note asking him to preach the sermon the next day. Graciously he accepted the "invitation" and conducted the service. As he left the church, he asked one of the lay leaders, "Just who is this woman who orders presidents around?"

The lay leader laughed and told him.

These were the contacts that prompted President Tubman to investigate this audacious nurse more thoroughly and eventually led to her first decoration, along with Dr. Earl Reber, for "outstanding performance in midwifery and medicine."

(2)

When Esther went down the path to Harrisburg in May of 1946 for conference, Phebe Hospital was in turmoil. For three reasons.

One, Phebe was being closed, after all these years.

Two, Dr. Earl Reber and his wife Anna Mae were expected to arrive from the States in July. He would supervise the closing of Phebe, then would go up the path to Zorzor where he would be permanently stationed. One of his first major projects at Zorzor would be to continue the construction of the new hospital started by Dr. Moore and Rev. Flora, half a mile closer to the town, using the funds left by Sarah Curran almost ten years before.

Three, the nursing school at Phebe would be transferred to Zorzor, to be staffed by Dr. Reber and missionary nurses Esther Bacon, Hazel Biederbeck, and Marianna Bunger. Miss Biederbeck, who would be in charge of the school, was already in Liberia, but had been seconded temporarily to Sanoyea where she was serving the dual role of re-organizing the clinic and waiting to deliver a child of Mrs. William Welmers.* Miss Bunger had not yet arrived in Liberia.

This was all exciting news to Esther, though she had heard rumors in Zorzor for months. After conference she could hardly wait to get back to her hospital to begin preparations for Reber's arrival.

But Earl Reber did not arrive in Liberia until Labor Day and did not get up to Zorzor until late December. He had been scheduled to fly the New York-Belem-Monrovia route on the China Clipper but all the Clippers had been grounded due to a structural problem. An engine had fallen out of one plane over Boston; in a separate incident in Reading, Pennsylvania, the crew had been trapped by a fire and almost lost.

Earl was most anxious to get to Liberia, so he maneuvered his way onto a DC-4 chartered by Firestone Rubber Company and flew for three long days and nights to Liberia via Gander, Goose Bay in Labrador, Shannon, Lisbon, Casablanca and finally Liberia. Anna Mae would follow later.

Cautioned about the rainy season by his aunt and uncle, Harry and Bessie Heilman, whom Esther had visited on her first trek through Sanoyea in 1941, Reber arrived with boots and umbrella. He laughs now as he says, ''The Firestone people were dressed in light Palm Beach suits and panama hats and we looked so dowdy.''

He would soon doff his dowdy duds and appear in a white shirt and bow tie or in a neatly pressed intern's blouse with buttons across one shoulder and up the neck. Often in the cool season he would also wear

---

*Wife of the Dr. Welmers who did the Kpelle language work.

a short white jacket. New to the tropics, he would continue to wear a white cork sun helmet for another couple of years.

Earl Reber was a highly trained, exceptionally motivated, dedicated Christian doctor. He had gone through Temple University Medical School during the war in three years, graduated with honors, then interned at the Episcopal Hospital in Philadelphia. He studied pathology for two years and public health for one year at Johns Hopkins. Later on he would do research on shistosomiasis for a year and a half at Columbia School of Public Health.

After almost four months at Harrisburg, supervising the closing of Phebe Hospital and the packing of medications and other equipment for delivery to Zorzor, he traveled up-country with Anna Mae, Hazel Biederbeck and two Liberian nurses — and ran head-on into Esther Bacon.

He says, "I finally arrived in Zorzor a little before Christmas and Esther was ready to put me to work at the hospital the moment I arrived. I told her that I was going to unpack my things and I would appear at the hospital on the first day of 1947. So that was the first problem I had with Esther. She was ready to put me to work on my arrival. I did tell her that she could call me if there were any emergencies."

The only record of Esther's reaction to this came in a letter to Aunt Nora a week after the arrival of the Rebers and the three nurses. She wrote, "Pray for us that all may work together according to His will."

It is easy to picture the scene: Esther has been at Zorzor since 1941, working without a doctor and, in her first term, without adequate obstetrical skills. She has prayed daily that a doctor be sent to Zorzor. Now one has been in Liberia for 3½ months, finally comes to Zorzor, and says, "I need another ten days to unpack my things and get settled in my house."

But Esther need not have worried (if she did) because Earl Reber would work at Zorzor until 1963, longer than any other doctor in the history of that hospital.*

The Rebers moved into Gertrude Buschman's house on the hill and Buschy moved into the guest house across the compound. The thatch had been replaced with "zinc," but the sides were still wire screen and netting with slatted, roll-down, bamboo curtains for privacy. Earl would come to love the house, especially the fireplaces in every room, and described it as the most comfortable house he ever lived in, and says he would return to it for the rest of his life if necesssary.

One of the things Dr. Reber unpacked was a carton of chloroquin tablets. While "champing at the bit to get to Liberia," he had read a newspaper

---

*Other doctors who would work with Esther: Dr. Lowell Yund, 1949-52; Dr. Franklin Keller, 1952-65; Dr. James Stull, 1959-65; Dr. Paul Mertens, 1963-72.

report about the new drug. The Council for Malaria Studies sent him 5,000 tablets which he carried to Zorzor, the first mission in Liberia — and probably Africa — to convert to chloroquin from quinine and atabrine. Only Bertha Koenig at Kpaiye balked at switching, but this didn't bother Earl because "she was just one of these older people who are more or less immune to malaria."

He also brought streptomycin, newly introduced in the States for the treatment of tuberculosis. But the complication rate with streptomycin used alone was high and he wisely deferred using it until the complementary drugs PAS and isoniazid were brought out by Esther when she returned from furlough in 1948.

(3)

The first six months of Earl Reber's first term coincided with the last six months of Esther's second term. It was a time of adjustment for Earl Reber and readjustment for Esther Bacon.

Esther had been the only medical missionary at Zorzor for five years. No one had told her what to do. She accounted to no one except herself and her God. She had established a pattern which worked for her and which had begun to turn things around in Loma-Kpelle-land. She *ran* the hospital and the clinics.

Dr. Reber was a product of a highly sophisticated medical system where doctors ran the show and nurses did what they were told. He was far from overbearing. In fact, Esther's first reaction was, "Both he and his wife are very fine, all and more than we could have expected." But he had definite ideas about practicing medicine and there were moments of conflict in those first months while Esther and Dr. Reber sorted things out.

On January 1st, 1947, Dr. Reber came over to the new hospital to begin his work. He found Esther passing out medications on the porch of the hospital. Not aware that Esther knew everyone there, he wondered how she picked out the ones who needed medications. He watched for a while and decided that, yes, there was some kind of order, but not his kind.

As he and Esther stood talking, he asked about the barn-like building up where they were cutting an airstrip out of the jungle.

"Well," she said, "that's the dispensary but it was built by a doctor ("Skipper" Moore) who the only thing he knew how to build was a barn."* She gave him her lop-sided grin, her eyes twinkling.

---

*Author's note: Not literally true. According to Roslyn Sadler, when Moore had first arrived, he said, "The only thing I've ever built was a barn."

He returned the grin but was not put off the track so easily. "Well, Esther, why don't we use it?"

"The people won't come there."

"If they want to see me, they'll have to come to the dispensary."

She didn't like lining people up to see the doctor, but had no problem accepting the edict. And it was not long before she saw that this new kind of order was necessary to handle the large number of people who started coming to the outpatient clinic.

Before long Esther began devoting her efforts to the hospital inpatients after the morning surgery was completed, while Dr. Reber ran the out-patient clinics up at the "barn." He sat at a table with a money-box for collection of fees, which were paid over to his assistant-interpreter and placed directly into the box, a routine that would persist for three more decades. Then he examined the patient, gave out the proper medicine, scheduled surgery, or perhaps sent the patient for laboratory tests.

After Esther made rounds at the hospital she came to him with her prob-lems. He told her what to do, or went down to see the patients with her. "This was one of her strong points," Dr. Reber recalls, "that she knew when to come for help. And the doctors in turn knew that when Esther came for help, they should help."

Then he added, "She was a quality person. She was the kind of person who could work with you, and with me, and she accepted our differences. She was a unique person, a hard-working, dedicated nurse. If she had any defects it would be that she worked too hard and at times did not recognize when she was tired. And it would be at these times that prob-lems would arise and she would have a hard time facing a death. She had given so much of herself to the survival of the individual that she couldn't look upon the loss of the patient as anything but her own inability to cope. So when a thing like this happened she would cry, but even that would not cut her off from her work for very long."

(4)

Just two weeks after his arrival, Earl Reber was initiated rather abruptly into the life of a missionary doctor in roadless Africa. A runner came up from Fassama with word that Roslyn Sadler had begun to bleed. She was now 6½ months pregnant with her second child. A month before she had bled rather vigorously and Esther had had her brought up to Zorzor by hammock, where she stayed for ten days.

Esther took off immediately, knowing the way, while Dr. Reber gathered together porters to carry the big tin trunk of medical equipment and other materiel.

As he struggled up the ridges and scrambled down the slopes on his way to treat his first missionary patient, Earl remembered a discussion he had had with Dr. Heilman. Uncle Harry had said that one of the problems on the mission field was that the missionaries often were unkind to each other, that they made rash statements and even false accusations, that sometimes the doctors acted as if they had come out only to treat sick Africans, not sick missionaries. Earl had resolved at the time that he would not be like that and he would prove it in time. That time had come.

A more pressing thought was the immediacy of Roslyn Sadler's problem. What could he do out in the jungle for a threatened sponaneous abortion? Mentally he reviewed the possible causes and ticked off the few weapons in his armamentarium. This exercise did not make him very happy.

A third thought was more reassuring: Esther Bacon would be there, was already on her way.

Esther arrived first, shoes in hand, having walked the ten miles through the high forest over steep ridges and through swamps in less than three hours. She was immensely relieved to find Roslyn not *in extremis* but waiting patiently in bed. In fact, Roslyn took one look at Esther and said, "Esther! You didn't walk here in your bare feet!"

Esther tossed her shoes in a corner and said, "They got in the way."

"Oh, Esther, what are we going to do with you? Why didn't you ride your horse?"

"I couldn't catch him in the dark and there was no time to fool with him!"

Earl Reber arrived shortly, breathless and anxious. Together he and Esther succeeded in stopping this second hemorrhage and threat to Kumbe's developing life. From the signs, symptoms, and history, Earl was sure that he was dealing with a "placenta praevia," a premature separation of the placenta, because he thought he could feel the placenta covering the cervical canal. He decided that Roslyn should be carried to Zorzor the next morning by hammock so she would be under constant supervision and could be delivered by Caesarian section if necessary. There was no argument from Wes or Roslyn.

So he and Esther stayed overnight with the Sadlers. As the others sat sipping cool drinks, Roslyn said from the bed where she lay flat with the foot propped up, "Thank you so much for coming, Dr. Reber. It isn't every doctor who'd make a house call three hours away." Then added, with a chuckle, "On foot."

They talked of many things that evening: the relief of finally having a doctor on the field, Wes's full-time work of reducing Loma to writing, Esther's work in the villages (which was already beginning to bother Earl Reber), Roslyn's frustrating attempts to save the motherless babies brought to her.

The return trip the next morning was slow but uneventful. Wes walked behind Roslyn's hammock to Zorzor but returned to Fassama after lunch. Dr. Reber placed Roslyn in the nurses' dormitory with Hazel Biederbeck, up on the hill near the Floras' house and only a hundred feet from Esther's. He ordered Roslyn to stay in bed and not sit up without help. Her baby was not due until the end of March and it was now only mid-January. But with Hazel in the house giving her 24-hour nursing care, and with Esther so close, Roslyn felt safer than she would have in the States.

Earl Reber decided that Roslyn should have a Caesarian section as soon as the baby was big enough to survive. What he didn't have was an operating room on the new hospital compound. So he got his men to work moving the operating room from the old hospital.

Roslyn, from her house on the path between the old compound and the new, watched the parts of the operating room go by. "First the roof," she recalls, "then the windows and frames, and so on. There was a race on to see who would win — Earl Reber and his operating room transplanted to its new location, or the baby."

The baby won.

A month later, on the evening of February 13th, before the new operating room was ready, Roslyn began to bleed again, this time seriously. Roslyn tells the story: "It was a long night for everyone. Mr. Helm from Firestone was having dinner with the Rebers. He grabbed a flashlight and headed for town to gather his workmen. Earl examined me and took off for the hospital. Mr. Helm's men and the hospital staff moved everything needed from the hospital to the living room of the house where I was staying. I believe every lamp and lantern available was brought to the house. Certainly every medical worker possible and all the missionaries and Mr. Helm were there. It was the most public birth possible in the dark of an African night!

"I was moved from my bed to the table in the living room — I was losing a great deal of blood. Earl talked to me about his inability to use ether because of the kerosene lamps. He said that the less sedation used, the better chance my baby had, since he was going to be premature. I told him I wanted my baby, do what he had to do.

"The novocaine helped with the *first* incision. The 23rd Psalm and my request for someone to play the record player helped some during the rest. I felt so sorry for Earl and Esther, working with hunting lights on their foreheads, while other missionaries held flashlights and all prayed for my life and the baby's. I remember Buschy at my head, wiping sweat from my face, Miss Biederbeck watching blood pressure and doing what nurses do at such times, the shadows on Earl's and Esther's faces as someone wiped away the sweat.

"I remember looking at the Congo mats used for the ceiling, studying the design of the weaving, and thinking all we need now is a stampede of rats up there to shake down stuff from up there. And the never-ending PAIN — until I heard the baby cry and someone exclaimed, 'He looks just like his brother.' It was 11:45 P.M. according to Zorzor clocks, on February 13, 1947."

And then Hazel Biederbeck announced the good news, "He weighs six pounds. Esther, we won't need your incubator after all."

(5)

The next major conflict between Esther and Earl Reber came when Reber made it clear that he thought Esther belonged at the hospital, not out in the forest at all hours of the night and day, sometimes for days at a time.

One day as he sat on a low stool dressing leg ulcers, he said to her, "Esther, you're tiring yourself too much on these long trips into the bush. You've done the job you set out to do — getting the women to come in, and to bring their babies back for pediatric care."

He took off his wire-rim glasses, polished them with a white linen hand-kerchief, and looked up at Esther with his sharply intelligent eyes. "That job's over. Now we need you here."

She didn't argue. There wasn't much she could say. But there was much to think about.

She was still dealing with this proposed major change in her life when she went to Monrovia in July, 1947, en route to the States on furlough. The church offices in Monrovia were busy. After 87 years of Lutheran mission work, the Evangelical Lutheran Church of Liberia was being formed. Dr. Luther Slifer had come to Monrovia in 1946 for the express purpose of organizing the Church. Rev. Louis Bowers was preparing the read the new constitution at the Constitutional Convention. Significantly, the new Church would still be under the iron control of the Lutheran Mission Conference, a separate body comprised of missionaries. Another twelve years would pass before Dr. Earl Erb would come to Liberia to reorganize the church and write another constitution to give Liberians a say in their own church.

Esther left Liberia by ship, which she preferred to flying because it gave her a chance to recondition herself to the amenities of civilization — like regular meals, bathtubs and indoor plumbing, time to read, time to think.

As she sat in her deck-chair or lay on her bunk in the tiny stateroom, her thoughts constantly returned to the people and her work in Zorzor.

Several things were apparent. She wasn't ready to give up her village work entirely. Far too many pregnant women *would* wait until it was too late to come to the hospital. Far too many men *would* forbid their wives to come to Zorzor until the zoes, midwives and sandplayers had done everything they could. Though country illnesses were slipping one by one across the zo-drawn line and becoming hospital illnesses, the process had not yet affected the baby business much.

If only Hazel Biederbeck would help in the hospital more, Esther thought, then I could keep going to the villages. But Hazel had decided that since she was the designated teacher for the nurses' training school, she was not going to take part in the medical care in the hospital. Esther agreed with Dr. Reber that Hazel couldn't teach student nurses properly unless she could cope with the problems in the hospital.

She smiled inwardly: Earl was stubborn all right. If he'd give a little and go ahead and order his workers to straighten out the path by the hospital that Hazel didn't like, and enlarge the pharmacy like she wanted, maybe *she'd* give in and come down to the hospital.

But that wasn't Esther's problem now — Earl and Hazel would have that ironed out one way or another by the time she returned.

Another thing was obvious. She was going to be Dr. Reber's right hand man (woman?) in the operating room. Dr. Reber was not a surgeon by training, but there was much surgery to be done and he had already started to do it. He *did* do very competent surgery, Esther thought. Like Ros's C-section. A man who can do *that* under *those* conditions, has got to be much more than just adequate.

So she was concerned about her own competence in the operating room. She hadn't worked in a *real* operating room for over ten years, and that had been as a student. There were certain things you never forget, but there were other things you do forget, and furthermore, there were many things she'd never learned. Oh, well, she thought, time will tell.

(6)

When she arrived in the States, she went on retreat to a lakeside Bible camp, Mt. Carmel, on Lake Carlos near Alexandria, Minnesota. Aunt Nora came to visit and brought all the news of home. When Nora left, Esther moved into a small cabin with two other young women. One was Mavis Felin, a Luther College girl who was very shy and retiring, but friendly and full of questions about missions. She planned to go into nurses' training to prepare herself for mission service in Columbia, South America.

The other was Miss Hansen, a supervisor at the largest civilian hospital in the world, the 3500-bed Cook County Hospital in Chicago, where one-third of all U.S. doctors then practicing had had part or all of their training.

Miss Hansen was active in the Christian Nurses' Fellowship and had been mailing packages to Africa for years. Esther helped her with practical suggestions about what was really needed on the mission field. And Miss Hansen vigorously supported Esther's idea of working in a Stateside operating room to learn the nurse's role in modern surgery.

So when Esther returned to Sioux City, she immediately looked for a place to study. She walked into the operating room at Mercy Hospital, introduced herself to the supervisor, Gladys Holm, and told her she would work for nothing in return for all the instruction she could get. Gladys was so intrigued by this quiet yet forthright young woman that she arranged for her to work for two months under her own supervision and with some of the more active and learned doctors.

Gladys remembers that Esther's concern was always for the welfare of the patient. She says, "I would have other people griping about the length of time surgery was taking and what we had to do in the cleanup, but never from Esther."

To everyone's surprise, Esther established a routine which, though common practice now in the better ORs, was almost unheard of then. She went down to the wards the day before surgery to get acquainted with the patients and learn what their problems were. On the morning of surgery she went with the orderlies to bring the patients to the operating room. After surgery she followed their progress on the ward for several days. She treated each patient as a person, not as just another unconscious body on an operating table. Nor was it her way to send them back to the ward and then forget about them.

She learned a great deal in the operating room, both as "scrub nurse" at the Mayo table, and as circulator. But she was also a great help to Gladys Holm with the students.

Gladys says, "Our kids were a little in awe of her because here she'd been out in Africa where they were doing all these things. She talked about not being able to have lights for the surgery and about a lion* that had torn a person and she had had to deal with that — and did — and the person lived. They (the students) were really not so sophisticated and it kind of threw them. She would spend her time with her patients and not goofing off like some of us do!"

---

*Actually a leopard. In a letter to Aunt Nora from Zorzor she had told about the new intermission radio and a few other modernities creeping into her life. Then she added: "In the midst of civilization descending upon this hinterland — a leopard caught a man this week, and we sewed and sewed."

The doctors quickly realized that they were dealing with someone out of the ordinary. All took a great interest in her and helped her in every way they could. One of the doctors said to Gladys Holm one day, "We've got to get her *here.*"

"She's a missionary, Dr. Down."

"Oh," was all he said. He hadn't realized that she was going back to Africa, but he was always glad when she was on his team.

It was a time of rapid change in antibiotic treatment. She had been amazed at Zorzor as Earl Reber told her what was happening. Now she saw it on a larger scale. Doctors used penicillin widely and some were already worried about indiscriminate use. For the first time in history, drugs (streptomycin, isoniazid, and para-amino-salicylic acid) *cured* TB. Patients with pernicious anemia took Vitamin B-12 shots now instead of eating a pound of liver a day. Cortisone cautiously used for rheumatoid arthritis produced dramatic relief of symptoms. Esther not only watched all this with awe, but collected as much medicine as she could to take back with her.

She also watched carefully to see what new "hardware" was being used and gathered together what she could. She packed away some boxes of polyethelene IV tubing and some new kinds of needles. She was intrigued by a newly popular form of anesthesia called "continuous spinal" and learned enough about it that she was able to teach the technique to Dr. Reber when she returned. She got the formulae for new kinds of IV solutions and knew that she could make almost all of them right in the Zorzor hospital. She was amazed that mouth-to-mouth respiration was just gaining a foothold because she had used it for years in Africa.*

(7)

It wasn't all hospital work on that furlough. She went to church on Sundays with Nora and afterwards ate lunch in one of the hotels. One Sunday, after lunch with Nora and Lucille Anderson, she said, "Let's go by the church and see how many people are planting flowers."

Lucille remembers the day: "The church people were supposed to come and plant flowers that day. And there was hardly anybody, two or three people, so we get out of the car, we leave her aunt in the car, while we

*Author's note: According to my father's diary, my sister Elsie, born in 1923 in India, was kept alive for *six hours* by the doctor "breathing into her the breath of life." Winfred Harley, wife and biographer of Dr. George Harley, interprets I Kings 17:21,22 as the use by Elijah of mouth-to-mouth resuscitation. So much for modern medicine!

planted flowers. Then came a downpour, oh yuck, and Esther's shoes were all wet and muddy and she just turned the outside faucet on and washed her shoes off and put them back on.''

For Esther, that was nothing new. In Zorzor she often tied the laces together and put her shoes around her neck, as she did on her trip to Fassama to help Dr. Reber with Roslyn Sadler. When she got where she was going, she'd wash her feet and put the shoes back on. This was something the people of Sioux City couldn't understand.

She was also called upon to speak in churches, to missionary societies, and to other groups. As good as she was with patients, as comfortable as she was when talking with mothers and pregnant women, and as forthright as she was in teaching students in Gladys Holm's operating room, she wasn't an eloquent speaker.

Eleanor (Carlson) Raynie comments, ''She spoke fast but very low and in a monotone. She didn't use much expression. I had to listen very intently to hear what she was saying.''

Lucille Anderson remembers: ''It was very disappointing to hear her talk. Very soft voice and sort of a shyness there. 'Course having no microphones then made it even worse. Here she had a fabulous background to tell us about, her work and everything, and yet she just didn't have that little flair for presentation that would lend itself more to the audience.''

Gladys Holm agreed. ''In the nurses' lounge when they were visiting she was very quiet, she listened all the time, she didn't miss a trick. When she was teaching my students, they learned things that I wouldn't even know how to teach them, and believe me she was not shy! And they really looked up to her. But then I'd come down to the church and see people not paying attention when she was speaking...!''

(Many years later, Bob Dettmer, a Peace Corps Volunteer, also agreed: ''She was hard to engage in conversation except on medical questions, but the medical students raved about how much they learned from her.'')

Gladys also heard Esther criticized by a church lady for not wearing lipstick and for not getting a permanent to wave her straight hair. Gladys was furious. She said to the woman, who was a nurse, ''I *envy* her, all the things she's doing out there, and boy, I'd like to see *you* handling an operation with just a mirror reflecting in the sunlight — and keep *your* uniform so clean under those conditions.''

Esther was not unaware of all this. She of all people could sense the nuances and recognize the restlessness in the gatherings. She was unhappy with the situation but didn't know what to do about it. Someone suggested that she take Kodachrome slides of her work in Liberia and on her next furloughs do audio-visual presentations. (She did do this and her programs were much more enthusiastically received.)

None too soon her furlough was over. Already she had reached the stage that many expatriates do, especially missionaries: her real home was now in Liberia, its people her people. Bertha Koenig's exclamation, "I can hardly believe I'm almost home," was a thing of wonder no longer. For no longer was Esther at home in modern-day America. There was no one, except other returned missionaries, who truly understood the kind of a life she led at Zorzor.

She couldn't talk to *anybody* about horseback rides into the forest to deliver twins or to bring back a man dying of tuberculosis. Or about raising chickens so there would be eggs to mix with coconut milk to feed motherless babies. Villagers who would't take smallpox vaccination and so died needlessly. A hospital without an X-ray machine and none closer than 200 miles away. A newborn baby convulsing from tetanus because the umbilical cord had been smeared with cow dung. A three-year-old who wanted to eat newly hatched chicks because he was so hungry for meat. These and a thousand other things she could not talk about bcause no one would understand.

There was another factor.

Esther had grown up in Sioux City. She had been gone for only seven years. Her aunts, uncles, cousins and friends remembered when she climbed house roofs and put live earthworms in her mouth. They liked her, loved her, admired her, but they did not understand her. It is unlikely that any of them ever entertained the thought that this quiet young girl would ever do anything *great*.

And Esther Bacon was the last one to sing her own praises. She was not one to stand in the pulpit — or in the Carlsons' living room in Hawarden — and say, "Hey, look, when I went to Zorzor. . ." and then describe the changes that had taken place in Loma-Kpelle-land directly due to her presence.

She felt the same estrangement Christ had when He returned to Nazareth. He taught in the synagogue and everyone was astonished and asked if this were not the carpenter, son of Mary. And Christ could do no mighty work, but marveled at their unbelief and said, "A prophet is not without honor but in his own country, and in his own house."

This is not to say that Esther returned to Africa like a dog with his tail between his legs. But in her reaction to the experiences of this furlough can be seen the human side of Esther Bacon. It *did* bother her that her work was not fully appreciated by family and friends.

While stranded on the M/V Del Campo off Recife, the farthest east point of Brazil, she had a lot of time to think and to write. She set down a long dissertation on II Corinthians, part of which stated: "Change your attitude in regard to friends. Give up fretting about their state, and thus poisoning your own. Commit them to God and BELIEVE; He loves them more than you do. Change your attitude toward them and pour out upon them all the love and kindness your heart can show, for they need all the love you can give them."

Then, pointedly, poignantly, she wrote a poem:

> Men may misjudge thy aim,
> Think they have cause for blame;
> Say thou art wrong!
> Hold on thy quiet way;
> Christ is the judge — not they;
> Fear not! Be strong!

This poem was in a letter addressed to Aunt Nora Leander in Sioux City, Iowa, on April 28, 1948.

It was also addressed to the heart of Esther Bacon.

(8)

As Esther sailed for her African home on the M/V Del Campo in April, 1948, she was, like almost all missionaries, acutely aware of world events. In January she had gasped in horror at the assassination of Mahatma Mohandas K. Ghandi. She had watched with more than casual interest the establishment of the World Health Organization in Geneva, and wondered in what ways it would reach out into the interior of Liberia.

Now, aboard ship, she talked with the captain about a new Liberian Maritime law which would be profitable to the Liberian Treasury. Edward Stettinius, former U.S. Secretary of State, acting now as a private citizen, had proposed that an International Bank and Trust Company be set up in Monrovia which would make it possible for ships from any country to register under the flag of Liberia at a rate favorable to the ship owner. Esther was particularly interested because medical missionary Dr. George Harley at Ganta had been selected by Stettinius to explain the advantages to President Tubman.

Momentous political events occurred in 1948. It was the year of the Berlin airlift, the establishment of the State of Israel, the coining of the term "cold war" by Bernard Baruch. Justice was served when Alger Hiss was indicted on evidence Time editor Whittaker Chambers had hidden in a hollowed-out pumpkin on his farm. Justice was outraged when Jozef Cardinal Mindszenty was jailed in Hungary for making anti-communist statements. Poetic justice triumphed when Harry Truman was re-elected president of the United States despite the Chicago Tribune's headline proclaiming Thomas Dewey the victor.

It was the year that the electronic transistor was invented, ushering in a minia-turization revolution that would render obsolete Dick Tracy's "impossible" wrist radio.

At an Amsterdam auto show the British introduced the Land Rover. In Germany, Volkswagen designer Ferdinard Porsche introduced his new sports car.

It was in 1948 that Walt Kelly's Okefenokee 'possum Pogo first tickled the world with his political satire, then grabbed it by the throat with, "We have met the enemy and it is us."

And that world, still decontaminating Hiroshima and Nagasaki, and bull-dozing ruined cities in Europe, continued to be flagellated by its authors: Norman Mailer's The Naked and the Dead, *Irwin Shaw's* The Young Lions, *Carl Sandburg's* Remembrance Rock, *Truman Capote's* Other Voices, Other Rooms, *Graham Greene's* The Heart of the Matter, *Alan Stewart Paton's* Cry the Beloved Country, *Albert Camus's* State of Siege, *and Tennessee Williams'* Summer and Smoke.

But there was lightness too, in 1948, as Ed Sullivan hosted a new TV show that would air for twenty-three years, Ted Mack brought laughter and even some talent into his "Original Amateur Hour," and Ray Bolger enchanted millions in "Where's Charley?"

(9)

Yes, the world was changing as Esther sailed for "home."

This time she had sixty-two chickens with her. She kept them in her shower. They were beginning to lay, so she sent two eggs up to the captain for his breakfast. The next day the following announcement appeared on the passengers' bulletin board:

NOTICE   NOTICE
Fresh sea eggs for sale   Fresh sea eggs for sale
                              Sea Miss E. Bacon
Eggs are guaranteed strictly fresh and are excellent for making scrambled a La Del Campo eggs. Eggs are gathered and packed carefully by the owner herself, to insure quality. Owner possesses the best layers in the world and they are grain fed. Eggs are also guaranteed to be good hatching eggs in any incubator.

The crew loved it. They loved her. She was one of them, full of fun and mischief. When they tied up at Pernambuco, the Second Mate made a special trip to town to find an egg just ready to hatch and slipped it in with Esther's chickens. It hatched that same night and greeted her the next day. She had great fun first finding the culprit who had played the joke, then trying to find a hen to mother the little orphan. She carried it around in her pocket until it was big enough to take care of itself. Finally a rooster "mothered" the chick and everyone was happy.

At another port she stood with Bertha Koenig on the fantail of the ship and watched with amusement as cattle were unloaded with a sling and pulley. They wondered, with chuckles, if they looked like that in the mammy chairs at the Monrovia harbor.

Days of sunlight and warm breezes brought them to the coast of West Africa. While the ship was off-loading at Dakar in Senegal, Bertha and Esther hiked into town on Sunday morning and found a Protestant church service. They were seated by a beaming black usher who handed them a hymn book — in French. The two missionaries then realized that the service was in French, but the music was lively, the scripture readings recognizable, the ambiance worshipful.

At Monrovia Esther was greeted warmly and her chickens with much laughter by Hazel Biederbeck and the Rebers. Dr. Reber had come down to Monrovia because so many missionaries were sick, including three of the four nurses. Hazel was on her way to the States for furlough.

Esther stayed at Harrisburg for almost two weeks to attend the Church Conference at the Mission House in Monrovia and Annual Conference at Harrisburg. She was pleased to see so many Liberian Christian leaders at the Mission House: Rev. Diggs,* Mr. Morris, Miss Amanda, Rev. Ezra Keller, and Miss Smarte.

While attending the conferences, she put her chickens in care of an old African man. One morning he killed a seven-foot blacksnake in the chicken house after it had killed three chickens and eaten five eggs. She had him cut the snake up into thin slivers to feed the chickens, though she admitted that her "books on chicken feeding have no information as to whether snake meat is satisfactory chicken feed!"

Just before Esther went up to Zorzor, Rev. George Flora arrived from the States with his family, and, to everyone's astonishment, a jeep, a small portable home electric plant, and an electric washing machine. There already had been talk about putting in a light plant at the Zorzor hospital, but George Flora had not waited for that. With great good humor he took the ribbing from his envious colleagues. With calm reassurances he took the well-meant chastisement from the older missionaries who "knew" that these things were not meant for the interior of Liberia.

---

*At this writing, Rev. Diggs lives in retirement at Belefani, while his son, Rev. Ronald Diggs, is Bishop of the Liberian Lutheran Church. It was Bishop Diggs who mediated the talks in Monrovia during the 1990 civil war.

Esther was pleased and also somewhat surprised to learn that the radio-telephone network had been expanded to almost all of the mission stations, including Zorzor, and that they worked most of the time. She marveled: "Buschy said 'hello' to folks at the coast a few minutes after arrival in Zorzor! Imagine it!"

Then came the biggest surprise of all. She travelled by station wagon with Mrs. Flora, the three little Floras, and two other passengers to Suakoko, near Gbarnga. Then they all *flew* to Zorzor in less than an hour with her typewriter, suitcase, and pressure cooker. There was no room for her new $80 sewing machine, nor her chickens, but George Flora, with a wicked grin that almost belied his vocation, promised to bring them up in his jeep.

Esther was enthused by air travel and would champion its expanded use. After her first flight to Zorzor, she wrote Aunt Nora, "If that isn't a marvel — you can't imagine the thrill of the trip over the trees among the hills, just at sunset. How small the people, thatched roof villages, and tall palms looked below us. In a few minutes we could see the other side of the mountain at Belefani, and then the St. Paul River, and the road wending its way in and out among the irregular contours of the land. Clouds reflecting the light of the sunset made a softly colorful background... then bath water at Bunger's (hadn't had time for two days — shhh!)."

(10)

She was welcomed home by the entire village, it seemed, but her eyes were for her children. As on her return in 1945, they surrounded her and took turns jumping into her arms. Also as before, Esther spent hours on her first day walking the lanes of Zorzor and the paths in the high forest.

In some ways it seemed as if she'd never been gone. The people snapped fingers with her in greeting on the paths. Young girls with firewood on their heads waved gaily and called greetings to her. Mothers held up their babies for her to kiss. Young lads, grinning broad welcome, stepped off the path to give her room to pass. When Esther scratched Lizard's ears, he stood patiently as if she'd never left. Chickens pecked at insects in the tall grass.

The deeply muddied streets of Zorzor wound indolently among the white-daubed and conical-thatched houses. Dark smoke from cooking fires in the houses crept lazily around the clay pots and drifted straight up in the heavy, still air. Buckets and pans ringed the houses, catching the rain when it fell.

The high forest beckoned with its golden birds and creeping vines and deep shade. Blue-breasted kingfishers, almost a foot-long from beak to tail, whistled "piou-piou-piou," starting high and decrescendoing to a fade-away.

Little green bulbuls, often heard but seldom seen in the thick leafy growth, entranced Esther with their songs almost as much as her bird-books' description of it: "A jumble of gutteral chuckling notes followed by a rigorous, rich warbling and ending with a loud and characteristic tri-syllabic phrase."

Senegal coucals, brown wings flashing and bodies shining like green velveteen, bounced ahead of her in the clearings. The big casqued horn-bills straggled in a ragged, undulating formation through the forest and laughed weirdly as they settled into palm trees.

As she followed the path into the bush she watched a ten-year-old boy literally walk up a palm tree, one foot in front of the other, using a crude oval climbing hoop around the trunk to pull himself along. Men stood or squatted in small groups, arguing about their work. Men and women laughed and sang and danced in the fields as they planted their rice, stimulated at least partly by the palm wine brought by a special delegation who collected it early in the morning at the palm tree source.

Two little girls knelt beside the path, heads bowed, while their mother snapped fingers with Esther. Esther admonished the woman not to let her children do that, for it was a sign of submission, almost of worship. The woman answered, "We do worship you, Bayka."

(11)

But some things had changed during the year she'd been gone. Dr. Reber and missionary builder Paul Weiss were still busy rebuilding the hospital. The Lutheran Hospital at Zorzor was now known as Curran Memorial Hospital.

The roof was still off one end, greatly crowding the other end. Paul Weiss was reinforcing the walls with fieldstone and would eventually put on a "zinc" roof. After all the years of mud, wattle and thatch in the old hospital, it was a joy for Esther to see buildings going up that wouldn't wash away a little with every rainstorm.

The patient census had continued to climb. Hazel Biederbeck had come down to help out on the wards. Marianna Bunger had worked in surgery and now with Hazel gone had taken over the nursing school, which was operating at capacity with three girls and four boys.

Esther was disappointed — but not surprised — to learn that neither the nurses nor Dr. Reber had been going out into the villages. That part of the ministry had suffered, at least according to Esther. She couldn't let it go: it was the cornerstone of her work. At least until there was a revolution in communications in Loma-land.

(12)

That revolution began three weeks later.

In retrospect, 1948 would be recognized as the watershed year, the year Rev. George Flora drove a jeep to Zorzor.

He and Rev. Homrighausen drove north from Monrovia to Ganta, then northwest through "the French side," paralleling the Liberian border in French West Africa, to Koyama. There they crossed the Mounie River to Yella, Liberia, then south to Zorzor. In one five mile stretch they removed over thirty fallen trees which had been blown down in a storm just before they came through. Two of Esther's chickens were killed when their crate flew off in a rough spot, but her sewing machine made it unscathed.

George Flora apologized profusely for losing the chickens, but Esther, with a sparkle in her eyes, said, "I didn't really expect to see *any* of them again!"

One morning at the regular 6:30 A.M. radio broadcast, Rev. Flora proudly parked the jeep outside the radio room window and loudly honked the horn to prove to the unbelievers in Monrovia that he really had brought it all the way to Zorzor. It was, of course, the first automobile that most of the local people had ever seen.

It would be ten years before a "real" road would penetrate to Zorzor, a road that trucks and other two-wheel-drive vehicles could navigate. But local village chiefs working with their people soon widened paths, built log bridges and constructed rock fords to accommodate George Flora's jeep.

George Flora directed his own efforts to the five-mile stretch from the end of the "French road" at Koyama to Zorzor. This route cut through five swamps, crossed many creeks and one fair-sized river. Across the river and the creeks, and through the swamps, he and his men built stick bridges tied together with native vines. On the ridges between they cut branches down and dug roots up to smooth the passage. Even so, four hills were so steep that the jeep climbed only in the lowest gear, and occasionally had to be winched through the worst places, especially when the track was muddy and slippery. A successful roundtrip to Koyama, ten miles, was one that took only three hours.

But George Flora's jeep was a forerunner of the changes preparing to sweep into the high forest. With a working jeep — and everything else happening in Loma-Kpelle-land — the pace of change began to accelerate.

(13)

George Flora soon got his electric plant working. He ran insulated wires under the back screen door into the utility room and plugged in his wife's new electric wringer washing machine. Gradually in his spare time he wired the entire house and moved the access wire up onto the side of the house. Within three months he had electricity for several hours each evening.

They put the jeep to work. Three days a week Earl Reber used it to haul rocks from Kiliwu for the hospital.* When roads, bridges, and ferries allowed, the jeep hauled missionaries and supplies and patients to and from Zorzor and other accessible villages. Rev. Flora used the jeep occasionally to hold services in some of the villages.

The trip to Fisebu, an hour or more on foot, took fifteen minutes to drive; to Salayea, five hours on foot, an hour to drive; to Belefani, a long two-day hike, six hours to drive, if they could have gotten the jeep across the St. Paul River. Everyone was impressed with the increased effectiveness of the pastors and medical personnel, now spending far less time just getting to and from churches and clinics.

George, Esther and Earl began to envision a time when clinics and services could be held in the towns on a regular basis, but this was far in the future.

Earl Reber got a new microscope and began putting to use his Johns Hopkins' pathology training. Many nights he could be seen in his house studying slides taken during the day. He was now working an average of 12 hours a day, from seven in the morning until seven at night, sometimes with a little break for lunch at noon. He rued the fact that he had to haul rocks for the hospital, but there was no one else who knew how to drive except Paul Weiss. And Paul really needed to stay on site to supervise the construction because most of the workers knew little or nothing about stone buildings.

---

*Author's note: he should have hauled more! As late as 1989, the last time I drove to Kiliwu, the "road" was still so strewn with rocks and boulders that only a high, four-wheel-drive vehicle could pass.

Esther had never learned to drive. Neither her mother nor Aunt Nora had ever had a car, and few of her classmates had one. It is unlikely that she would have gone out in the jeep at any rate. She did begrudge all the time that Dr. Reber had to devote to non-medical activities. She fretted in a letter to Aunt Nora, "It is too bad that Dr. Reber can't do more of the work that he does so well."

Earl Reber's plan for Curran Memorial Hospital was to incorporate the main adult ward into the central spine so that the hospital could eventually be expanded into an H-form. This was well under way when Esther returned from furlough in 1948. Twenty years later, Dr. Paul Mertens would oversee the expansion in just the way Reber had envisioned, building new wards in the shape of an H, and then converting the adult ward into library, conference room, office space, pharmacy, X-ray, and outpatient examining rooms.

A curious thing occurred when the old hospital was dismantled in order to utilize the bricks and the shuttered windows. During a lapse in supervision, the shutters were all turned on their sides when being reinstalled, so that one shutter swung upwards and the other downward. They remained that way for almost twenty years, "a constant reminder," Dr. Mertens comments, "of what can happen if the supervisor of unsophisticated workers does not closely keep his eye on what is happening."

Despite the building program at the hospital, or perhaps because of it, patients came in increasing numbers. One memorable day sixteen new patients were admitted to the hospital. The nurses and doctors in the dispensary now treated between one and two hundred outpatients daily. Prenatal and postnatal clinics ran between forty and fifty. Patients began to put up mud-and-stick houses on the hospital compound where they could stay while waiting for surgery. At one time there was a list of sixty patients waiting for hernia repair.

One little girl of seven was brought in by her mother from Koyama, the town in French West Africa just across the Mounie River from Yella. She weighed eleven pounds, a scrawny, living skeleton. Her mother had taken her to the zoes several times. A particularly powerful female zo had gone into the forest, brought back hand-picked, carefully chosen leaves, and mixed them with a certain bark in a pot in the corner of the house. Then she added palm oil to make the concoction liquid and poured it down the little girl's throat. She warned that if this didn't work, there was an evil matter involved.

It had not worked.

The zo told the mother that her daughter was not human and should be sacrificed to the Spirits of the River. In other words, drown her. She did, indeed, look hardly human with her stick-like limbs, great staring eyes, thinning pinkish hair, and protuberant belly, all signs of kwashiorkor. As Esther put the whiny little thing into the baby scale, her mother disappeared and never returned. Earl Reber and Esther examined the girl and found nothing specifically wrong except gross malnutrition.

Esther took the little girl into her home and named her Ruth. She fed her milk, bananas and vitamins. Within a month she was walking. In three months she had doubled her weight and in four months was considered well.

She would live with Esther for the next ten years and would take the name Bacon. Esther never formally adopted her but this made little difference to Ruth, who says now, "She was my mother, and I never went back to Koyama to see my other mother. Bayka treated me as her daughter. I didn't know anybody except her. Anything I needed, she used to give to me."

(14)

Air mail was now commonplace. On January 6, 1949, Esther sent her first "Air Letter." In block capital letters was a warning: IF ANYTHING IS ENCLOSED THIS LETTER WILL BE SENT BY ORDINARY MAIL. Occasionally a letter came from Aunt Nora in less than two weeks.

Workmen lengthened and widened the airstrip at Zorzor to accommodate a four-seater Cessna. In July, Rev. Stelling came back from furlough with his own plane, a two-seater Piper Cub, but the Board in New York forbade him to fly. Esther was very unhappy and in a fit of pique wrote to Nora, "Of all dumb things! I hope they straighten it out soon. Plane is the *safest* method of travel here, besides saving time. If they think it takes time from his work they had better inquire into how much time missionaries have spent in transportation. Going down to Monrovia and back recently took four days of Rev. Bowers' time. The same amount of travel could have been less than one day, with no sweating on bad roads." Apparently she had forgotten about once writing, "No planes, cars, trains, etc., however, I love it the way it is. . ." (Stelling later received permission to fly the plane for his personal use, but it was never used for church-wide transportation.)

One thing hadn't changed. Esther still preferred to ride Lizard out to the villages to deliver babies for women who wouldn't come in, or whose husbands forbade them to come in. Often she would be gone for several days.

Earl Reber didn't like this. He still thought she should be at the hospital where she could take care of many more patients, much more efficiently, than she could out in the high forest. One time he said to her, "Now look, if you want to go to the villages, if you must go to the villages, I'll drive you there and see that you get back."

He recalls with somewhat grim amusement one time when he did just that — and spent four hours lying on the hood of the jeep waiting for her to talk the midwives and zoes into letting a laboring woman go to the hospital. She was finally successful, but by the time they arrived back in Zorzor they were all exhausted and the woman died anyway.

"She was burdened by the death," Dr. Reber says, "and came to me almost apologetically. I told her that this was a difference that she and I had and we would have to work it out between ourselves."

He went on to say, "Sometimes the missionaries in Zorzor felt that I was a little hard on Esther in trying to make her conform to the idea of giving many people care in a prenatal clinic and doing many deliveries under safe conditions rather than spend a couple of days out in the village and then losing the patient anyway. But even to this day I never felt that there was a great degree of difference between Esther and myself."

But, for Esther, there was more to her forest treks than just going out to do deliveries and bringing back sick people. She just liked to walk in the high forest and not only observe but participate in the life there. She loved the contacts she made with the people.

In an article for *Lutheran Woman's Work* in 1951 she made it quite clear why she was drawn to the high forest and the villages out there:

> The road back to the hospital led through Fisebu — a typical village town. It being Sunday, the Christians were coming from the service conducted by the village evangelist, David Harris. Other people were busy about their work. The heavy part of the farm work is over now until rice cutting, so most of the people were in town. Some of the women were spinning cotton; another was weaving a mat; another threshing rice with her feet; another watching the food cooking over the fire on the floor; a man was busy weaving his cloth; children were playing in the streets.
>
> In one hut there was sorrow; the people were mourning a child who had died recently from dysentery. But in spite of grief and blindness the grandmother took time to welcome strangers into her home. The old lady, who herself was a zo, listened carefully when we told her that the mission doctor could remove the cataracts from her eyes so she could see again.
>
> After speaking to the evangelist about her, he asked us to see another old man who was blind — an old man named Goveaboo. We saw him sitting on the floor in the doorway of a small dilapidated mud and stick thatched hut. He was old and alone. His feet

were swollen badly with jiggers in all ten toes. He was troubled by these itchy little creatures, and was trying to fix leaves in a pot for medicine for them. We saw no food; his clothes were dirty shreds of what they had been. His face told of pained resignation without hope.

He had been told about other old men and women with the same sickness in their eyes who had come to the mission doctor, and through his trained skill had learned to see again. He responded with a questioning look of half hope and half doubt. His reply was that if help comes, he knows it is only God. Arrangements were made with the evangelist for a few coppers for food. The old man's face took on a look of surprised happiness that hardly seemed possible to one in such condition as his.

Plans were made to bring him to the hospital as soon as the doctor returned from his trip down coast. Meanwhile David Harris will continue to visit him with the message of God's care to bring sight to his soul. It is hoped this old man may be restored in body, mind, and spirit so that he may enjoy his few remaining years, and be able to take care of himself again. Even if his sight is not completely restored, the light of Jesus' Gospel will shine in his soul.

(15)

There was another reason that Earl didn't want Esther off in the high forest more often than absolutely necessary. He needed her in surgery. Not knowing that he would be the only doctor in an isolated hospital, he hadn't planned to do much surgery in Liberia. He had done very few operations on his own in his Episcopal Hospital internship in Philadelphia. Now he had to do emergency surgery for strangulated hernias, Caesarian sections, hysterectomies and a wide range of other operations.

In those early years he prepared for surgery by reading the book, and then telling Esther to be there. He states very honestly, "With Esther there, you had the feeling that you could do just about anything because she was by your side. One time we had a patient with a very large goiter and Esther said that her doctor back in Iowa would do them under local. I tried to resist the idea but with Esther you didn't resist very much. The best way to get her off your back was to cooperate. So with her pushing, I went to the book and I read how I could do a thyroid under local and I was able to pull it off, chiefly because Esther was there. If it weren't for Esther I certainly would not have accumulated the vast experience I did have in surgery."

At first, Esther scrubbed in on all the cases, utilizing the knowledge she had gained under Gladys Holm in Sioux City. Marianna Bunger, also a trained operating room nurse, began scrubbing when she could be spared from the nursing school and the wards. Esther also taught some of the brighter Liberian students in the art of the Mayo nurse. So gradually Esther scrubbed less and less, and served more often as the circulating nurse. This allowed her to run out and look into other emergencies as they arrived.

Most surgeons are uneasy when the circulator absents herself from the room for more than a few seconds at a time. But Earl Reber never had the feeling that he had been abandoned: Esther always seemed to be there when he needed sutures or packs or help with anesthesia. Dr. Reber was the first, but not the last, to feel that Esther had an uncanny sixth sense which called her back to the OR when she was needed.

Jeanette Kpissay says flatly, "When you were thinking of sending for her, she'd *come*...just sort of show up. Or, sometimes you'd send for her and she *wouldn't* come — and then things would turn out alright."

Esther never credited herself with extraordinary powers, except those that came from her trust in the Lord. She knew her doctors, she knew her nurses and her midwives, she knew her patients, she knew her surgery and medicine. And she knew her Lord. What more did she need to know?

(16)

And so the months of Esther's third term moved swiftly by. She and Earl Reber developed a very close professional relationship that would grow ever more fruitful as the years passed.

For Earl Reber it was a very pleasant association, though he adds a caveat: "It doesn't mean that I wasn't angered once in a while because she could climb on any doctor's back. I don't know of any doctor who has been up there who didn't experience the time when Esther climbed on his back and he would have to shake rather angrily to get her off. But that was the nature of Esther: the patients, the people came first. And sometimes her tenacity would wear rather thin on the person who had to absorb it."

For Esther it was a time of re-adjustment to some sort of routine which took into account Earl Reber's wishes. She admitted to Aunt Nora that she would miss the total freedom in which she had worked, but it was a small sacrifice compared to the higher level of medical care her people now had available.

Up at 5 or 6 A.M., she showered, dressed, had breakfast, then visited her children on the old compound, always wishing for more time just to play with them. Morning devotions began promptly at 7 A.M. in a small room above the operating theater (the site of a murder to be described in a later chapter). After devotions, the staff shared administrative and housekeeping problems.

Then Esther went down to the wards for a quick appraisal before going to surgery. A newly-arrived nurse once said, after watching Esther on her early morning rounds, "It looks like she's just wandering around." Not so. Casting a loving and searching eye on everyone and everything, she quickly sorted out the sicker patients and did what was necessary for them at the moment. She checked to see if the proper treatment and medications had been given to new patients admitted during the night.

Meanwhile Earl went down to the old "zinc house," the original operating room, again a storeroom, and gave out the supplies for the day. Also at this time he was known to be available to talk informally and privately with any emotionally disturbed individuals, usually nurses, school teachers, or other educated Africans feeling the pressures of living a modern life in an ancient culture.

Then to surgery. Esther was really in her element here. She came bustling in, full of energy, well before Earl Reber's arrival. She sent one student for the first patient, set another to boiling water, made sure the proper surgical pack was ready on the back table, checked over the anesthesia equipment if a spinal was to be given. If ether was to be used, she punctured the rounded aluminum top of a pint can, inserted a grooved cork and cotton wick, then secured a gauze over the wire-screen mask.

Then Dr. Reber came in, donned cap and mask, and scrubbed his hands over a basin on a chair in the corner. A student nurse stood close by with a pitcher of cold water, watching carefully to catch the signal (cupped hands) to pour more water onto Earl's hands. Also watching him out of the corner of her eye was Esther. As he finished his scrub, she handed him a sterile towel with sterile pickups. Earl dried his hands, held them in front of him with fingers together until they were quite dry, then put on the gown and gloves himself.

He painted the already-scrubbed surgery site with zephiran chloride, placed sterile towels and drapes around it, then stepped back to allow the Mayo nurse to move in with the Mayo table.

When all was ready, he quieted everyone with, "Let us pray."

With his gloved hands resting lightly on the drapes, he prayed for a quiet heart and a skillful performance of the proper surgery. He felt that such a moment of silence was necessary because until then everybody was running around and there was need for calm. He says, with a laugh,

"And I guess part of our effort was to get Esther to quiet down as well because she could be very, very busy and at times a bit noisy and it would disturb..."

After surgery, which was usually done three days a week, Esther went back down to the wards to make more thorough rounds. Many people who worked with Esther recall the shock waves that emanated from the wards as she swept through them. She moved quickly from patient to patient, flipping through the chart to check the vital signs and other pertinent material. To the nurses she spoke, as Betty Stull describes it, "in rapid, quick, fragmented statements, as though her mind was going a mile a minute... talking with her was sometimes a little difficult."

But with each patient she spent a little time. She greeted each one by name, then took time to explain a new treatment, or reassure the patient or relatives that all was well, or perhaps to chat for a brief moment with a mother about her other children back in the village. To the patients, the hustle and bustle was but an illusion, for she treated each patient as an individual. They almost always got as much of Esther's time as they demanded.

Dr. Reber comments on this. "Esther's life was not one of order but it was one of trying to be everywhere at once. I think it was a good life to live, a style that really helped the patients more than if she had been more 'orderly.' She gave them a feeling of comfort and support. She was a good bedside nurse."

The perfect accolade: "She was a good bedside nurse."

(17)

Most afternoons, when not occupied with emergencies, both Esther and Earl taught classes in the nursing school. Earl enjoyed classroom teaching. Esther did not, for she knew she wasn't good at formal, structured teaching. Paul Mertens says, "It could not be said that Esther made an excellent classroom teacher or an excellent clinical teacher. However, as an example of devotion, determination, tireless effort, uncanny knowledge and skill, and a real love for her patients, she was an outstanding example to students and staff alike."

There is considerable evidence that Paul was right about her inadequacy in the classroom, just as she had been inadequate in the pulpit in Sioux City. But there is also much evidence that he was wrong about her clinical teaching. Liberian nurses, missionary nurses, and later, a succession of medical students and doctors (including Paul Mertens himself) positively rave about how much Esther Bacon taught them in the delivery room, operating room, and on the wards.

Dr. Franklin Keller always told newly arrived medical students, "You listen to Esther Bacon. She's the nurse, yet *listen* to her! She'll save you a lot of work."

After classes, Earl and Esther went back down to the hospital and made evening rounds, restarted IVs, checked drainage bottles, re-evaluated doubtful diagnoses, ordered lab tests (many of which Esther herself would do) for the next day, changed dressings, examined new patients, and did whatever else was necessary to ensure that the patients would go through the night in comfort and safety.

Earl Reber returned to his home to eat supper with Anna Mae and then pored over his microscope or his books. Esther went home for supper, usually alone, and often went back down to the hospital once again to make sure everything was all right. Always she visited her little children in the "orphanage," sometimes staying an hour or two if there were no emergencies or really sick people at the hospital.

Emergencies seldom came in at night in those early years, for the fear of what the darkness held was great. But occasionally a villager braved the terrors to bring in his hemorrhaging wife. Or perhaps a patient with a bad fracture arrived from a village connected to Zorzor by a path easily traveled in the darkness. And sometimes now a runner lighted his way with bamboo torches through the green darkness to get Earl or Paul Weiss and the jeep to bring in an injured patient or a laboring woman. Then Earl and Esther could be up all night or most of it, and of course still be present at morning devotions at seven in the morning.

(18)

But it was not all work, even for Esther. One of her chickens laid nine big brown eggs in a ten day span. She kept a duck in her bathtub but it was unhappy there and she ended its misery by eating it. A big box of toys from the Mabel Dysinger's Circle at Trinity arrived two days before Christmas. President Tubman came up for Easter services and afterward capped the graduating class of nurses. Two Swiss traders opened a store in Zorzor to sell, among other things, cheese.

Missionaries visited from other stations. Church leaders came from the States and other parts of the outside world to see Curran Memorial Hospital in action. Others, in government or business, came and went. Esther complained about all the activity but there was a sense of enjoyment, too, in being the hub of Lutheran medical work in Liberia.

There was, each year, the Annual Missionary Conference, and a General Conference of all the Lutheran Church leaders in Liberia. After one of these latter, Esther again made special note of the national leaders arising in the church: Teacher Morris from Salayea, Miss Amanda from Sanoyea, Pastor Diggs from Belefani, Father Abraham from Fisebu, and many more.

George Flora was called to Monrovia, where he took over as the mission business manager, leaving the Zorzor parish unfilled for many months. Mrs. Flora complained in a letter to Esther that her children were swimming and canoeing in the lagoon where they often saw crocodiles. Esther laughed and wrote back, "At least you don't have to worry about pygmy hippopotamuses down there!"

Esther felt the hand of God in all these things. She wrote:

> Love leading — shall I question where?
> Nay, Lord, I shut my eyes,
> And place my hand within Thine own
> To ope with glad surprise,
> To find where'er my lodgings be
> The Saviour, God, abides with me.

(19)

In May of 1949, Earl and Anna Mae Reber went home for their first furlough. For three months, Curran Memorial was doctor-less. In early September of 1949, Dr. and Mrs. Yund arrived in Liberia and within two weeks came to Zorzor. After 3½ months without a doctor, the nurses had accumulated a formidable backlog of cases to be evaluated by a doctor. So Lowell Yund was put right to work. 306 patients welcomed him the first dispensary day and over 200 the second.

The Yunds fit into the mission station very quickly. Lowell, born in Kpolopele, Liberia, of missionary parents, had a well-remembered child's-eye view of living under primitive conditions in the tropics. He was tall, lean, had very black hair always meticulously combed with a natural wave, wore horn-rimmed glasses which corrected his myopia and gave him a wise-owl look. He almost always wore a neat white intern's blouse buttoned up the shoulder and side of the neck.

Lowell Yund brought with him a drug which would revolutionize the treatment of leprosy.* The drug was the first generation of sulfones and for the first time in the history of this gruesome disease most cases could actually be cured.

---

*Author's note: we are now urged to drop the term "leprosy" and call it Hansen's Disease after the researcher who first identified the causative bacillus. This, to me, is a clumsy euphemism and I mean no pejorative intent when I speak of lepers and leprosy.

Yund sent word to all the chiefs that he was starting an in-patient leprosy treatment center. Nine lepers came in the first group. They built a
dormitory close by the abandoned and crumbling mud-and-thatch buildings of the old hospital. The patients were given a year to build themselves
houses on the compound. John Dorbor, one of the first nine (and still
living in the village in 1989), built his in the first month.

The village was soon dubbed "Little Ganta" after the large leprosy compound at Ganta under the direction of Methodist missionary doctor
George Harley.

Thus it was that tuberculosis and leprosy came under control at almost
the same time. They are closely related, both of the genus Mycobacterium,
and indistinguishable under the microscope. Earl Reber brought streptomycin in 1946, Esther Bacon brought isoniazid (isonicotinic acid hydrazide)
and PAS (para-amino salicylic acid) in 1948, and now Lowell Yund brought
sulfone.

After four months of watching Yund work, Esther called him a top surgeon who loved his work and enjoyed being in Zorzor. He also enjoyed
working with his hands in other ways: he'd been there a very short time
when he decided to convert some old motorcycles into a small electric
plant for the Operating Room. It worked. For the first time an electric
light shone down on the operative field in the Zorzor operating room.

Ruth Yund, an RN, helped her husband in the operating room on surgery days and worked the wards on non-surgery days. She was a very
pretty young woman with a neat trim figure, a flashing smile, and a readi-
ness to do anything and go anywhere. She had proved this already by
coming to Zorzor with Lowell.

(20)

In the remaining months of Esther's third term, the hospital compound
was awhirl with activity. Mr. Weiss was still working on the hospital and
sometimes "borrowed" Lowell Yund and occasionally Wes Sadler to help
get supplies down from Koyama. Wes and Roslyn now lived in Wozi,
twelve miles north, fulfilling Esther's half-joking prediction that the empty
house in Wozi was for Wes to live in while he worked on the Loma language. He had worked on it, and had completed his Loma grammar in 1948.

Paul Weiss stored his cement bags wherever he could: he filled the classroom, then one room of Esther's house, and more came with every trip.
Eventually they used 1500 bags to pour the first concrete floor the hospital
had ever had. The patients were unhappy because they could no longer
build fires on the mud floors to cook meals and keep warm.

Surgical patients were still pouring in faster than they could operate on them. Dr. Yund did hernias (and pulled a two-foot-long living worm out of one, which almost made him sick but fascinated Esther), thyroid-ectomies, vesico-vaginal fistulas, hysterectomies, fractures, and everything else that came in. He began doing cataract extractions, something entirely new to the area. The first one was on a young woman still nursing a baby. Esther wrote, "You should have seen her smile when she discovered she could see something."

Edith Curran's prosthesis, the one Pauline Ziegler had gotten for her eight years before, was sent to the States for repairs. It came back just in time for her to lend her crutches to Paul Weiss when he drove a nail through his foot and then got a reaction to tetanus antitoxin.

In January and February of 1950 the midwives delivered twenty-two babies in the hospital, including four sets of twins, all of whom lived. It is certain that there was a twinkle in Esther's blue eyes as she and Edith Curran reminisced about the old days when *no* babies were delivered in the hospital.

Lowell Yund, impressed also with the continuing flow of motherless babies, asked Esther to count those who had come during those same two months. Esther told him, "Don't have to count. Nineteen. Five died. And they were moribund when they got here." The salvage rate was therefore almost 75%. In 1942 it had been about 33%. The difference was due to education of the villagers. The "educator" was Esther Bacon.

Dr. Yund examined the 280 students on the campus of the Lutheran School. He found, among other things, that three-fourths of them had malaria, half had shistosomiasis, and one-third had intestinal parasites of one kind or another.*

Just before Esther left for a short furlough in mid-1950, a power plant came up by truck through the French side to replace Lowell Yund's jury-rigged machine, which had worked (most of the time) for two years. And, "wonder of wonders," exclaimed Esther, "they brought a well-used portable GE Army field X-ray machine in working condition."

Even more wonderful to many, including Esther, was the system of running water installed in the hospital, although the water was at times a bit muddy. For the IV solutions she mixed, Esther continued to get water from a clear, cool pool at the far end of the half-mile-long swamp that encircled the hill where the old mud-and-wattle hospital and her first-term house had stood. It was at least a mile from the present hospital.

---

*Author's note: not a startling finding. Twelve years later, in 1962, in Tanganyika, I examined 100 school children and found enlarged spleens (indicating parasitic invasion) in all but one. And it was unusual to find *any* African with a bowel free of worms.

Every doctor who came to Zorzor always wondered just what electrolytes and other substances were in that water, but none could find a better source, and no harm ever seemed to come to the patients.

It had been an eventful term: the radio-telephones, the jeep, the airplane, the new Curran Memorial Hospital with running water and electricity, the rapid increase in both inpatients and outpatients, and especially gratifying to Esther, the rise in in-hospital deliveries. Time had passed so quickly that it seemed to Esther that she had just gotten back from furlough and was not yet ready to go.

But the staff had enlarged to the point that she herself didn't have to stay to maintain the proficiency of the new Curran Memorial Hospital. Nurse Elizabeth Wiley had arrived from the States and was busy in the nursing school. Nurse Mabel Hosterman would soon come down from Wozi where she was taking language study under Wes Sadler. Edith Curran and Frances Leonard were becoming ever more invaluable in maintaining a continuity of nursing care. Three graduates of their own nursing school had remained with them: Miss Massaquoi, Miss Rogers, and Mr. Johnson. Dr. Yund would be staying for at least two more years. Earl Reber would soon come back from furlough. Then there would be *two* doctors at Zorzor. Incredible.

Esther no longer felt indispensable. If she ever had.

Mission Cessna four-seater aircraft on Zoror airstrip, circa 1952.

Chapter Six

(1951-1958)

(1)

When Esther returned to Zorzor in January, 1951, after a four-month furlough, the Korean War was underway. Six months earlier the North Koreans had swept down out of the mountains into the breadbasket around Seoul and had driven the South Koreans into a tiny perimeter defense of Pusan. United Nations troops, 90% of whom were Americans, reversed the tide, and drove the North Koreans back to the Yalu. Now in early 1951, the Chinese were on the peninsula in support of the North Koreans. Esther no doubt wondered what would have happened to her if she had gone to China in 1939 as she had originally planned.

Also in 1951, Winston Churchill at age 77 was re-elected Prime Minister of England. Traitors Burgess and Maclean fled England for the Soviet Union. Traitors Julius and Ethel Rosenberg were found guilty of selling U.S. atomic secrets to the Soviets, and would be executed in 1953. The world's first thermo-nuclear reaction was set off and the first power-producing atomic reactor was built. In South Africa, apartheid was given an even sturdier footing when every person was color-coded and forced to carry proof of his registration.

On the lighter side, the first coaxial (cable) transcontinental TV program was aired and the first direct dial telephone was put into use. Hank Ketcham's Dennis the Menace was launched and within months was seen in 750 newspapers. Center-

fielder Mickey Mantle played his first game for the New York Yankees.

Three books, now classics, were published: J. D. Salinger's Catcher in the Rye, *James Jones'* From Here to Eternity, *and Herman Wouk's* The Caine Mutiny.

"The African Queen" launched Bogart and Hepburn down a dirty river and into glory. "A Streetcar Named Desire" carried Brando to new heights. "The King and I" made school-teaching seem an adventure.

The U.S. population reached 153 million, slightly more than half of what it is today.

Esther Bacon was now thirty-four years old. In her first nine years in Liberia she had revolutionized medical care in Loma-Kpelle-land, especially in maternal and child health. If she had left the field then, the impetus of that revolution would surely have continued. She would have been remembered as the lady with the lantern, the Nightingale of Liberia, the first nurse to go to the villages — on a horse called Lizard — to deliver babies that the midwives had given up on, the one person in the history of those tribes whose love for God and people successfully invaded the power of the zoes.

She would have been remembered with awe, with reverence, with love.

But she remained a part of her own creation for the next twenty-one years. Her genius sought other avenues of expression.

(2)

As usual she returned with keen enthusiasm. And as usual, she received, as she put it, "a grand welcome back. Surely good to be here." She moved back in with Elizabeth Wiley, who had now served at Zorzor almost a year, and who Esther found to be "a grand person to work with."

Elizabeth's primary responsibility was to the nurses' training program, so much of her work was in the classroom. But her real love was bedside teaching, which pleased Earl Reber greatly after his recent battle to get Hazel Biederbeck to come down to the hospital with her students.

The new hospital, nearly completed, nicely painted brown and green inside, looked lovely to Esther. Everyone — except Paul Weiss — had gotten used to shutters that opened up and down. New metal beds were en route from the Methodist Hospital at Ganta to replace the old wooden ones. The electric plant was working well and lines had been run to all the houses on the station.

There were now two doctors: Lowell Yund and Earl Reber. They shared surgery and all other hospital duties. Reber had received a set of orthopedic instruments and was becoming recognized country-wide as one of the better surgeons in the operative treatment of osteomyelitis.

In general, the hospital was supplied better than ever before — with drugs, dressings, linens, and instruments. Mattresses had been put on the beds for the first time. A new delivery table came, finally replacing the one that Roslyn Sadler and the carpenter had built using the picture in Esther's OB text. While they were admiring the new table, a rooster walked in, flew up onto the table and sat there as if he owned it. But the table was soon put to its intended use by Esther, Elizabeth Wiley, and the other midwives, with a flood of deliveries, many of them preemies.

Among the many triumphs at the hospital was an occasional disappointment. One that Lowell Yund remembers vividly started out with great expectations. Yund examined a chief who had been going blind slowly for years. Yund was very optimistic when he saw that the chief's problem was cataracts. He informed the chief that if the optic nerves were still functioning, there was every reason to believe that his eyesight could be restored. They made an appointment for the following week.

The chief didn't keep it.

Months later Yund saw the chief and was horrified to find him now permanently blind. He had been persuaded by a powerful zo to undergo a traditional "cure" first. His head had been secured between two heavy stones. The zo struck first one eye and then the other with a rounded rock held in his fist, hoping to rupture the lens capsule and dislocate the opaque lens. It had not worked. The chief was now hopelessly incurable.

(3)

The Yunds, a little discontented with the musty smell of rotting thatch and the pitter-patter of little rats' feet all night, had the roof torn off their house and replaced with aluminum. They reported somewhat sheepishly that it was now much hotter in the house, but claimed it was dryer, easier to keep clean, and in general much nicer.

Keeping house still presented frustrating little problems. One day Esther decided to bake a cake for a party. The wood was wet and the stove wouldn't get hot enough. While she was out looking for drier wood, one of her boys put kerosene on the wood and the stove blew up. The thatched roof caught on fire but the boys climbed up and put it out with water. After 2½ hours the stove finally got hot enough, then too hot. While she was mixing the frosting, she got a call from the hospital, jumped up and tipped more water into the bowl. When she returned she had to thicken the frosting with more cornstarch.

Lowell Yund, Harvey and Wilbur Currens, and several Loma men from Zorzor went on an elephant hunt near Salayea. Ruth Yund went along and stayed with Lana Bartolomei. While they were gone, Esther "baby-sat" their 3-foot boa constrictor, which she described as being very bashful and spending most of its time in a bowl of water. The first report drifting back from the big hunt was that they were unsuccessful, but later on Dr. Yund and Wilbur Currens showed up with pictures and elephant meat to prove that they had indeed "caught" an elephant.

With much sorrow, the station gave Gertrude Buschman a farewell party. She had been in Liberia since 1915, thirty-six years. Esther in particular owed much to Buschy's steady hand and loving counsel during the early 40s when Esther so often seemed to be fighting a losing battle.

In January of 1952, Esther went down to Monrovia in the Wozi jeep with Paul Weiss and his three little girls who were going back to school after the Christmas holidays. Elizabeth Wiley came down a day or two later in the Zorzor jeep with the young Currens, Gerry and Ginny. For the first time they stayed on the beach at the new mission hostel (which is still in use), with sixty other missionaries. Esther loved the beach and reported to Aunt Nora that she had "several pleasant dips in the ocean — even entertained marines and sailors at a weiner roast on the beach when their ship was in port."

The main reason for the trip down the road was the Annual Missionary Conference. Esther was not ordinarily very enthused about these meetings and this one was no exception. She wrote to Nora, "I'm anxious to be back up country. Wish I were there *now*!" But she was fair about it. She knew there had to be meetings like this and she wrote, "On the whole, the Mission Conference went well and many a problem was resolved; some heated discussions, yet love remained among fellow missionaries."

A second, more exciting reason for the trip, for Esther anyway, was the inauguration ceremonies for President Tubman, recently re-elected. Esther liked him personally, liked the way he was opening up the country, especially for women. And, of course, he had never forgotten *her* and the way she "ordered presidents around." The ceremonies were well-attended, very colorful, the men in their best clothes, the women all dressed up in their finest ankle-length gowns, the flags flying and the honor guard marching with the big drums booming.

A week later, on the last day of the Mission Conference, Esther attended the divine worship services of His Excellency's inauguration at the Methodist Church. The big church was filled and many had to be turned away for lack of room. Tubman was a popular president.

While in the "big city," she went with Elizabeth Wiley to two concerts. One was piano and strings with Kontorowitz on the violin, the other by singer Etta Moten. Music appreciation was not one of Esther's best suits — in high school it was the only subject in which she did poorly. She wrote to Nora, "I could have settled back and slept nicely, only I was sitting next to Norma (Bloomquist?). Wiley thoroughly enjoyed it and wished for her own violin here."

Elizabeth Wiley was a great letter writer. She kept after Esther to write oftener to Aunt Nora, and often wrote to Nora herself even though she had never met her. After one long letter she added, "The foregoing paragraphs were not, of course, written by your niece, although some of the wording and all of the ideas were hers. You, knowing her much longer than I, will appreciate how hard it is to force her down at the typewriter. I have insisted that she write at least a few words herself. Yours respectfully, E. Wiley, amaneunsis." Esther added, "I'm quite sure you can appreciate the fact that Wiley is quite an asset to Zorzor."

She *was* an asset. She was an excellent teacher and the students loved her. Outside the classroom she was always busy. When the metal beds came down from Ganta, she painted ten of them green and five blue. Then she went ahead and painted the treatment cupboard and the chairs in the nurses' dining room. She had the queer habit of eating three meals a day, about which Esther said, "I think it's a nuisance at times!" She was good at keeping the kerosene fridge in working order, which meant spending a couple of dirty hours once a month or oftener extracting and trimming the huge ring-wick. She took her turns at devotions and always produced thoughtful meditations.

But in April of 1952, she became quite depressed and attempted suicide. Esther and Earl Reber brought her safely out of her nembutal-induced coma. She returned to the States with the Yunds, who were due for furlough, and never returned to the mission field. Dr. Reber feels that she had had personal problems which had been overlooked in the States.

There was still another factor which in retrospect may have played a part in Elizabeth's breakdown. Earl Reber now thinks that part of Elizabeth's problem was Esther Bacon. Esther was so superior in her abilities, in her single-minded dedication, in her endurance. She set such high standards for herself and for the nurses working with her that some of them just couldn't cope.

Most of them did, of course. Jeanette Kpissay says, "I think we all knew we couldn't be Bacon, we couldn't be like her. But it's a struggle to see somebody who's so completely selfless, so giving, and then acknowledging that you're not like that." Reber thinks that Elizabeth Wiley was one who couldn't cope with Esther's standards and lost that struggle.

Whether or not this was a factor, it does illustrate an ongoing problem. Paul Mertens says, "Esther Bacon, in spite of her great store of knowledge in how to treat and salvage patients, both obstetrical and medical, and her skills in anesthesia, was not a nurse who was readily and generally accepted by all the other nurses, simply because of her disorganization, and her lack of fitting into their scheduling."

Margaret Miller at Wozi also recognized this. She says that other people, especially the nurses, saw Esther working long hours, not adhering to any nursing shifts, and doing things that weren't strictly her responsibility. They criticized her for this because they didn't want to work and live like she did. But it was clear to Margaret that Esther wasn't looking for special recognition: it was just her way. As Earl Reber says, "Esther was Esther."

Bishop Roland Payne saw through the facade to the true emotions of the other nurses and frankly calls it jealousy, a term we might perhaps modify to "envy." But he strengthens his argument with this story:

"Esther was in the States on a short furlough. The Director of Nursing at Curran was proudly boasting to the wife of another missionary how in the month of November thirty babies were born in the hospital. She ended her remarks by saying: 'And I didn't have to go to a village to tell the women to come to the hospital to have their babies; they came on their own.'

"I recognized the sarcasm and impetuously retorted: 'Yes, you're right. You didn't go to any village to bring them. But someone before you made it possible and easy for you not to go to a village. Someone went on horseback to bring them to the hospital. Someone waded through flooded creeks to bring them. Someone risked her life in the jungles, fearless of snakes, wild animals, and storms, to bring them. Someone who didn't care for material possessions, but gave all she had to save a life, made it possible for you not to go to a village. And finally, someone filled with genuine Christ-like compassion laid the groundwork and made it possible for you to have them come to the hospital on their own. Do you want the name of that someone?'

"The answer, of course, was, 'No.' "

(4)

In October of 1952 Esther moved into a big new house that had been abuilding for almost two years. One side had been occupied for almost a year by Miss Holl, a missionary nurse, but Esther had not pushed the finishing of her side because she had doubts about the size and the "luxury" of such a dwelling in Zorzor.

It was called "the duplex," and sat on a low hill about a hundred yards above the hospital. Most of the giant trees had been saved but the brush had been cut away to allow grass to grow. Also saved or planted were flowering shrubs, grapefruit, pawpaw, plum (mango), and banana. The effect was that of a park.

It was not really a duplex in the conventional sense. It was actually one large house that had four bedrooms, two on each side of a large, common living-dining room. This common room was 24 feet wide, 40 feet long, and 13 feet high. A huge central fireplace opened onto both sides. The kitchen, also shared, was in a small separate building reached by a covered concrete walkway. It had a sink with running water, a kerosene refrigerator, and a wooden table with four straight-back chairs.

On the other side of the duplex now lived Maebelle Hosterman, about whom Esther said, "She's a pleasant, tenderhearted young woman with a good way with patients."

On Esther's side, the south side facing away from the hospital, were two rooms and a bath. She chose the smaller for her bedroom and used the larger as an office. The floors of the bedroom were painted rose ("not bright," Esther assured Aunt Nora), the drapes green with a white figure, the chairs wicker. The bathroom was blue, had running water and a flush toilet. The office walls were buff, the woodwork white, the drapes plaid striped in red, grey, and greenish yellow; it was furnished with desk, cupboard, and a newly varnished dresser. Rev. Gerry Currens had selected the material for the curtains and Anna Mae Reber sewed them. Apparently Esther had little or nothing to say about decorating her house. It is likely that she had neither time nor inclination to bother with it.

With rather obvious ambivalence, Esther wrote, "It doesn't feel quite like home yet; it seems rather fantastic!" But it would become home and she would live in this house for the next twenty years.

(To this day that house is still called the "Bacon House" by everyone at Zorzor despite its many other occupants during the last nineteen years.)

It never contained anything of monetary value. No radio, phonograph or tape recorder. No vases or pictures or carvings. On the window ledge of the kitchen rested her lantern. In her closet, five or six dresses and two or three pairs of shoes. Margaret Miller, who was in the house many times, says, "Her bedroom did not bear the marks of much living and certainly none of enjoyment. It was a place to change clothes, park papers, and hang uniforms."

Esther's kitchen was the place of enjoyment, the center of her home. It was here she entertained everyone from a little child with a hungry look, up to President Tubman, who dropped in on Esther one day and was given refreshments. The "convivial cannibal from the downcast hinterlands" and the "outlaw for God" shared a great many goals for the people of Liberia and were comfortable with each other.

(5)

In early 1953 she spent three months at Sanoyea, replacing Kirsten Marie (Ma) Jensen, who was home in Denmark on a short furlough. Her primary responsibilities were the "orphanage" and the dispensary. There were eleven "little folks" of preschool age, nine boys and eight girls of school age, a few bigger girls who helped take care of the little ones, and several adult workers who made up the "family."

One of the little folks was Kirsten Jensen, named after Ma Jensen. There was something special about her and Esther recognized it almost immediately. A bond formed between the young white nurse and the little black girl, a bond which was never broken, and about which much more will be said.

Esther had a very pleasant time at Sanoyea. She called it "a blessing, almost like a furlough with no speaking to worry about!" There is no doubt that one of Esther's reasons for disliking furloughs was her obligation to do deputation, that is, to speak in churches that supported her work and in others assigned by the Board.

When she returned to Zorzor she began to feel at home in her new house. The bugs liked it, too: cockroaches, spiders, and several varieties of ants. She found several hundred ant eggs in her office cupboard. One evening she was invaded by an army of driver ants.* She was writing Aunt Nora at the time: "I see driver ants have come to visit us — packed on the porch and inside the office just two feet behind me — also in my bathroom. I'm not sure I'll take my bath and wash my hair just now. All the spiders are scurrying by in the dining room beating a hasty retreat. I've moved to the other side of the house now until the little guests go. I planned to mimeo a couple more reams of temp sheets tonight but the mimeograph is surrounded. Now my bath tub is full of ants. They will leave again when they get ready!"

The size of her house, the size of her household, and the size of her heart added to the legend of Bacon of Liberia. Everyone has a story or two about her hospitality and the menage she maintained. Two or three people lived with her at all times. Frequently there were half a dozen and sometimes even more. Her letters home mention houseguests literally dozens of times.

One group was, of course, patients. Her motherless babies remained a priority and she had one or two there all the time. They stayed with her until they were out of danger of dying. Then they returned to their

---

*Voracious, carnivorous ants that periodically migrate in the tens of thousands, undeterred by any physical structure.

village if they had family or to the "orphanage" on the old compound which Esther still maintained with her own money.

But she frequently housed adult patients, too. When Louise Faust visited with her for a week in 1966, she had three accident patients in the living room, one of them with a broken pelvis. In one of her bedrooms she had a badly burned little boy who needed frequent skin grafts. Since the boy's relatives lived so far away and there was no room for them in the hospital, they too lived with her.

She was also taking care of a schizophrenic man who lived in her chicken coop. This man had tried to cut his throat and when he recovered from that Esther invited him to live up on the hill behind her house in the revamped chicken coop. When asked why she took him in, she said, "Well, he helped with the smallpox cases, when nobody else would do it. He did it. Who helped me bury them? This schizophrenic guy. We had an epidemic of 22 cases of smallpox and of course many of them died. No one would touch the bodies except this man."

Later on she taught him how to do woodcarving, one of her favorite ways to calm disturbed people. She taught him how to help in X-ray, how to do gardening, and how to help around the house with tasks like carrying water and wood. He had two sons, so Esther helped one of them with his school fees.

Louise Faust says of this man, "I have no doubt in my mind that he loved Esther Bacon and would do anything in the world for her. She prompted this from the Africans. But the Europeans and other missionaries thought she was a nut. They respected her and they loved her but they all acknowledged, 'I could never do that.' "

Louise paused for a moment, then said thoughtfully, "I don't do that at my own station in Tanzania. But this is *Esther Bacon*. This is the woman that Esther Bacon was. I don't know of any other person who lived so totally for other people as she did. There's that verse about laying down your life for a friend. She laid down her life for sure. And that's what she *wanted* to do. That was to her the normal way to live. Esther Bacon went the whole nine yards with her life and everything that she did, and that's why she went after every single thing with such intensity."

Esther also took in missionaries who needed medical treatment but didn't need hospitalization. It seems that almost every missionary in Liberia stayed with her at one time or another. Margaret Miller, for example, came down from Wozi and lived with her, getting intravenous injections twice a day for a month. Lana Bartolomei stayed with Esther for two weeks when she developed cerebral malaria. And when Dian Marquardt came up from Toteta to have Adam, she stayed with Esther before and after the baby was born.

She also opened her home to Liberian nurses who had moved elsewhere, gotten ill, and come back to Curran for treatment. Irene Morris says, "And she always had food ready for any stranger or visitor who came around. She *always* had food ready. And all the nurses who were sick or people that she knew lived in her house. If I was sick, I came to the hospital and she would say, 'Let's go to the house,' and I stayed at her house."

When medical students began coming to Curran regularly from the States for three-month training in tropical medicine, they stayed in the other side of the duplex. Esther mothered them. They had one complaint: Esther's rooster began crowing at unpredictable times, such as two A.M. They claimed that Esther was so off-schedule that the rooster was never really sure when to wake up and start crowing.

Esther's guests never knew for sure when Esther would be there to eat with them or to visit with them. Often she invited them for supper and then didn't show up until Subasu, her cook, had fed them. Then she showed them where to sleep and asked, "When do you want breakfast?"

The guests usually asked in return, "Well, when do you serve?"

"Oh, any time between 4 A.M. and 11 A.M."

Esther, of course, was serious. It just didn't make any difference to her.

It was clear by the time Esther's fourth term was up, in 1953, that Curran Memorial Hospital in Zorzor had gained the confidence of the Loma and Kpelle people. In that year, 127 women delivered in the hospital. The general wards were full to overflowing. The outpatient and specialty clinics were jammed every day.

But its reputation had spread beyond the local tribes. People came from all over Liberia. Mrs. Liberty, wife of the District Commissioner, came down from Voinjama for a checkup. The Jensens, Assembly of God missionaries from Chien, came to have their baby. Jean Elinor Slifer, granddaughter of Lutheran Mission President Dr. Slifer, was born at Curran. Mrs. Louis Bowers from Toteta delivered Marguerite Ann, the 18th delivery at Curran that month, and the first girl for Mrs. Bowers after four boys.

They didn't all come just because Esther Bacon was there. Dr. Reber was there, an experienced and trusted doctor. Dr. Yund was there, a capable and caring physician. The Liberian and missionary nurses were competent and caring. The laboratory was as good as any in Liberia and better than most.

But for most of the pregnant women, Esther was the main reason they came. Childbirth, anywhere in the world in those years, was not viewed quite so complacently as it is today. These women and their husbands knew that if they had trouble during delivery, they would get from Esther

Bacon, Earl Reber, and Lowell Yund, as good obstetrical care as they would get anywhere in Africa.

So, in July of 1953, when Esther flew out of Robertsfield for New York, she left with a feeling of sadness that she couldn't stay to continue the work. Even knowing that Dr. Franklin Keller would be arriving any day, she had written Aunt Nora a month before, "Continue to pray for those I left behind at Zorzor. There is much work to be done."

(6)

Esther's furlough after her fourth term was for almost a year. For most of that time she lived with her Aunt Nora at 1514 Jackson in Sioux City. But she did spend a few weeks in California with friends and declared, "I'm firmly convinced this traffic is more dangerous than anything in Liberia!"

High on her list of priorities was a college degree. She now pursued this again by taking another semester at Morningside College from September of 1953 through January of 1954. She was avant-garde in this as she was in so many things. She felt strongly that nurses should get more than "just" a three-year diploma. It would be twenty years before nursing schools in the States took the first serious steps toward baccalaureate degrees.

She also made another statement: in an era when "older" students were rare, the 37-year-old Esther was not afraid to go back to school even though she often felt she should be teaching rather than studying.

The editor of *Lutheran Woman's Work* encouraged her to do a story about the women of Zorzor. She happily complied. She saw this as another opportunity to share her concept of the African people with her American readers. The first few paragraphs from the May, 1954, issue are reproduced here.

The women of Zorzor? Typical village women, they know both the hard work of scratching and tending their rice farms, and the joy of cutting the rice at harvest time. They are accustomed to carrying wood from the farm to the village to cook the evening meal, and know how to bring the pans of water gracefully balanced on their heads. There the fire is started between the logs on the center of the earth floor. Rocks and perhaps an iron ring hold the cooking pots of clay or iron. A little dried fish, greens, and

palm oil are cooked in one pot to make soup for the rice in the other pot. The meal is served in a pan from which several people eat. The men are offered the best; then the women and children eat.

In the evening the women spin cotton and "tell tales" as they sit on low stools or mats around the fire in the hut. Now and then the listeners join in with a singing refrain. (Can you picture a Christian mother or grandmother telling about Christ and His way there?) The young girl is learning to spin; later, more practice will make the thread come strong, smooth and even without breaking. Soon the people in the hut go to sleep on grass mats on the floor or mud bed.

A young mother in the hut tends and loves her little one. She hopes that the bit of monkey skin medicine tied on the child's neck will soon end that whooping cough. She inspects the baby's mole (fontanel). Grandmother offers the advice that the baby's head should be hotpacked and medicine applied, and proceeds with the treatment. Sorrow for children they have lost is a common experience. But the young mother is anxious that this one shall live and be well and walk soon. If only she knew the One whose love is for all men!

Esther Bacon tried so hard to make it clear that her African friends were *people*. They work, they cook, they "tell tales," they sing. They agonize over a sick child. They grieve for lost children. The grandmother offers advice. *Real people*. Not ignorant savages boiling missionaries in a pot!

On her way back to Liberia she visited first in Dayton with Marianna Bunger and Pauline Ziegler, then went by train to visit Ethel Emerick in Beaver Falls, Pennsylvania, near Pittsburgh. Spring was in the air and Esther revelled in the bright sunshine, the blooming flowers, and the budding trees. She had hoped to see Elizabeth Wiley, but could not.

As usual she tried, but this time in vain, to take chickens back with her. She knew that after a year's absence most of her chickens at Zorzor would be scattered, or more likely, eaten. She wrote Nora from Boston, "Now I have no chickens nor feed. Ferrel Lines' passenger agent couldn't agree. It's a big boat, too."

(7)

When she returned to Liberia in May of 1954 she was assigned to Sanoyea, where she would stay for two years. Although Ma Jensen was still able to do much, she was now 63 years old and needed help.

Of at least equal importance was the Board's feeling that it was time for Esther to do at Sanoyea what she had done in Zorzor ten years before — on a lesser scale perhaps because no one envisioned a full-scale hospital for Sanoyea. Dr. Franklin Keller had arrived at Curran Memorial to work with Earl Reber. There were missionary nurses and Liberian nurses up there who could handle the load. Now the Board felt that the Sanoyea work needed Esther.

It would be interesting to know Esther's personal feelings on this matter. Did she wonder if she had joined the ranks of all those people in politics, revolutions, education, medicine, science — indeed, in every field of endeavor — who had been shunted aside once the groundbreaking (and back-breaking) work had been done? The only clues are in two letters to Nora where she says, in one, "It was a bit surprising," and in another, perhaps a little wistfully, "Some of my stuff is still at Zorzor, some at Belefani, some at Toteta, some here. I hardly know where I live."

Sanoyea was still almost as isolated as it had been when she first passed through in December of 1941. It was even more isolated than Zorzor had been when she first arrived up there. Halfway between Salala and Suakoko (which were on the Monrovia-Gbarnga motor road), a primitive track took off to the north through the high forest to Sanoyea. As the hoopoe flies, it was ten miles. On the track, which could sometimes be navigated by jeep in the dry season but was impossible in the wet, it was nearly twice as far. Esther was glad now that during her last furlough she had finally taken a driver's course. Then in Monrovia she had practiced with the mission jeep and passed her driver's test. Later she would greatly rue her decision to learn.

This was Kpelle country. The language was close enough to Loma that Esther could understand it, but dissimilar enough that the people had a hard time "hearing" her Loma. An interpreter came to the dispensary each morning, but patients came at odd times when no one was available to translate from Kpelle to English or Loma. Even the village and town names seemed suddenly foreign after thirteen years in Loma-land. Names like Maivangpeleta, Stephentaa, Zawngkai, Gbangagilengta, Bgawnawkalai. So one of her tasks, no fun for her at all, was to learn Kpelle.

Besides Esther and Ma Jensen, there were two other missionaries on the station. Ni Connie, a Bible woman, worked in the villages and led the dispensary patients in prayer just as Buschy had done in Zorzor for so many years. Elsie Otto worked in education in the Girls' School. There was no missionary pastor, but the Reverends Bowers, Spehr, and Ehrhart took turns coming in for services, usually by plane.

Esther and Miss Jensen lived together, an arrangement that worked out fine for both. The house was of mud and stick with a cement floor and a "zinc" roof. Esther loved the sound of rain thundering on the roof, sometimes so loud that it completely drowned out normal conversation. If it was a daytime storm, she loved to stand at a window, listen to the thunder crashing overhead, watch the wind lashing the great trees in the forest and the water running in little red rivers down the paths. Certainly she remembered the line, "I see the stars, I hear the rolling thunder, thy power throughout the universe displayed." And then her soul would sing, "How great Thou art."

She had more time now to herself, especially in the evenings. She loved to go down and play with Ma Jensen's children. Ma Jensen's namesake, little Kirsten, was growing up nicely. No one had come to take her home, so she was still there. The love-bond between her and Esther slowly strengthened during these two years.

Esther also had more time to read, write, and study. Miss Jensen remembers Esther sitting on her bed, typewriter between her legs and a lantern on a little table at her feet, typing out reports and letters. She also remembers that Esther was always studying, a habit that Irene Morris has also noted.

Esther's work load was considerably lighter than at Zorzor. Dispensary patients varied from forty to ninety on Monday, Wednesday, and Friday. She had no surgery except for the usual lacerations to be sutured, abscesses to be drained, and skin grafts to be done on slowly healing leg ulcers. Dr. Keller came down from Zorzor regularly, usually by plane, and Esther lined up her problem cases for him. Her only help at the dispensary were two part-time school boys, a dresser, one young girl who was a willing worker but untrained, and two part-time pregnant women.

Miss Jensen spent most of her time with her children. After forty years in Liberia, it is not surprising that Ma Jensen's reputation was widespread: motherless babies and children came to her as iron filings to a magnet. They came on the backs of ten-year-old children, in the arms of fathers who had no one to nurse them, or were perhaps left, literally, on her doorstep, in a plaited rice-straw basket.

One incident stood out in Esther's mind.

It happened on a Sunday morning. She and Ma Jensen had gone to church to hear Rev. Louis Bowers preach. After the service, they stood talking with him in the bright morning sunshine. An old grandmother and a man with a trunk on his shoulder came out of the forest toward them. They thought he was bringing supplies. Rev. Bowers was just about to tell him where to take his delivery when the man set the trunk on the ground and propped open the lid with a stick.

Inside the trunk were two tiny babies which Esther guessed could not weigh more than 2½ pounds apiece. The grandmother knelt before Ma

Jensen and begged her to take them. Just at that time Ma Jensen had so many babies she hardly knew what to do with them. She said to the man and old woman, "I've got to think and pray about this."

She and Esther went up to their house, talked it over while they had a cup of Danish coffee, then prayed for guidance. Esther was mildly amused because she knew what would happen as soon as Ma Jensen started to pray for guidance. Of course she would take the babies.

And she did. Both little girls survived. And both grew up in the Christian faith and went on to college scholarships in the United States.

(8)

Esther faced up immediately to the same problem she had fought and solved in Zorzor: the reluctance of the women to come in for prenatal care and delivery. She tackled it with a proven technique: she went to them. As in Zorzor, it worked. It worked because she developed the confidence of the people and they began to trust her.

Bishop Roland Payne remembers the specific incident which was the turning point. A man came to Esther from Kilibai, about four hours walk from Sanoyea, deep in the high forest, and said, "My wife has been in labor for three days. The zoes have finally relented and want her brought here to Sanoyea. But the creeks are in flood and I'm afraid she'd deliver on the path and then I'd lose them both."

Then, just as Flumo had said so many years ago in Zorzor, he said, "Will you come with me?"

As she said to the man, "Let's go," she thought to herself, yes, history repeats itself, God's plan is ever old, ever new.

The man started out carrying Esther's bag of supplies and medicines, but before long he tired and suggested a rest. Esther replied, "Kpai, kwillii, dii na," a mixture of Loma and Kpelle that meant, "No, let's go on now." So she took the medical kit and struck out ahead of him.

She arrived at the village long before he did and had no trouble finding the right house. With the midwives and zoes all around she worked on the woman for an hour, successfully delivering a breech baby.

The grateful family named the baby boy Bayka.

Esther knew enough of tribal superstition to understand the significance of this.

Ordinarily the child is named at birth in a highly derogatory fashion such as "Dirt" or "Good-for-nothing" so that the ancestors aren't inclined to call the baby to them. Then later, after the Poro or Sande Society initiation, when it is safe, the child is given his rightful name. She knew one child who was named "No Ground Left," suggesting to the evil spirits of the ancestors (witches that eat babies) that there was no more room in the ground for another baby and therefore they should leave this one alive.

So when this boy was named immediately, Esther knew there was immense respect for her "magic." She was both pleased and disturbed. She did not want to be known as a magician. But this was a first step: their acceptance of *her*. Later would come the acceptance of her faith. She knew this, for did not God work in mysterious ways to perform His wonders?

They brought her a woven bamboo mat to lay on the mud floor for her bed. Early the next morning men carried the mother and child in a hammock to the clinic in Sanoyea.

"And from that time," Bishop Payne says, "everybody was coming to the clinic at Sanoyea."

Then, with a twinkle in his brown eyes, he added, "And then the local government made a law that no one was to deliver in the villages. If you don't deliver there (in the clinic at Sanoyea), they fine you. Esther established that in Bong County."

In August of 1954 the Reverend Dr. and Mrs. Wolff and their four children came to Sanoyea by plane after trying by jeep off and on for a month. Esther was grateful for the presence of a pastor on the station. Though her personal religious life was strong, she got special joy from congregational worship, especially when she could understand the pastor's sermon, and when the sermon contained significant content.

The Wolffs made themselves right at home. Within a few weeks the children had acquired a chimpanzee, two monkeys, a squirrel, an ant eater, a baby bush hog, a dog, and a cat with three kittens. One of the monkeys, Diana, went to church one Sunday, jumped on Miss Jensen's shoulder and wouldn't get off until Rev. Wolff interrupted the service to carry the monkey outside.

The monkey was not the only non-human visitor in church. Dogs wandered in and lay down in the aisle. Chickens frequently followed their owners to church and had to be shooed out. One time when Dr. Franklin Clark Fry, President of the United Lutheran Church in America, was preaching, a snake turned up on the altar during the Thanksgiving service. (Though Dr. Fry's reaction is not recorded, it is unlikely that he was overly enthused. It is well known that he considered Liberia to be the biggest waste of time and money with which the Lutheran Church in America was involved. He was opposed to pouring in more money when there were so many other places where no work was being done. Also in a series of articles, he blamed the national leaders for the lack of progress being made in the church. A few years later, he would be totally negative about the "new Phebe Hospital" being envisioned to replace Curran. To be fair, he did alter his stance in 1965 when the church became autonomous.)

(10)

Esther's tour at Sanoyea coincided with the heyday of missionary plane travel in Liberia's interior. Interest in airplane transportation had actually begun in the late 20s with Dr. Erwing Lape, who had been an aviator in World War I and recognized the pregnant possibilities for the then-road-less Liberian interior. Though promised a plane by the same Mr. J.B. Franke who endowed the first Zorzor Hospital, he never got it. Rev. Stel-ling in 1949 brought his own plane out but it was never put into general use. In 1953 Rev. Louis Bowers received a Cessna Skywagon four-seater from the Incarnation Lutheran Church of Columbia, South Carolina.

Now in 1954 it was the Skywagon, piloted by Paul Knecht. Esther had appreciated the airplane when she lived in Zorzor. Now she depended on it for six months of the year when the jeep track was impassable. She was unhappy when there were rumblings about cutting back on service or when she or other missionaries were forced to spend long days on the roads.

During the rains in her first summer in Sanoyea she describes one day's itinerary: "The plane came from Zorzor to Toteta, brought Mr. Perella (builder) here, took Doctor Wolff to Palaquelli, the pilot Knecht returned here where he and Mr. Perella fixed the light plant for radio broadcasting. Then Mr. Knecht went back to Palluquellie (sic) and brought Dr. Wolff home. The plane did eight days travel in one, and gave the men time to work besides."

For six months of the year she was completely dependent on the plane to bring Dr. Keller in for dispensary visits. Even during the six-month-long dry season the doctor saved a great deal of time by flying down from Zorzor. Keller also flew to Toteta, Belefani, Salayea, and many other dis-pensaries to supervise them and to see patients who could await the per-iodic visits of a doctor. Reber, the senior man, remained on the Zorzor station most of the time, but did occasionally use the plane for dispensary visits and to get to Monrovia for meetings.

Esther described a day on which the plane brought Dr. Keller in for a dispensary visit, took Edith Curran and her new baby to Zorzor, re-turned to pick up Dr. Keller and take him back to Zorzor, and then went back to Monrovia the same day. She calculated that this itinerary would have taken twenty people-days without the airplane.

One weekend she flew up to Zorzor to cover the hospital while both Reber and Keller were gone on business at the same time. This would have been impossible without the plane; in days past, the hospital just would not have had someone there with Esther's skills.

The pastors also used the plane a great deal. In the old days they had to travel by foot, or as in Wes Sadler's case, by horse. But they knew it was inefficient use of their time, spending days just getting to one isolated village. Now with the airplane they could cut down tremendously on travel time, allowing them far more time for the really important business of evangelization.

Local village chiefs readily gave the church permission to land the plane in their fiefdoms. They vied for the status an airstrip brought and conscripted their men to clear the land. The ground was then smoothed by twenty-five men dragging a giant tree over the surface.

George Flora's jeep had revolutionized local transportation around Zorzor. Now Louis Bowers' little Cessna revolutionized transportation in the interior jungles of the entire country.

By 1957, when Esther had returned to Zorzor, a plane came in almost daily to bring supplies, people, and mail, and to take people and patients to other stations. Part of this traffic was engineers and supplies for the new all-weather road being pushed north from Belefani to Voinjama. It was then that Esther exclaimed, "Airplanes buzz in and out at Zorzor — every now and then two arrived in quick succession. Civilization is here for true! Some other things don't progress as rapidly as the transportation! And the contrast is quite striking!"

Earl Reber remembers one time when he was at a meeting of the Executive Council at Muhlenburg. By radio came word of a surgical emergency back in Zorzor. Reber drove a jeep to Monrovia where the plane was waiting to fly him to Zorzor. It was, of course, Esther who had admitted the patient, examined her, made the diagnosis of a ruptured uterus, gave her blood and other fluids, meanwhile sending word to Muhlenburg that Dr. Reber was needed.

As soon as she heard the plane, she transferred the patient to the operating table and anesthetized her. When Reber arrived breathlessly in the operating room, the patient was ready for the incision. After surgery he left the post-operative care to Esther and flew back to Monrovia and then jeeped up the road to Muhlenburg where he continued the meeting.

This incident also illustrates another point which has been made before but can bear repeated emphasis: the total faith Earl Reber had in Esther Bacon's diagnostic skills.

This heyday of air travel lasted about five years, from 1953 to 1958. The planes had been used before that, and they would be used after that. But within a year after the "all-weather" road to Zorzor was opened in June of 1958, the missionary plane would be sold and Pilot William McKay would go home on furlough. However, the road proved not to be as all-weather as anticipated, so within another year Pilot Eston Wilkins would come out and another plane bought. But the heyday was over.

(11)

It was while she was at Sanoyea that Esther first met Roland Payne. Roland Payne was thirty-four years old in 1956 when he came down to Sanoyea to visit his wife's parents, who were native to the area. He says now, "There I met Esther Bacon for the first time and I was just impressed with her. I fell in love with the woman because she was so dedicated. I just admired her dedication and commitment."

Roland Payne would become the first native-born Liberian to be elected President of the Lutheran Church (and later, bishop). During his high school years at the Methodist College of West Africa in Monrovia, he worked at Firestone to earn money to put himself through. Then through the efforts of Rev. George Flora he got a scholarship in 1952 to Midland College in the United States, Flora's alma mater, where he received a college degree as well as training as an X-ray and laboratory technician. He returned to Liberia in 1956 and was assigned to Zorzor, where he would spend the next four years doing the lab and X-ray work.

The future for Roland Payne was bright and developed in this way: in Zorzor he became increasingly disillusioned with his contribution to the Church as a laboratory technician. So, in 1960, after four years at Curran, he returned to the United States and then to Waterloo, Ontario, halfway between Toronto and London, where he got his Bachelor and Master of Divinity degrees. Upon his return to Liberia in July of 1963 he attended the church convention, expecting to be assigned to a parish. Instead, he was elected president.

With a great guffaw he says now, "They even elected me before I was ordained. I was elected at 10 A.M. in the morning and at 7 P.M. I was ordained." He remained as head of the church for the next twenty-one years, first as president until 1965, then as bishop until June 10, 1984, when he consecrated Pastor Ronald Diggs as the new bishop.

This transition from lab tech to bishop is one of Dr. James Stull's favorite stories. He says, "It's a vignette of the type of change that took place in the leadership (during those years). When I went to Zorzor in 1959, Roland Payne was my lab tech and ended up being my bishop."

In a later year, at a Church Convention in the United States, Payne said, "I was born in heathenism, full of superstitions, negations, fears, and witchcraft. The light of civilization which I enjoy today was made possible by the American Lutheran Mission. I can assure you that we the aborigines do appreciate the valuable services the mission is rendering our people."

But this was all ahead of him in 1956 when he first met Esther Bacon at Sanoyea just before she went home on furlough and he started his work as a technician at Zorzor. She told him, "When I come back from furlough, you have me transferred to Zorzor!"

She had enjoyed the relative peace and quiet at Sanoyea. As usual she had made her mark. By the time her term was over, she had gotten busier and busier with babies and deliveries. For long periods of time she had even had to sleep at the dispensary most nights. But she was not joking when she asked Roland Payne to transfer her to Zorzor when she came back. He of course didn't have that authority at the time, but when she returned, she did indeed go back to Zorzor.

(12)

Esther's furlough this time was for a full year, from July of 1956 to June of 1957, time enough to finish her baccalaureate degree. She was already thinking of going on for a master's degree in Public Health on a subsequent furlough.

Her studies at Morningside were almost interrupted by a solemn event back in Zorzor. On December 8th of 1956, a young nurse, Elaine Bradfield, who had been at Curran Memorial for only five months, died of encephalitis.

On December 12th, Esther wrote Dr. Reber: "I will gladly return to Liberia the end of next month, to be at whatever station seems best. It does not seem urgent that the other semester be completed this time."

Earl wrote back immediately: "We willingly accept the added tasks so that you may complete your studies." Later on in the letter he writes: "Your earlier experience here, your willingness to assist and your capabilities in teaching in the Nurses' Training School, your convinced spirit as to the importance of nurses' training, make it mandatory that we bring you back to Zorzor."

So Esther continued her schooling. She was grateful to Earl Reber for his willingness to do without her for six more months and pleased by the complimentary statements in his letter. Now, after three separate sessions years apart, she finally got her Bachelor of Science degree. She was forty years old.

Esther was also informed of another sad death back in Liberia in 1956. Up in Wozi, where the Sadlers and Margaret Miller lived, Chief Mamolu died. Fifteen years earlier, when Wes and Roslyn were walking and riding horses to the villages from Zorzor, the chief had graciously loaned them a house in which to stay and his court house in which to hold services. Later, when the Sadlers moved to Wozi, he gave up his chief's medicines and status to join the church. When he died in 1956, Roslyn furnished the artistry, and his people the material and muscles, to make a grave marker with a raised cross on it. He was buried in front of the Wozi church, the old court house.

Esther found time to go out to Brush, Colorado, where her father now lived in the Ebeneezer Lutheran Home. A year before, he'd had a stroke and was only slowly regaining some strength in his paralyzed extremities. When he died a year later, on September 16th, 1957, at age 79, Esther was glad she had seen him one more time.

(13)

Again she was asked to do a short piece for *Lutheran Woman's Work*, this time on ''The 'Good News' in Liberia.'' In a simply written but moving story she described how the gospel came to the old, the new, and the young in Liberia.

The ''old'' was Mama Vaba, an elderly lady whose first contact with Christianity came at Esther's dispensary in Sanoyea. She had an incurable disease and Esther was unable to do much for her body. But her soul was receptive to the gospel. Before she died she was taught the meaning of salvation by Liberian evangelist Louis Stevenson and missionary Bible woman Ni Connie. Her grandson read to her from Kpelle literature, pieces translated from English by Dr. William Welmers just a few years before. After her baptism by Pastor Wolff, Esther wrote, ''She lived on to enjoy the rice harvest. She knew that as a Christian she could not expect her people to feed her spirit when she died, but she remained cheerful and happy in the faith she had found.''

The ''new'' was Knowae, a pregnant young woman who had lost five little ones already and came to Sanoyea to get help from Esther to bear a child who would live. While under treatment, she became interested in a Bible class taught by Kpelle convert Miss Amanda, one of the strong Christian lay leaders rising in the Lutheran Church. After her baby arrived safely, Knowae continued with instruction, learned to read, and was baptized.

The ''young'' was Dolikwi, a nine-year-old who had had an accident and was treated at the Zorzor hospital. He became enthused about the Sunday School, saying, ''They don't teach anything like that at my home.'' Precocious and intelligent, though still illiterate, he learned the Lord's prayer and many of the hymns in Loma. He began conducting Christian services for both adults and children. Esther concludes her article with, ''Now he has a desire to go to school. Will there be a way next year, and what will his future hold?''

(14)

When Esther returned to Africa in June of 1957, she sailed from Brooklyn on board the S.S. Tana, a Norwegian boat flying the American flag. There is just a hint of nostalgia as they cleared New York: "There was a lovely sunset last night as we bid goodbye to Statue of Liberty and New York." She had worked in Africa most of the past sixteen years. She had done much in those years but there was much more to do. So she fretted about time wasted in Monrovia as she checked her baggage — including a wheel-chair — through customs, then struggled with petty officialdom to renew her residency permit and nursing registration.

Finally she got away, up the familiar, muddy red road through Kakata, Salala, Toteta, Gbarnga, to Belefani, where the all-weather, all-vehicle road ended. From there on it was the equally familiar jeep track across the St. Paul River and up through Gorlu, Salayea, Gbangoi, and at last to Zorzor.

Her car dipped down the hill past the open market, crossed on the causeway through the swamp-rice fields, climbed the hill past the hospital and the airstrip in a wide loop back to her house. People swarmed, hands outstretched, voices calling out, "Bayka, Bayka, Bayka."

As the car stopped at her house, a man rushed up to her. "Bayka," he said, "will you come to the hospital? My wife is very ill and no one knows what to do."

Esther looked around her at the skilled doctors and nurses who she was certain knew exactly what to do. But she didn't hesitate a moment. Ignoring all the others, leaving her suitcases on the porch without even going into her house, she followed the man down to the hospital. Only after she had checked the patient and reassured the husband did she return home to unpack and settle back in.

She moved back into the duplex with Maebelle Hosterman. The house had been rescreened to keep out rats which had been entering the house through holes they had eaten in the plastic screening. Daily rains soaked the bedrooms, but nothing could be done until the rains ended in October. Esther complained that it was much more complicated fixing the aluminum roof than it ever was when they had thatch. She did like the refrigerator and kerosene stove, but she wrote Aunt Nora, "I do miss some of the old things."

In her next letter she described "the cutest little squirrel" in her oven, eating gingerbread, and told of a snake killed in the Operating Room during emergency surgery. Apparently enough of the old things remained to keep her happy.

There was in fact a constant mix of the old and the new. The electric plant was on from 6 A.M. to 10 P.M. They now used a small electric autoclave to sterilize syringes and instruments. When the autoclave gave "humbug," the doctors worked on it and Esther philosophized, "It's rather nice to have others worry about such matters!"

Esther used an electric blender to mix what Earl Reber called the keystone of their baby clinic. He had gotten from Church World Service a supply of six million atabrine tablets for which they had paid $41, including shipping. In the blender, Esther mixed it with cod liver oil (Vitamin D) and ascorbic acid (Vitamin C).

The baby clinic was "taking off." Reber comments that in the end it was too much of a success. They sometimes saw as many as 500 children on clinic day. But he recognized quite clearly that the children who came in half-dead and often died were those who had never attended clinic.

In Esther's three-year absence missionary nurses Alberta Holtzinger and Maebelle Hosterman had established working hours at the hospital. Every nurse was now off duty every third weekend and either Saturday or Sunday on the other two. Call was every third night. The Liberian nurses — including Edith Curran, Frances Leonard Morris, Nora Howard and Grace Howard — were taking more responsibility.

(15)

In September of 1957, Dr. Keller returned from furlough. Franklin Lloyd Keller was 27 years old when he first went to Liberia in October of 1953. He was from New Kingston, Pennsylvania, and took his undergraduate training at Gettysburg College. After attending Lutheran Theological Seminary in Gettysburg, where he got his Bachelor of Divinity degree, he went on to the University of Maryland School of Medicine in Baltimore for his MD degree. He was ordained a pastor in March and commissioned a missionary in August of 1953, then went almost immediately to the "University of Wozi" with his wife Sarah Ruth to study Loma with Wes Sadler.

Keller and Esther had not yet worked together much. Esther was home on furlough during Keller's first year at Wozi, at Sanoyea during his second and third at Zorzor, and then Keller was on furlough when Esther returned to Zorzor. They had worked together one day a month during her term at Sanoyea when he came regularly to hold clinic. Once she had heard him speak at a conference at Toteta, and another time at Annual Conference when he had shown slides of a Nigeria trip.

But this was the first time she had a chance to work with him regularly. They were a perfect match. Keller was interested in surgery, and would later take a surgical residency and return to the new Phebe hospital as a board-qualified surgeon. He was a perfectionist about techniques and compulsive about record keeping, the latter bringing him into frequent spats with Esther.

But he respected her immensely, and she reciprocated the feeling. Louise Faust says, "Franklin Keller was a perfect person for her to work with because he respected *her*, he respected her opinion, he never questioned it, he figured she knew as much or more than he did. He would go along with all this bizarre behavior because he figured the ends justified the means."

Keller told Louise Faust, "Whatever she puts her hand to, God is with her. If she says operate, I operate. If she says no, I don't. She's never wrong. We doctors would be poring over the symptoms of some strange malady and more often than not Esther would come up with the answer and it would turn out to be some obscure tropical disease."

Keller was also impressed by Esther's tenacity, as were all the other people who ever worked with her. He tells a story in which her tenacity and her astute judgment were combined.

He was in the operating room doing a Caesarian section. "Everything was going well," he says, "and Esther was not needed. She was nowhere in sight. I delivered the baby and started to close. In a few seconds the patient's blood pressure dropped, her breathing stopped and her heart failed. I put down my instruments.

"What sixth sense told Esther there was trouble, I'll never know. But suddenly she was there, forcing her breath into the patient's lungs, frantically willing her to live. I plunged a cardiac stimulant directly into the woman's heart. There was no response. Still Esther kept on trying to breathe for the woman.

" 'It's no use, Esther,' I said. 'She's dead. There's nothing more that can be done for her.'

Esther looked up at me in anguish.

" 'But, Doctor,' she pleaded. 'You can't give up.'

"I'm very sure she didn't tell me to do this, but suddenly I found myself with the scalpel in my hand making an incision in the chest wall. I reached in and massaged the heart. The organ throbbed under my fingers and started beating again.

"I was off on a week's trip after that, but at least once a day I thought of that woman and wondered if she had really survived. The first person I met in the hospital corridor when I returned was my resurrected patient, alive and smiling, her baby in her arms."

Earl Reber was one of the first to comment on Esther's ability to get people to do things they really didn't want to, like teaching in the nursing school, or giving blood. A classic example occurred during Franklin Keller's second term.

A bus went off the road and seventeen people were brought to Curran, many of them with lacerations needing suturing. When Esther came into the emergency room and saw how wild it was, she marched back into the obstetrical room where one of her own nurses was in labor. "Come help us," Esther said.

"I'm having a baby!" the woman cried.

Esther had examined her just a few minutes before and knew she had a long way to go. "It's all right," Esther said, "you still have plenty of time."

So the astonished nurse got up and helped until all the patients were cared for. Then she went back to her room and delivered her baby.

(16)

Curran Memorial Hospital had never been staffed so well. Two doctors: Reber and Keller. Seven Liberian nurses. Four missionary registered nurses: Esther, Dorothea Greiner, Maebelle Hosterman, and Alberta Holtzinger. Dorothea now had charge of the operating room and doubled as a teacher in the Nursing School.

Esther herself had ten hours of classroom work a week. The three-year Registered Nurse school now averaged twenty students, six or seven in each class. Much was made of the capping ceremonies at the end of their first six-month probationary studies. Esther once complained that "tonight we have capping, so will have to polish my shoes and press a cap!" One year the new caps for the probationers did not arrive in time for capping, so Esther spent most of the night before with pillow cases: cutting, starching, shaping, and pressing caps for her students.

There had been two doctors at Zorzor once before, from 1949 to 1952, when Lowell Yund was there with Earl Reber. But local transport was so poor then, and the nursing staff so small, that little could be done to upgrade medical care in any but the closest villages.

Now there were double the number of nurses, plus the jeep and frequent plane service. The doctor and a nurse or lab tech Roland Payne could make clinic visits 25-50 miles away more easily than Dr. Yund made a trip to Kiliwu four miles away.

As one example of the new medical outreach, Reber and Keller took on the project of supervising a young public health worker in Sukolomu, a town of 175 houses a few miles down the road from Zorzor. One weekend neither doctor could go, so Esther went down with Roland Payne and some of his students. Esther organized the patients, explained the proper process for collection of specimens, then turned them over to Roland Payne, who worked all weekend checking stool specimens for parasitic worms.

This weekend was a nostalgic trip into the past for Esther because she spent the night in Sukolomu, her first night in a village in a long time. Transportation had improved so much that on the infrequent occasions when she went out to a village, she was easily able to return to Zorzor the same day. But Sukolomu was a two-mile walk off the motor road. Since she had had visitors and movies at her house three evenings the past week in Zorzor, she really appreciated having no classes, no laundry, no social life, in a village like those of her early years.

(17)

In June of 1958, the Raymond Concrete Pile Company opened the all-vehicle, all-weather road to Zorzor, replacing the jeep track which often had been impassable during the six months of heavy rains. The trip to Gbarnga now took three hours by public bus or private vehicle. The jeep trip over a dry track had taken a full day, the hike during the rains, three days. One day the fun-loving and impetuous Esther took off by bus from Zorzor on a friend-visiting spree. First straight through to Gbarnga, back up the road to Belefani, Gorlu and Salayea, and back to Zorzor by 8 P.M., having visited for an hour or two in all four towns.

The bus was — and still is — called the money-bus. No one seems to know why. Many Liberians got into the transport business by buying mini-buses, toppered pickup trucks, and anything else capable of carrying 15-25 people.* Drivers vied to invent the most distinctive names for their vehicles: AFRICAN BOY BACK TO TOWN, PUT ME TO TOWN, TO LIVE IS TO STRUGGLE, BINGO — M. BAYO, TRY YOUR BEST, V.D., GOOD NEVER LOST, BE CAREFUL, and many, many others.

Shortly after the road reached Zorzor, and while the Raymond Company was still encamped about fourteen miles away on the Via River, a seriously ill patient came in from a village by hammock. Dr. Reber was on a short vacation and Dr. Keller had gone down the road to Monrovia for a two-day meeting.

Esther examined the lady and within a few moments made the diagnosis of a ruptured uterus. Quickly she rounded up the relatives and the carriers and drew blood from each one whose type was right. She started a unit slowly and sent one of the carriers up to the Raymond camp to get the company physician.

---

*Author's note: I once rode to Borkeza in the back of a Toyota pickup with 26 other people, several chickens, two dogs, and one goat.

He came down willingly, examined the patient, then informed Esther in a very polite but slightly condescending tone, "This can't be a ruptured uterus. Those patients are always in very serious condition. This lady would've been dead by now if your diagnosis was correct." He refused to operate and left, saying, "But if she gets worse, you can call me again."

Esther didn't bother to call him again. She titrated blood infusion to stabilize the vital signs without causing further bleeding. She maintained fluid intake, monitored urine output, administered antibiotics — all night she stayed with her, and into the next afternoon, keeping her alive, waiting for Dr. Keller to return.

When she got word that he was back, she put the patient on the operating table and sent a runner for him. He didn't doubt her for one moment. He opened up the abdomen, found a ruptured uterus and of course a dead infant, and did a hysterectomy. The patient survived.

(18)

During her years in Liberia, Esther was involved many times with smallpox, a disease that remained dormant for years and then broke out in seemingly random fashion. Three specific episodes illustrate three different facets of Esther Bacon's character. The first was described in Chapter 5, Part 2, when she introduced mass inoculation to Loma-land.

The second involved Franklin Keller. By the time he arrived in Zorzor the large-scale epidemics were uncommon because of the increasing number of people who had been vaccinated. But some cases still popped up. One old man was brought in near death and isolated in a mud "kitchen." His relatives feared to come close to him while he was alive, and adamantly refused to carry him away when he was dead.

Without anything more than a "Shall we?", Esther and Franklin Keller wrapped the body in woven grass mats, a traditional Loma custom, slung the body onto their shoulders, carried him up to the cemetery, dug the grave, and buried him.

(19)

The third was an amusing incident started by a rumor reaching Esther that smallpox had broken out across the border in Guinea. She took her briefcase and some medicines, caught a money-bus to Yella and walked across the Mounie River on the log bridge to the Guinea customs house. Her passport was in Monrovia. She tried to talk her way across the border. The Customs official refused to let her pass.

Undaunted, Esther walked out of sight down the Liberian side of the river, waded across, and found a path that led her back to the road well beyond the customs officer. A money-bus soon picked her up and took her to the village.

The rumor of smallpox was untrue, the cases all being severe chicken-pox, so she started back to the river on another money-bus. She intended to get off well before it reached the customs office, but she was foiled when officers stopped the bus long before it reached the river.

Esther could hardly hide, a white woman in a sea of black faces.

The senior customs man spotted Esther immediately and walked down the aisle toward her.

But before he reached her, he broke out into a broad smile. "Bayka, what are you doing here?"

"I heard there was smallpox over here and that's why I came."

He smiled again. "Bayka," he said, "do you remember you delivered my wife just a few weeks ago in your hospital? Welcome to Guinea."

He took her off the bus and drove her across the bridge in his own car. Roland Payne, commenting on the incident, says, "She didn't need a passport. Her passport was herself."

(20)

Tetanus was another disease on its way out in the mid-1950s. Franklin Keller is very candid about the reason. He says, "The year I came to Zor-zor, Esther was home on furlough. That year we did not save one baby with tetanus of the (umbilical) cord. The following year, after Esther's re-turn, 64% of the tetanus babies lived. That was 2% better than Cook County Hospital (in Chicago) did that same year with all their modern equipment."

Tetanus of the cord was very common, primarily because traditional treatment included smearing the end of the cut cord with cow-dung. Tetanus spores lie dormant in animal dung for long periods of time and then are activated by warmth and moisture. The freshly cut cord was a prime nutrient broth for tetanus bacilli.

Franklin Keller tells a story illustrative of Esther's perspicacity in diag-nosing tetanus and her tenacity in treating it. One baby-clinic day the line of people stretched along the entire length of the hospital. Esther walked along the line to pick out the sickest ones to examine first. She came to a eight-month-old lying on a cloth in a small basin. One glance told her he had tetanus. She picked him up and began treating him imme-diately. There are numerous witnesses to the fact that on this child she did mouth-to-mouth breathing periodically for *eighteen hours* with one uninterrupted six-hour stretch before she would admit to herself that the child was lost.

Earl Reber also had recognized early that Esther possessed not only the knack of early diagnosis in tetanus but an uncanny sense about how to treat it. In the early years, before valium, they had mephenisine, a drug related to meprobamate which would come out much later. The drug was a sedative and muscle relaxant. As with all soporific drugs, if used too sparingly, convulsions and suffocation continued; if used too heavily, respiratory paralysis ensued.

To the casual observer, it seemed that Esther knew instinctively just how much drug to use. The truth is that she watched her little patients so carefully that she could detect nuances in the signs that foretold the need to give more drug or less drug in the next dose. In the total absence of more sophisticated monitors, she used her five senses to evaluate what was happening.

There was, of course, more than just her own personal care involved. After all, she couldn't stay at the hospital 24 hours a day, though sometimes it seemed as if she did. "So," Earl Reber says, "Esther's way of teaching the national nurses made it possible to save more tetanus babies."

One of the national nurses she taught was Priscilla Payne, Roland's wife. She came up to Zorzor specifically to learn Esther's technique of saving tetanus babies. She did learn it, and helped spread it throughout Liberia.

(22)

Zorzor was still growing. Esther wrote home, "I guess we could say the *City of Zorzor* now! The rural village has given way to the road. There are two gas stations in Zorzor now. Also we sometimes buy fresh apples and pears, as well as cold meats, and ice cream in the stores in town; also fresh butter and cheese. Name anything you want, and there's a good chance you can get it at one store or other; notions, ready-made clothing; canned goods, record players, clocks — in fact, Zorzro is mostly stores. Watch out for the traffic, too! There have been tremendous changes in community life. Hardly a week goes by without some kind of an accident. But a good thing patients can now come to the hospital via motor vehicle who would not have had a chance to come in years gone by."

And the hospital wards were crowded with adults, babies and children. There was hardly space to walk around the mats which were placed between the beds in all the wards. In January of 1959 there were 39 deliveries, three of them by Caesarian section. The clinics were overflowing.

Curran Memorial was a far cry from the Zorzor Hospital that Esther had come to almost twenty years before. But she was the first one to disclaim any credit for the miraculous turn-around. She wrote, "None of my work has been alone. Liberian co-workers, particularly nurses and medical assistants, have had a large part in anything I might seem to have accomplished. Fellow-missionaries have stood with me and encouraged me. Friends in the United States supported and prayed.

"The Great Physician has been ever with us."

The new hospital at Zorzor, circa 1950, renamed "Curran Memorial Hospital" in 1948.

Chapter Seven

(1959-1967)

(1)

To end her sixth term, Esther took a ten-week vacation from August 7th to October 21st in 1959. When she returned to Zorzor, both Dr. Keller and Dr. Reber were on furlough. In their place was young Dr. James Stull, newly arrived from the States.

He may have been young, but he was one of the strongest personalities to come onto the field for many years. He would have a profound effect on Curran Memorial Hospital and its personnel, especially Earl Reber and Esther Bacon.

James Stull, the son of Rev. and Mrs. Maynard Stull of Youngstown, Ohio, grew up knowing he was going to be a missionary pastor. He took his Bachelor of Divinity degree at Wittenberg College. While in seminary he met two people who would influence his life: a very pretty young lady whose crowning glory was brown hair that shone with red-gold highlights in the sun, Betty Ann Laughner, whom he married, and a young Chinese Christian who convinced him that health care on the foreign mission field was a more meaningful approach than verbal evangelism.

So. Rev. Stull went to Jefferson Medical College in Philadelphia, intending to go to China as a doctor. But as it had for Esther Bacon, the door to China closed for him, too. (The door marked "Exit" opened widely for

151

nearly all missionaries in China in those years.)

Close to the end of Stull's senior year, two Mission Board secretaries came to him in Philadelphia and said, "China is not available to you. But for many, many years we have been trying to get a new, modern hospital started in Liberia. It's name will be Phebe, after the old hospital at Muhlenberg."

Stull laughed and said, "Yeah, I remember as a Luther Leaguer I bought a brick for a dollar for Phebe Hospital."

Following internship at Mercy Hospital in Springfield, Ohio, Stull spent a year at the Kennedy School of Missions in Hartford, Connecticut. There, Dr. William Welmers introduced him to the Kpelle language.

Jim and Betty Stull and their four children, Paul, Sydney, Susan and fourteen-month-old baby Mary Carol, arrived in Liberia on the 20th of July in 1959. They were carried up the road to Toteta, a town on the main motor road between Monrovia and Gbarnga, where they began the study of Kpelle.

After two weeks of pleasant settling in to their modern, western-style, cement-block home, Jim was ready "to find out where Phebe Hospital planning stood, whose court the ball was in, who was doing what and who *thought* what, and why the planning seemed not to be moving forward." He found to his dismay — if not surprise — that the people on the field were waiting for decisions from the New York Board, and the Board was waiting for the field to move.

In October the Stulls interrupted language study to cover Curran Memorial in Zorzor for the three months that both Keller and Reber would be gone. It was then that Esther Bacon returned from furlough and met the Stulls for the first time.

On December 15th, 1959, after only two months at Zorzor, Stull wrote to Dr. Herman Gilbert, then Liberia Secretary in the Board of Foreign Missions in New York: "Great amounts of time, labor and love have made Curran the place it is, and the marks of many personalities are left here. But. . .most of the facilities are taxed beyond their capacity. The work here has grown tremendously, and more so since the motor road was completed. There has also been a more rapid change in the attitudes of the people toward the type of medicine we practice. The point is that we (have) out-grown the present facilities."

A month later, in January of 1960, the Board in New York made the definitive decision to build the new Phebe — at Suakoko, near Gbarnga ("Bahng-ah"). The prospective cost: $950,000. The chairman of the hospital planning committee: Franklin Keller.

(2)

When Reber and Keller returned to Zorzor, Jim and Betty Stull went back down the road to Yanekwelle for eight more months of language study. Jim saw a few patients each day and periodically flew to Sanoyea or Kpolopele to visit the dispensaries there. Betty also started a garden and spent some of her time doing sketches and water colors. But the language occupied most of their time.

Stull would never regret those months. He noted that "there is something that happens between the doctor and the patient when the doctor is willing to try to converse with the patient in his own language."

Meanwhile, up in Zorzor, Keller, Reber, and Nurse Alice Dietz met on most weekends to discuss the new Phebe. Stull made the journey up the road to Zorzor as often as he could to sit with them. But he began to feel as if he were standing on the side-lines while big things were happening elsewhere. After all, *he* had been sent out to get Phebe moving. Well, he had gotten it moving and now he wanted to *keep* it moving.

Alice Dietz, who had arrived on the field in June of 1960, had been given the primary responsibility of upgrading the nursing school at Zorzor. She actively crusaded for a significantly larger nursing staff for the new Phebe, and for nurses who had at least a bachelor's degree and preferably a master's degree in nursing. Jim Stull agreed wholeheartedly with Alice's ideas and backed the plan to transfer her to Phebe as Director of Nursing.

(3)

Earl Reber was emphatically opposed to a drastic increase in staff at the new Phebe Hospital, arguing that the size of the project he envisioned did not merit it. It was not that he was opposed to a new and larger hospital. He long had been aware that Curran Hospital was like an overloaded electrical circuit without a fuse box. For years he had been working evenings and weekends on pencil sketches for a new Phebe with missionary pastor/builder Paul Lewis.

Stull says now that Reber's and Lewis's plans "just didn't look like they were very powerful hospital plans to me." Then he adds somewhat pensively, "Looking back, maybe some of the things they wanted to do may have been more useful than the way we finally went. But I've rehearsed this whole scenario so many times and I think the only way it would ever have gotten *going* was like the way it happened, in spite of the serious flaws in the final product. At least we got it up and got it going."

Stull also thought a non-MD hospital administrator should be recruited. Reber, who had matured in the Liberia setting, felt strongly that administration should be done by a doctor, which was the current policy. (It may be that he saw himself in that role at Phebe.) Stull, however, knew that every hour a doctor spent on administration was an hour stolen from patient care. His goal was to have every patient seen by a physician. Later he recognized the impracticality of this and worked to train non-MD physician extenders.

So Earl Reber, the Old Guard, with long years of experience in a bush hospital, did see the need for a new Phebe, but thought it should be built and staffed along proven lines. James Stull, the Young Turk, had been challenged by the Board to build a hospital new not only in buildings but in concept.

The Stulls finished language study and went back to Zorzor in October of 1960. Stull covered pediatrics and general medicine, Keller obstetrics and surgery, Reber the out-patient dispensary. Since the clinics were so over-loaded, all three doctors helped with them. They rotated coverage of the hospital on nights and weekends. Reber maintained the decision-making role of Medical Director.

(4)

Meanwhile, Esther had been asked to go down to Sanoyea for the last six months of her 7th term. She readily agreed and began to pack a trunk. When Jim Stull heard about this, he wrote to Dr. Gilbert in New York, ''We are feeling the pinch of fewer nurses and I believe we are all in for something of a shock when Esther goes to Sanoyea. None of the other nurses have the diversity of ability that Esther has, and I'm sure we don't realize how much we depend on her for various things.'' But he forsaw that Esther's leaving would have its good side: the Liberian nurses would have to take on more responsibility and he considered this good.

Esther had always been cognizant of both the shortage of national nurses and the need to integrate them more fully into responsible positions in the hospital. There were two problems. One was that few stayed long enough to earn a job such as department supervisor. Some, like Irene Morris, who one day would become co-chief of obstetrics, had just graduated a year before. Some, like Nora Howard and Jeanette Kwekwe who had new babies, just went back to their villages. Some moved to other stations when their husbands were transferred. Others, usually unmarried young people, sought the bigger towns like Monrovia.

The other problem was that the older nurses like Frances Leonard Morris and Edith Curran, simply just weren't qualified because they had had only 6-12 months training at the old Phebe school.

But what worried Esther now was the fate of Curran Memorial Hospital. She saw clearly that when Phebe opened, the services and the staff at

Curran would be drastically cut unless a great many new people were found. The "worst-case scenario," which Esther could hardly grasp, would pull *all* the doctors and nurses out of Curran, relegating Curran Hospital to the status of dispensary.

But the work went on. Franklin Keller was doing many thyroidectomies as the people began to realize they didn't have to go around with big lumps in their necks. Deliveries were increasing by almost geometric progression. One day Esther did six deliveries with her students on the same day that Keller worked for hours on a difficult strangulated hernia and Reber plated a badly fractured leg and then removed a ruptured uterus.

The patient census regularly ran over 100 in a hospital that held twenty-five beds. Under each bed was a mat for pediatric patients and their mothers. Men and women were separated by movable partitions. Only the most acute cases could be kept in the ward. The other 60-70 patients were assigned beds in huts built of mud and thatch behind the hospital.

Esther was happiest when she was the busiest. But Keller would order her to go home when he thought she was over-extended. Sometimes she actually obeyed him.

But Roland Payne remembers the times when she didn't. "Sometimes," he says with a rumbling chuckle, "she would come into my laboratory and ask to hide until Dr. Keller was occupied elsewhere, and then she would go back on the ward to finish up some task or treatment that Dr. Keller had interrupted."

Then, as the Bishop's eyes shifted off into a remembered past and saw again the mischievous young Esther Bacon hiding in his laboratory, he added, "Yes, she was an outlaw. An outlaw for God. She was a genius — that woman was talented and gifted — she didn't go for any plan — her main idea was just *'go'!*"

Roland Payne left with Priscilla for seminary in Canada in September of 1960, again leaving Curran short-handed in the laboratory. No one begrudged Payne's move. Everyone knew that he would be much more effective in the over-all work of the Church when he returned as a pastor.

But it did emphasize the need for recruiting technicians and Stull was quick to see it. He wrote Dr. Gilbert: "It may be alright for each doctor at the present time to take his own X-rays, set up for many of his procedures, do a good bit of his own lab work, and search out medicines himself from the drug stores as he has need. But when you . . . think in terms of roughly four times the number of patients (at Phebe), the individual doctor won't have time to do all that, and still render the services he should as physician."

(5)

Before going down to Sanoyea, Esther took a full day off: she went to church in the morning, had two guests at her house for lunch, visited friends in town after lunch, cleaned her house thoroughly (she enjoyed this), typed up and mimeographed an exam for her students, relaxed with a book for an hour, packed for Sanoyea, walked out to a farm to see a former patient who was now a good friend, drove down to Salayea in the evening for more visits with friends, one of whom was Lilliana Bartolomei, who still remembered vividly that Christmas Day emergency in the bush.

Late that night she came home to write a few letters. Since her Aunt Nora would be retiring soon, Esther invited her to join her in Baltimore in 1963 — still almost three years off — when Esther planned to get a master's degree in Public Health. She also urged Nora to come out to Zorzor and stay for six to twelve months in order "to really get the feel of the place." Esther thought Nora's secretarial skills would be a very valuable asset to the station.

Leaving the stew of the new Phebe simmering in Zorzor, Esther flew down to Sanoyea just before Christmas in 1960 to switch places with Dorothea Greiner. She was mellowing a bit. She actually enjoyed the change and the reduced work-load compared to Zorzor. She even began to enjoy Ma Jensen's mid-morning coffee hour, though it always seemed to catch her in the middle of doing something. "But," she said, "she always has some good Danish cheese."

While she was at Sanoyea, she lost two people close to her heart. One of her adopted children, Ben Bacon, who early on had developed a debilitating illness, died in Zorzor Hospital, an event emotionally charged for everyone present.

And in February of 1961, Frances Leonard Morris, who had accompanied Esther on her first walk to Zorzor way back in 1941, became seriously ill with kidney failure. Esther went up to Zorzor to be with her but she was in a coma and died without regaining consciousness.

At Frances's funeral, Esther was struck by a rare attack of nostalgia. She rarely looked back, but she did now, and she compared the Zorzor hospital of twenty years ago with the hospital now. Then there had been no doctors, only one fully-trained Registered Nurse (herself), two or three Liberian nurses with training varying from six months to a year, no medical assistants, no X-ray, markedly limited laboratory services. And, of course, only dying patients in the wards and almost no deliveries in the OB section. There was no School of Nursing; there could be none, for there were few patients and no teaching staff.

Now there were three doctors, Reber, Keller and Stull. There were four missionary nurses; Dorothea Greiner, up from Sanoyea; Fran Brouse who had come out in 1959 from the Lankenau School of Nursing in Philadelphia, and then spent a year in Wozi studying the language; Alice Deitz, in both the hospital and nursing school; Janet Reinbrecht, teaching in the nursing school.

Despite the turn-over in Liberian nurses, there were now four at Curran, and one or two medical assistants. There was a small, almost new, 15 milli-ampere X-ray machine, and a greatly expanded laboratory.

The hospital was jammed with surgical, medical, and obstetrical problems of all kinds. The obstetrical suite was delivering over 500 women a year; in the previous year (1960) there had been 553.

The School of Nursing and Midwifery was flourishing. Esther's midwifery class was delivering at least one baby a day; one student did eleven deliveries in his first two weeks on 24-hour call.

So once again, as Esther went on a short furlough in July of 1961, she recognized that the Curran Memorial Hospital in Zorzor, though taxed to its limits, was in good hands.

(6)

When Esther returned to the States in July of 1961, a great many things were happening in the world. The Cold War had been intensified by two major incidents: the Bay of Pigs fiasco in Cuba, and the Wall built by the Russians to seal off East Berlin. On the other side of the world, the Chinese signaled their disillusionment with Russian-style communism when Premier Chou En-lai walked out of a Soviet party congress in Moscow.

In the same year, President Kennedy created the Peace Corps; soon volunteers would be working in most of the developing countries, including Liberia. Tanganyika gained independence from Great Britain, and in a few years would join in a political alliance with Zanzibar to form Tan-zan-ia. Russia's Yuri Gagarin was the first man to circle the globe in a spacecraft, followed three weeks later by the U.S.'s Alan Shepard. In Germany 302 deformed babies were born after their mothers had taken thalidomide, a drug banned in the U.S. while studies continued. Newton Minow coined the term "vast wasteland" to describe TV programming. Ray Kroc bought the McDonald brothers' franchise in California and soon the golden arches rose over 3,500 cities. Roger Maris broke Babe Ruth's home run record, but purists smugly noted that the Babe's ball was heavier and he played in twelve fewer games.

If Esther had her radio on, she heard the first recordings of The Supremes and heard Bob Dylan stirring the hearts of civil rights activists with "Blowin' in the Wind."

(7)

Esther's plane was met in Sioux City by Mrs. Ruth Shuldt, Trinity Church secretary, and cousins Ken and Jean Carlson. It was late at night, but they were all anxious to hear Esther's news. Within five minutes, she was sound asleep in the back seat. They arrived at Hawarden at about 2:30 A.M. and Esther went right to bed at Aunt Nora's. Nora had moved to Hawarden after retiring.

Much to Jean's surprise, but not out of character at all, Esther rang Jean's doorbell at eight the next morning. She had already examined her Aunt Nora and was able to tell Jean about Nora's blood pressure, pulse, and all the other pertinent information needed to establish that Nora was healthy enough to go back to Liberia with her.

Even though her doctor had told her she was healthy enough to make the trip, she said to Esther, "I'm 74 years old, too old to go, and I don't want to go, and that doctor doesn't know my condition that well anyhow."

Jean Carlson explains why Esther wanted Nora to go to Zorzor. "Esther felt a responsibility to Aunt Nora as she aged. We were here to take care of her, but Esther felt that *she* should, but there was no way that she could, unless Aunt Nora went to Zorzor."

Esther's enjoyment of her two months in Hawarden was enhanced by not having any speaking engagements. She was able just to relax and enjoy living where you could buy fresh and tender meat without flies crawling on it, packaged cereal and flour without weevils in it, and literally dozens of other things that she had not really missed at Zorzor but now thoroughly appreciated. She became fascinated with cake mixes which, although not new, were becoming much more popular. Jean Carlson says, "She made angel food cakes for everything that came along."

Once when they visited Jean's mother there was a dish of apples on the table. Soon Esther had an apple in each hand, taking a bite out of first one and then the other. In Zorzor apples were a dollar apiece, when she could get them.

She loved to prowl around in the Carlsons' grocery store. One time she found several thousand packages of Koolaid removed from shelves because of their cyclomate content and shipped the entire lot to Zorzor, saying, "It's already sweetened and I have so many people coming to my house. Besides, the cyclomate isn't going to do any more damage than the sugar." In one sentence the astute Esther predicted two things: that cyclomates weren't all that bad, and that sugar might be.

Jean drove Esther down to Sioux City to see a doctor about some problem she had had in Africa. The doctor wanted her to stay overnight in the hospital but she refused. She said, "There's no reason for me to waste that money by staying overnight in the hospital." Room rates then were about $20 a night.

So Jean drove her home. On the way they took a detour from the usual route because of a bridge that Jean considered too rickety. Esther pestered her all the way home with, "What's wrong with that bridge? There's nothing wrong with that bridge at all. That's really a good bridge. There's no reason you couldn't go across that bridge." For twenty years she had used monkey bridges, log bridges, and waded streams where there were no bridges. She was appalled that anyone would balk at crossing a "perfectly good bridge," thereby wasting time and gas.

She was always on the lookout for things to ship to Zorzor or take with her. This time she needed a part for a baby incubator which she hadn't been able to find in Liberia. She went down to the Hawarden chick hatchery and found just what she was looking for. Jean Carlson says, "Who in the world except Esther Bacon would have thought of going to a *hatchery?*"

She also found at a Sioux City hospital thirty jars of outdated sutures which she and Ken packed in an old wooden box he had in the barn. They took the box to the shipping station in Ken's brother-in-law's car. When they were ready to leave, the car wouldn't start, so the men lifted the hood and stood around wondering what was wrong. Esther looked over their shoulders for a moment and then said, "Could this be the trouble?" As usual, she was right.

It was on this furlough that Esther drove a car in the United States for the last time. They had been out to Elsie Leafstedt's farm for the day and on the way home Ken asked her if she'd like to drive. She said, "Oh, sure!" But she was used to driving slowly on Liberia's rough roads. On Iowa's smooth highways she didn't realize how fast she was going. Ken says: "I tried to get her to slow down as she turned to make a corner and she made a big wide sweep clear out into the ditch."

Esther spent two months in Hawarden, then went on a blitzkrieg people-visiting tour of the United States. She went to Omaha, Bennington, Chicago, New York, and then Baltimore where she spent a night with the Kellers who were home on furlough. From there she went to Silver Springs, then Washington, back to Baltimore, Philadelphia and finally to New York where she sat in on a Board meeting. In New York she roomed with Ma Jensen and then flew back to Liberia.

She was absolutely amazed when she realized that it was only a seven-hour flight from New York to Dakar. Although it was an overnight flight, she sat up most of the way and wrote letters, one of them to Nora back in Hawarden: "It is just after sunset. The moon is shining out over the darkness on the water below, but the clouds up here are silvery white, with a reflection of blue from the sky.''

(8)

Esther's two-year term from August of 1961 to June of 1963 was spent at Zorzor. She lived in the duplex up the hill from the hospital and at first had it to herself except for Alice Dietz's office. Later Margaret Leeper shared the other half. Fran Brouse was still at Curran, working in surgery, on the wards, and teaching in the School of Nursing. Electricity was on eighteen hours a day now, from six in the morning until midnight, and at night for emergency surgery or difficult OB cases.

One of her first OB cases when she returned was Dian Marquardt, wife of Rev. Bill Marquardt of Toteta. Nine months pregnant, Dian was flown to Zorzor. Dian recalls, "Up to the plane runs Esther. And she grabs me around the legs, this big pregnant woman, lifts me out of the plane — Esther was not a big woman, about my size — she's got me and walking over the airfield and I was saying, 'Esther, lemme down, Esther, lemme down. . .' ''

After the baby was delivered by Earl Reber and Esther, Dian stayed with Esther for a few days. Esther told her, "You sleep tonight and I'll get up and feed Adam." So she did. And, against Dian's protests, the next night, too. On the third night Dian insisted on getting up to feed the baby. Esther got up, too, so Dian gave her the baby. "That's what she wanted," Dian says, "so I went back to bed!"

Another case that illustrates Esther's perseverance, strength, and efficiency was witnessed by Margaret Miller a few months later. A young man was brought into the hospital claiming he had taken crocodile bile, considered by Loma people to be a prime poison. (There's actually a law that states that if one catches a crocodile, he must turn it in because of the danger that the bile might be used to poison someone.)

The young man was raving wild. Esther put him on a stretcher and in her business-like manner began to push down a stomach tube. He thrashed around, crying out, "No, Bayka, no!" Her assistants couldn't control the wild movements of his arms and legs and she couldn't take the time to show them how. By herself she subdued the man and got the tube down.

Margaret was greatly impressed with Esther's performance. She says, "Now that's hero qualities to snap into action like that, using the strength in your body with utter efficiency."

The irony in this case turned out to be that the young man had concocted the crocodile-bile story. He was due to be arriagned that day at the magistrate's office on a charge of embezzling $2,000 from his employer.

(9)

Plans for the new Phebe occupied much of the doctors' spare time, especially on the weekends. For Reber, it was getting out of hand. He had
been impressed with a new "Africa-type" hospital just built at Firestone
which incorporated many of the ideas he wanted to see used in the new
Phebe: simply but strongly constructed buildings as maintenance-free as
possible, large outpatient facilities, inpatient meals provided by relatives,
electricity only on an as-needed basis, and many other things.

But the plans now nearing the irrevocable stage, championed by Jim
Stull, Franklin Keller, Alice Dietz, and the Board back in New York, included 100 beds (considered minimal for a nurses' training school), air
conditioning, no windows in the operating room or labor-delivery rooms,
patients' meals catered by an in-hospital kitchen, electricity 24 hours a
day, huge laundry facilities, hot and cold running water, and a sophisticated sewage disposal system. The forecast for staff included 15-20
doctors and dozens of nurses. Jim Stull and almost everyone else felt that
the old "missionary mentality" was wrong and that everything should
be the very best.

In almost every instance when a decision had to be made, the vote was
3 to 1. Jim Stull says, "In meeting after meeting after meeting we just
voted Earl down on practically everything."

As Esther listened to the discussions following these meetings (to which
she was not invited), she felt that many things being planned on the pediatrics ward would have to be modified later, a gross waste of time and
money. She wrote to the Board and described what else she thought
would be needed: "Running water and electric lights. An adequate supply
of bottles, nipples and covers. An adjacent diet kitchen with refrigeration.
The ward should be well screened against flies and mosquitoes; beds with
sides for young children; wheel chairs for crippled children; toys, pictures,
books and handicraft materials to keep the children occupied and happy.

"I would like to see an adequate number of nurses trained to meet the
needs of sick children, including spiritual care, and how to help in the adjustment of family problems. I would like to see provisions for isolation
in cases where this is needed. A demonstration room should be provided
for the teaching of parents regarding diet and better methods of child care."

She was well aware that it was far easier to build things properly than
it was to modify them later. The planning committee knew this, too, and
were conscientiously trying to do things right. For $20,000 they had hired
a Swiss commercial builder from Monrovia, Pierre Antille, to draw up plans
for the hospital. He was the only one they could find who had the trucks
and the courage to go upcountry and build. He worked hard and honestly,

and met with the committee faithfully. Unfortunately the committee realized too late that he was not a hospital architect. Equally unfortunately, the Phebe committee members were not really hospital planners.

Finally, in mid-1963, after three years of meetings, the man who had been sent out to build Phebe Hospital, Jim Stull, suggested that the smartest thing to do would be to abandon the plans for the new Phebe Hospital and enlarge Curran Hospital in Zorzor. To their credit, the committee unanimously agreed with Jim Stull.

The committee sent their decision to the newly-elected President of the Liberian Lutheran Church, Roland Payne, who had just returned from seminary in Canada. Reluctantly, for he agreed with the committee, he said, "Well, it does make sense, but we can't do it. We've promised President Tubman a hospital. He's given us the land. We've built missionary houses and a youth hostel on the land. We *cannot* renege."

So Jim Stull went back to work. With the help of an American Hospital Association booklet entitled, "How to Plan and Build a Hospital," he wrote out a functional program of what kinds of health problems would be handled and how they would be addressed. He hired a hospital architect, Dane Morgan from the United States, for $34,000. He drew up a set of preliminary plans and specifications.

And Phebe Hospital was under way. Again.

It was a difficult time at Curran Memorial. There was more or less constant friction between Reber and Stull. In addition to their clashes in Phebe Hospital planning meetings, Stull felt that Reber in his capacity as senior medical officer at Curran was too arbitrary in his delegation of day-to-day duties, and in his capacity as Medical Director of the Lutheran work in Liberia too autocratic.

In looking back now Stull realizes that both Earl Reber's and Esther Bacon's philosophy of medical mission work had developed at a time "when they *were* the medical work, and there was so little else — there was *nothing* else — available."

Esther had adjusted by filling in whatever slot was assigned her and then doing whatever else she thought needed doing, "overflowing," Jim Stull says with a laugh, "into everybody else's time and space as well."

Earl Reber had not adjusted.

The tension built and came to a head in 1963. The Medical Committee of the Missionary Council voted to replace Earl Reber with Jim Stull as Director of Lutheran Medical work in Liberia. This left Reber with only the chairmanship of the Medical Committee which had voted him out of the more important position.

Reber's disappointment was so great that he resigned from the mission.

He and Anna Mae left almost immediately and Esther went to Monrovia with them to see them off for the States.

(When Reber returned to Liberia a year later he took a research position with the Liberian Institute for Tropical Medicine. He would remain in Liberia up to the time of this writing, working as a doctor for secular companies, including Firestone at Harbel, but always remembering with great nostalgia and love his seventeen years at the Zorzor Lutheran hospital.)

(10)

Understandably, Esther was reluctant to leave Zorzor for furlough at such a critical time. She wrote Nora, "Actually, I hate to think of leaving here a whole year. There is much to do." But she did, at the end of her 8th term on 6/28/63, and traveled home via Spain where she attended a midwifery congress for a week. After attending another meeting in Kenosha, Wisconsin, she went to Hawarden to be with her Aunt Nora and the Carlsons for two months.

She had enrolled in a master's degree program in Baltimore at Johns Hopkins Hospital. Aunt Nora, now 76, accompanied her out there. The plan was for Nora to do all the cooking and the housekeeping in their little apartment while Esther went to school full time.

When Esther arrived in Baltimore, she knew that the course normally took two years. She planned to do it in one. The professors, of course, got together and soon realized that this 47-year-old missionary nurse from Liberia had signed up for every course offered. They called her in.

"This is impossible," they said, fully expecting her to agree.

What she said was, "Let me try."

And so she did it. She did it by almost never going to bed for a year. Later, Nora told Jean Carlson about that year. Jean says with an understanding laugh, "Esther just about drove her batty by not getting as much sleep as Nora thought she should." At night when Esther got home from classes, she took a blanket and a pillow and lay down by the radiator and studied, then dozed, then studied some more, and then dozed off again.

She not only got her master's degree in one school year, but graduated with honors. She now had four degrees of higher learning: Registered Nurse from the Lutheran Hospital in Sioux City, Iowa; Bachelor of Science from Morningside College in Sioux City; Midwifery Certificate from the Frontier Nursing Service in Kentucky; and now a Master's Degree from the prestigious Johns Hopkins Hospital in Baltimore.

When she returned to Liberia in July of 1964 to begin her 9th term, Esther felt she was ready for any assignment, whether it be back in Zorzor, down in Sanoyea, or perhaps even a transfer to the new Phebe Hospital at Suakoko.

(11)

The first thing Esther did when she returned to Africa was to look up Earl and Anna Mae Reber in Harbel and spend the day with them. For seventeen years she had worked with him in Zorzor and had learned to love and trust him. She had spent many days with Anna Mae, working on projects for the hospital or walking in the forest. She may not have agreed with Earl's decision to leave the mission, nor with his reason for doing so, but the bonds which had formed between her and the Rebers could not be broken so easily.

During the two weeks she stayed down in Monrovia, she found that there was still a great deal of uneasiness about the new Phebe. Cost over-runs were horrendous. The $60,000 Phebe Hospital had grown first to a million dollars and was now projected at three million. Construction was far behind schedule. The projected opening, delayed time and again, was now pushed up into May of 1965.

The Episcopalians, who had been trying to back out of medical work in Liberia and had already closed their maternity hospital in Monrovia, promised to second Canadian surgeon Dr. John Stuart to Phebe. The Methodists promised a doctor but since Dr. George Harley had left Ganta after 35 years they had enough trouble keeping that hospital staffed and never would furnish more than a doctor's salary.

Esther was dismayed to learn that the mission planned to close down Curran Hospital completely, or at best convert it into a dispensary-like operation. Even with the Methodists and Episcopalians assisting with Phebe, there was neither money nor personnel to keep Curran going once Phebe opened. Esther listened, asked questions, listened some more, considered, thought and prayed for guidance.

To compound the medical problems, Jim Stull had developed hepatitis and was being treated at the Sudan Interior Mission Hospital in Monrovia. Franklin Keller was in a surgical residency in the States. This left the new doctor at Zorzor, Dr. Paul Mertens, alone in a hospital grown used to two or three physicians. But the Board in New York acted swiftly and found a short-term doctor to help out; Dr. Robert Bain, recruited by the Episcopal Church, arrived in mid-July with his family and settled right in. Like so many other recent arrivals, they quickly acquired a houseful of animals: a chimpanzee and the Stulls' dog and cat.

(12)

Paul Mertens, like most missionaries, grew up knowing that he was going into missions, preferably as a doctor. He was raised in a deeply religious family. His father even organized a Sunday School in his Robbinsdale, Minnesota, home to reach unchurched children.

After high school, Paul went first to the St. Paul Bible school from which he graduated in three years. Then he took his undergraduate work and medical school at the University of Minnesota. He demonstrated his motivation and his intelligence by getting a Phi Beta Kappa key with his Bachelor of Arts degree in 1959 and an Alpha Omega Alpha key with his Doctor of Medicine degree in 1962. He was very active in Christian organizations on campus. An avid camper, hiker, badminton and touch football player, he never let a hip stiffened by a childhood infection interfere with his athletics.

Donna, whom he married just after graduation from medical school, had taken her Bachelor of Science degree in Home Economics in 1960. On July 10, 1963, ten days after Paul finished his internship at Bethesda Lutheran Hospital in St. Paul, the Mertenses were commissioned missionaries. Three weeks later they bundled up three-month old Mark and carried him to Zorzor. Committed for a two-year term, they were told by the Board that they would work at Zorzor for a year and then go to Phebe for a year. But with Phebe so far behind schedule, it was clear from the start that they would remain in Zorzor for the entire two years.

They missed meeting Esther because she had left on furlough just a few weeks prior to their arrival. They worked in Zorzor for a year before Esther came back.

(13)

While Esther was in Monrovia renewing her nursing and midwifery licenses (a full days' work), buying supplies (another full day), and taking care of other details, Paul Mertens up in Zorzor awaited her arrival with some anxiety. Concerning that time he says, ''I had heard many stories about this Esther Bacon from our other American nurses, most of them emphasizing her lack of organization, her disregard in keeping records, and the way in which she could walk into a room, say a laboratory in which things were in order on the shelves, and in a matter of a half hour or so, completely disarrange the place in doing her own laboratory tests and then leave without putting them back in order again. So mentally I was prepared to defend myself and the hospital against this disorganized nurse with the cantankerous streak who paid no concern to order.''

She arrived in Zorzor on July 18th, by taxi. She disliked waiting for transportation to be arranged for her by the church and frequently hitched a ride on a truck, took the money-bus, or spent $5 on a taxi. Jeanette Isaacson Kpissay, a nurse-midwife who would come to Zorzor in 1966, says,

"Esther could never understand how people could stay in town for hours and never find a car. *She* never had any such trouble. And you'd lose your luggage (on an air flight). *She* never lost *hers.*" Shirley Schneider, a missionary nurse who idolized Esther and whose two children were both delivered by Esther in Zorzor, once said, "I think God has assigned two angels to Esther simply to arrange her transportation!"

Within 24 hours Esther was settled and back to full-time work in the hospital. Aware of her reputation, she decided to impress Paul Mertens with her ability to be organized if she wanted to be. Before she called Mertens to see a patient, she thoroughly reviewed the case history, wrote out a summary of the illness, and made a note of her own impression of the case.

About those notes, Mertens says, "The notes could not have been more concisely and clearly written by any physician referring a patient to another doctor. I knew immediately that I had found a nurse who had an understanding of illness and treatment equivalent to that of any well-trained physician."

In the press of the rapidly growing obstetrical service, this new Esther didn't last long, but by then Paul was so impressed with her skills that it no longer mattered.

Esther's obstetrical knowledge and skills impressed everyone, of course. But her capabilities were not limited to the OB ward. She was supremely competent handling desperately ill non-obstetrical patients. Shortly after her return, a patient came in dehydrated from a bacillary dysentery, perhaps cholera. Dr. Bain stood there amazed as Esther went right to work and within 24 hours had run in eight liters of fluids, more than two gallons. She had learned from her books and from her twenty years in Africa that you don't stop pouring in fluids until the patient's kidneys begin to work. Dr. Bain later said to Paul Mertens, "I think the man's kidneys just finally said, 'Esther, we give up, we'll start to work, don't push fluids at us anymore!' "

The School of Nursing had outstripped even Esther Bacon's fondest dreams. When the old Phebe Hospital at Muhlenburg was closed and the School of Nursing transferred to Zorzor in 1946, Esther Bacon and Earl Reber *were* the staff. What the students learned, they learned from Bacon and Reber.

Now, in 1964, there was a real faculty. The Director of the School was Alice Deitz, just back from furlough (and disappointed that Phebe wasn't ready for her). Margaret Legenhausen, Director of Nurses in the hospital, taught Fundamentals of Nursing, the backbone of the program. Sister Lina Jurgens taught Obstetrics. The physician instructor was Dr. Paul Mertens. Religion was taught by Rev. Clifford (Cliffy) Grosenbacher, pastor of the St. John's Lutheran Church in Zorzor, and Rev. Joseph Wold, pastor at Fisebu, who was already working on his book, *God's Impatience in Liberia*. Wold's wife, Arlene, taught History of Nursing.

In addition, in the hospital, Frances Brouse was Night Supervisor, Esther Bacon OB Supervisor. Both taught the students as they came through the program on the wards. James Stull, now fully recovered from his hepatitis, had returned as Medical Director. Then, when Franklin Keller returned from his surgical residency, there were again three long-term doctors at Curran.

The appearance of a healthy, functioning, Curran Memorial Hospital at Zorzor was, of course, false. It was anticipated by the Phebe Hospital committee that *everyone* would relocate at the new Phebe in Suakoko when it opened in May of 1965.

Alice Dietz was sure of one thing: she did not want Esther to make the move to Phebe with the rest of the medical staff. She was afraid that Esther would be, as Paul Mertens puts it, "more of a disruptive force than a complement to their organized schedules, with their hospital set up closely on the American pattern in which nurses were nurses and would not do the work of a physician."

Nor did Esther want to go to Phebe. She knew she would not fit in there. The nurses at Phebe would not be allowed the freedom to work as Esther had worked for over twenty years. So she came up with a plan that solved both the problem of what to do with Esther Bacon and what to do with the Curran Memorial Hospital. She suggested that Curran continue to function as a maternal and child health center with Esther Bacon remaining there to run it.

Shock waves of relief rippled out through the medical community, especially the Phebe planning committee. It was the perfect solution. No one was eager to challenge Esther Bacon. And furthermore, no one wanted to hurt her feelings by even suggesting that she wasn't "fit" for a place like Phebe. On January 13th, 1965, she was officially notified that she would be staying at the Curran Maternal and Child Health Care Center in Zorzor.

There are strong suspicions that Esther never expected that Curran Hospital would really be restricted to maternal and child health work. Paul Mertens says flatly, "Any of those who thought differently were grossly miscalculating."

There are many indications that he was right. In later years it was widely believed and frankly stated that Esther Bacon had saved Curran Hospital. Bill and Dian Marquardt, then in Toteta, are adamant about it. Bill was impressed with the way she functioned at Curran after she was abandoned by everyone else. He says, "What she did, she just became a doctor, too. When there was no doctor there, she just took over and kept it going."

Margaret Miller, who watched this whole thing from a ringside seat in Wozi, says, "They just wanted to close up everything in Zorzor except for this minor maternity clinic. She just fought for Curran in the teeth of all resistance." Then Margaret laughed as she added, "Well, she *could* be a nagger. She would run after you. You'd say, 'It's finished, Esther.' And she would just run after you and keep talking. And that's what she did with Curran."

One of the people she "ran after" was Bishop Roland Payne, who in 1965 had been back in Liberia for two years as head of the Church. He really didn't need any nagging. He was greatly disturbed by the thought of Curran's closing or even continuing operations in a limited capacity. After all, the hospital had been functioning in Zorzor for 39 years. The people of the entire area had become dependent on it for medical care.

He says now, with a great laugh, "Moving to Phebe was going to answer *all* our health problems. The people (Stull, Keller, Alice Dietz, and the Board in New York) had a utopian attitude about Phebe. And Curran was going to function as a public health center and for midwifery. But Esther Bacon and Dr. Mertens didn't want to go to this modern American hospital being planted in the jungle."

So he and Pewu (Howard) Moleyeaze got in touch with two important Liberian men in the district, Mr. B. K. Morris, later to be a representative in the State House, and Mr. Liberty, then District Commissioner and later to be Lofa County's first senator. These men approached President Tubman and told him of the problem. Tubman reacted in his typical fashion. He guaranteed Curran $15,000 a year from the government if the Lutheran Mission Board would supply a doctor and nurses. The church agreed. In addition, the six clans in Zorzor District canvassed the Loma community and collected a considerable sum. Then they hauled rocks and sand for new construction.

Another source Esther cultivated was Bong Mine. A German pastor by the name of Shultz had come to Curran looking for a place to subsidize. Impressed by Esther Bacon, he looked no further and began sending Deutsch Marks 10,000 a year, at that time approximately $5,000. (Since then the yearly contribution has doubled.)

Six Liberian nurses would stay at Curran to help Esther. A few of them were not wanted at Phebe. The rest simply refused to move in spite of considerable pressure to do so, among them Edith Curran, Irene Morris, and Grace (Howard) Moleyeaze.

But the problem was to find a physician for Curran.

(14)

The dedication of Phebe Hospital was scheduled for May 16th, 1965. Jim Stull, Franklin Keller, Alice Dietz, Margaret Legenhausen, Fran Brouse, and Lina Jurgens moved down to Suakoko in April.

Although it had been the Board's decision to transfer the Curran medical staff to Phebe, Jim Stull felt a definite sense of guilt "for having robbed the Curran situation of all of its people." He also sensed that many of the Loma people held him responsible even though it had *not* been his decision alone.

The dedication of Phebe Hospital was one of the truly big events on the international mission scene. Everyone who could get away from his own work was there. President Tubman was Speaker of the Day. From the States came Bishop Dillard Brown to represent the Episcopalians,

The New Phebe Hospital at Suakoko

Dr. William Brown the Methodists, and Dr. Rudolph Burke the Lutherans.

Phebe was designated a 60-bed, general, acute hospital with a daily out-patient capacity of 500. The School of Nursing opened with eleven students but had a capacity for 48 which Miss Dietz expected to fill in two to three years. The yearly operating budget was estimated at $150,000, of which the churches pledged $70,000. Fifty thousand was to come from patient fees and the remaining $30,000 from business firms. It was an overly optimistic financial projection, and by November of the first year the hospital was already in deep trouble.

Paul Mertens had assumed right along that Curran would be closed. Since his two-year term would be up by the time of the move to Phebe, he had sought and found a pediatric residency back in the States. Now he had a problem. Curran would *not* be closed down entirely, would still be functioning, though on a limited basis. However, he felt he had made a commitment to the pediatrics department at the University of Missouri which he could not abrogate. So he, too, left Zorzor about six weeks after the other doctors moved, feeling that a physician would soon be found to come to Curran.

No one was found.

(15)

Esther worked without a doctor from May of 1965 to August of 1966. She was the only missionary nurse until April of 1966, almost a year. It was, as Yankee catcher Yogi Berra said, *deja vu* all over again. 1942 revisited.
Except for one very important difference.
In 1942 she had struggled to get women to come to the hospital to deliver their babies. She had pleaded with the zoes to let sick people come. Her in-patient census had ranged from ten to twenty and she did no deliveries.
In contrast, during those fifteen months in 1965 and 1966, the hospital in-patient census ranged from 80 to as high as 170, and over 800 women delivered in the hospital.
Esther did what she could to keep everything under control. She was doing what she wanted to do. She had been given the task of running a maternal and child health care center. With a clear conscience she could have turned away everyone except pregnant women and children. She could not. She did not.
Instead, for fifteen months she never had an hour to herself, much less a day or a week. As usual, she followed no schedule. She was at the hospital when she was needed, which was most of the time. She lived in a chronic state of fatigue. Eyes red from rubbing, ringed with sooty smudges, dark bags forming underneath. Skin sallow and unhealthy looking. Hair stringy. Shoulders slightly slumped, hands in pockets.
She worked until she couldn't stay awake, then went up to her house "to rest small." Sometimes this would be for an hour or two, sometimes for as long as five or six hours. Then she returned to the hospital to make rounds, deliver babies, sew up lacerations, set fractures, drain abscesses, and do all the other hundreds of things that a nurse-midwife-doctor does. As if that weren't enough, she had clinics to supervise, outpatients to treat, and all sorts of administrative duties as head of the hospital.
Bill Marquardt didn't know just how right he was when he said she acted as a physician.
And, despite the fact that she was always tired, she impressed others with her seemingly boundless energy. When Roland Payne was asked what he remembered about Esther, one of the first things he said was, "She was moving all the time — fast!"
In August of 1966, before Paul Mertens came back, Louise Faust, on a writing assignment from her own mission in Tanzania, spent several days trying to keep up with Esther. Louise, herself a whirlwind of activity, a buzz-saw of efficiency, tells of those days:
"On rounds in the morning on the adult ward, where there were ninety patients, Esther went from bed to bed, knowing everyone's name, illness,

treatment schedule, family problems, and home village. She checked on the progress of each patient, wrote orders in the chart, changed dressings, and did all the many things necessary for the continuing well-being of each patient.

"In the pediatric ward there were eighty children ranging from tiny infants lying on towels in enameled basins, up to ten- and twelve-year-olds. And, of course, eighty mothers plus grandmothers and sisters. She knew them all. She had a tape recorder playing music on the pediatric ward, which she said was very calming to both babies and mothers, especially in the evenings.

"Wherever she went, whatever she was doing, she was interrupted by staff and patients' relatives with problems. She never brushed off anyone. She listened intently, hands in pockets, head tipped to one side, straight hair tucked behind her ears. She adjusted a salary for an unhappy worker. She listened to the nurses as they described a patient's problem, sometimes offering a word of advice, often taking off for the ward or OPD to see for herself. She made a suggestion to a workman doing some plumbing in the stock room. There was rarely any dissension or even discussion. She was more likely to be right than anyone there.

"She carried medicines such as headache pills in her pockets and doled these out as necessary (to staff, sometimes, too!)

"A little boy scampered up to her and whispered something in her ear. She gave him a quarter. I asked what that was for.

" 'He wants to buy a turtle,' Esther said with her eyes sparkling and her grin wide.

" 'What will he do with that?'

" 'Oh, he'll play with it for a while and then it'll end up in somebody's soup.' "

She made rounds every evening, mostly just to satisfy herself that everyone was all right. She carried her lantern, as she still always did wherever she went, probably more from habit now than from necessity. She walked slowly through the adult ward, saying a soothing or encouraging word to everyone who was still awake.

Soft voices called out to her in four languages, Loma, Kpelle, Mandingo, and Liberian English, "Bayka, Bayka . . ." She heeded them all, taking a hand here, readjusting a dressing there, offering advice or caution or hope, promising something for the morrow, slipping a coin or two into a pocket. (Irene Morris recalls that "when Esther got her stipend, she would change it into small coins, put them in her pocket, and go all around the hospital.")

On the pediatric ward there were women everywhere, sleeping on the beds with their children, under the beds on thin mats, propped up against the wall talking to each other. The lights were out but a kerosene lantern sat on the nurses' desk and another hung from a rafter near the back door. Esther's swinging lantern threw dancing shadows on the walls as she moved slowly through the ward. Hands on thin arms reached up to take hers or just to signal their awareness of her presence.

They could sleep now. Bayka was here.

(16)

She did, of course, have help with this tremendous load. Six Liberian nurses had stayed, four registered and two practical. As usual, any credit given her she displaced onto her Liberian nurses, saying that without them she couldn't do anything.

One thing she didn't have to do now was surgery. Nor did she have to supervise any major illnesses that could stand transfer. With road, mail, and radio communications so much better than in 1942, she could send the patients seventy miles to Phebe or get advice from a doctor there. The doctors at Phebe set up a rotation schedule so that one of them flew up to Zorzor at least once a week. Usually it was Jim Stull, Franklin Keller, or John Stuart, the Canadian Episcopalian. Dr. Stuart enjoyed very much going up to the famous "Esther Bacon jungle hospital" at Zorzor.

Esther also drove the station's Volkswagen bus down to Phebe with patients, often women needing Caesarian section. She had already done her last driving in the United States when she drove Ken Carlson's new car into the ditch. Now she had another accident which ended her driving in Liberia.

She had several people in the bus, including a woman going to Phebe for C-section. She came to the Gbarnga junction and started to make the sharp right turn to Suakoko. Her brakes failed. She was afraid that continuing the turn would flip the bus. So she kept going straight — directly into the Gbarnga police station. She broke her arm and the pregnant woman broke a leg.

The police quickly took the patient to Phebe where she had her leg set and her baby delivered. Later, Esther was brought into court by the patient's husband. The judge looked up as Esther came in, recognized her immediately, knocked his gavel on his desk, and said, "Oh, oh, this is our good lady, Bayka," and dismissed the case. In one of only two letters to Nora in that 15-month period, Esther wrote, no doubt with tongue in cheek, "The traffic officers and the judge were very considerate and the case is finished."

From that time on, the mission assigned a driver to take her where she needed to go. Because she was so consistently tired, some people thought she had fallen asleep at the wheel, but the evidence is clear that in this case at least there really was a mechanical failure. No doubt it was still a good idea to keep Esther from the wheel during that time.

In March of 1966 Esther had her 50th birthday. It was just another birthday for her, but her co-workers gave her a surprise party. Margaret Miller came down from Wozi with the idea of having everyone come as pregnant women with pillows under their dresses so Esther would feel at home. But the others vetoed the idea. Margaret says, "Wouldn't Esther have been delighted with me, a single woman, who'd turn up pregnant? She'd've been so delighted she'd've gone around and patted everyone's stomach."

Still it was a successful party. Someone baked a cake with the inscription: "Delivered 50 years ago — delivering ever since!" They had taken up a collection and gave her a very good set of dishes because she so liked to entertain and had given away most of her New York Macy dishes in the past twenty-five years. Margaret recalls, "It was something everybody joined in very happily and we don't do that for everybody."

(17)

Help arrived in April of 1966 when nurse-midwives Jeanette and Deanna Isaacson came out from the States to Zorzor. With them was Carolyn Miller, another young nurse-midwife, who joined the staff at Phebe. The Isaacsons were unrelated to each other, Deanna coming from Iowa and Jeanette from Kansas. They were classmates while getting their bachelor's degrees in nursing in Kansas City. They then went with Carolyn Miller for a year of midwifery school in Edinburgh, Scotland. Together the three young women went straight out to Liberia.

The Isaacsons stayed with Esther in the big house on the hill for a few days. Jeanette remembers that when they moved in they found it freshly painted and spotless. She says now with a laugh, "I never again saw Bacon's house spotless." Later they moved into a smaller house between Esther's house and the hospital.

That very first night Esther got them out of bed to go with her to the hospital for a difficult delivery. Deanna remembers that "it was more eye-opening to participate in the delivery and see the way it differed from what we were used to than to just walk through the hospital and see its structure."

Jeanette also remembers that first night in Zorzor when she and Deanna were at the hospital till 3 A.M. She says, "Esther didn't sleep very much and she couldn't understand why other people needed to sleep so much! Later on we finally had to decide to let her know when we wanted to come and when we didn't want to come. She began to accept the fact that we just couldn't be there all the time!"

Deanna was more interested in child care than midwifery, so she spent most of her time in the pediatrics ward with Edith Curran. Edith could help her quite a bit, but often she felt she had to get Esther to come to see the patient. This was often frustrating because, as Deanna says, "There'd be a hundred other things before she'd get to *us*. It meant you went back to her three or four times, and then she'd come and would be so surprised that I didn't know how to do something. She had this assumption that I knew more than I did! Then she'd take it and do it. She was not able to stand by and watch me do it. Or talk me through it. You learned by watching her do it, and you learned many things."

Jeanette echoes Deanna's thoughts, "I had learned midwifery theory in Scotland, but she really taught me. I would be doing a vacuum extraction and she would say, 'What position is it in?' I'd say, 'LOA.' And she'd say, 'You're sure?' 'Yes, Bacon.' Then she'd say, 'Is the occiput well down? You sure it's not deflexed? Are you sure you're getting it in the right place? Which way is the suture running now?' And she'd go on and on and on in that way, just drive you crazy. Finally on two occasions I can remember saying, 'Bacon, I know how to do this! I know what I'm doing! If you want to do it, come and do it!' And then she'd say, 'No, no, no, no, you can do it, you can do it, you can *do* it!' and rush out!"

Deanna remembers that "everybody went to her, *every*body in the hospital went to her, so it was always a battle for her time and you were tugging, pulling her, this way and that."

Deanna and Jeanette began to alternate night call in obstetrics. Irene Morris lived in town then and did not participate in the call system. And of course, Esther never fit into any call system because she just came and left any time she wanted to. But if she happened to be home, she readily came back when called.

Deanna's major frustration was that she herself liked order, liked to schedule things and follow the schedule, liked to organize the OR shelves so that when an emergency arose things were where you could find them. She says with a rueful smile, "The worst violator of any system I tried to create was Bacon!" Then she added quickly, "She's one of the dearest people to me, I love her dearly, and when we would clash it was never hurtful, it wasn't anything to hold in your heart and she didn't hold it either."

(18)

Early in those first weeks Jeanette was on call one night when a lady came in delivering twins, both breech. She had never delivered a breech. She called Esther. And "she didn't come and she didn't come and I delivered the first one. I said, 'Go back and tell Bacon that the second one is breech, too, and she should please *come!*' She still didn't come. The next morning when she came, I said, 'Bacon, how could you do that to me? You didn't come. What happened?' She said, 'I knew you could do it.' She knew I could do it!''

Jeanette also remembers that she felt some resentment in those early months. She says, ''We went through a lot of struggle.'' And most of the struggle was with the lack of organization. She couldn't get used to Esther's policy of just taking care of things as they arose, intervening when there was a crisis, making out the nurses' schedule for the week on Monday morning, and things like that.

Jeanette sums up the feeling of all of the missionaries who knew Esther: ''We all knew we couldn't be Bacon, we couldn't be like her. It's a struggle to see somebody who's so completely selfless, so giving, and acknowledging yourself that you're not like that. To keep comparing yourself and know that you can't *be* like that. To know that you really don't *want* to sacrifice what she has sacrificed to be like that.''

(19)

Paul Mertens kept in touch with what was happening at Zorzor and Phebe. He became increasingly disturbed as the months went by and no doctor was found for Curran, either from the States or from Phebe. So when the Board asked him to return to Curran he accepted immediately. He resigned from his residency, effective June 30, 1966.

In recalling that difficult time, Dr. Mertens says, ''It became a special challenge to me since it had been predicted that one physician at Zorzor would literally lose his mind from exhaustion and overwork.'' He knew that some people thought Esther Bacon would add to this problem ''with her idiosyncrasies and way of occasionally irritating physicians. However, Esther did not irritate me. I fully enjoyed her and her peculiarities.''

So on August 6, 1966, Paul and Donna Mertens arrived back at the Zorzor hospital, euphemistically called the Curran Maternal and Child Health Care Center.

The people of Zorzor greeted the Mertenses with great joy. They remembered Paul's compassionate care in the hospital. They remembered Donna's vibrant personality in the church and the school and the town. They would have welcomed any doctor after being without one for over a year, but Mertens was special.

(20)

Esther, of course, needed a rest. She was physically and mentally exhausted. Though she had never been overly concerned about her personal appearance, this past year had wreaked more havoc. Fran Brouse says that she really did care about her appearance but was just too busy and too tired to worry about it. And, Fran emphasizes, she never ignored her personal cleanliness and hygiene. Her straight hair, chopped off at collar-length, was always clean and swept back behind her ears, or caught back with a ribbon. She always came to the hospital in a clean uniform, though by late afternoon it invariably became spotted with blood or vomit or something indescribable. Of course, if she really got doused, she went home and changed immediately.

There are indications that she did take some pride in how she looked. Jeanette Isaacson tells of one day when President Tubman was expected. "Everyone was cleaning the hospital and people were whitewashing — we used to laugh and say if you stand still for as long as five minutes they'd whitewash you to your knees! But, anyway, Bacon went and put on stockings. She put on her cap. She put on lipstick. We said, 'What!!??' Tubman was three or four hours late as usual and the students kept saying, 'The O'pa better come pretty soon or the O'ma will soon run her stockings!' "

But it had been noted by almost everyone that gradually over the years she took less and less trouble about her personal appearance. She never actually looked slovenly, Margaret Miller recalls, "but the impression you got was of a person to whom it was not important if her slip was showing. And maybe she'd have something on inside-out, but we can *all* do that!"

Her appearance when she went home embarrassed the other missionaries, precisely because they loved and respected her so much. Dian Marquardt says with a gentle laugh, "When Esther went home, we tried to intercept her to look her over! On more than one occasion we caught her going home with her shoes untied and without socks — she never wore socks up at Zorzor — and we'd force her to do down and buy a decent pair of shoes and a pair of stockings just before she got on the airplane."

Sometimes friends bought yard-goods and had a dress made for her. They knew money given her for a dress would disappear into some needy patient's pocket for food or medicines. Fran Brouse recalls, "Trying to get Esther on her way on furlough was interesting. I recall her making herself a suit to travel in on the night before she left! Meanwhile several of us were helping her pack."

After Paul Mertens had been back for about a month Esther took a three-month vacation and went to Hawarden. She did get her rest there, but for the first time the Carlsons noted that Esther was looking old. She was now fifty, but she looked older. When Jean commented on how tired she looked, Esther said with the old twinkle in her eye, "Yes, you know, I just can't spend two nights any more with my patients, up all day and all night for two nights. I can only do it for one night any more.''

The congregation at Trinity in Sioux City apparently had awakened at last to the fact that they had in their midst a woman of unusual accomplishments. Writings by her and about her appeared frequently in many magazines. She treasured to the end of her life a watch given her by the Trinity congregation at a special service held in her honor. On the back was inscribed simply, ''Esther Bacon, 11-6-66.'' It was, in fact, the only object of any value that she owned when she died.

(21)

She returned to Liberia just before Christmas and marveled once more about the seven-hour flight from New York to Dakar. She remembered all too well the slow passage from New York to Belem and across to Lagos or Freetown, the journey often taking four, five, even six weeks.

This time, as she returned for her 10th term at the end of 1966, she apparently had taken to heart much of the overt and covert criticism of her personal appearance. She had bought an attractive pair of glasses with fancy scroll-work on the horn half-rims. She had gotten a permanent wave. She had gained weight, and complained about it, but it filled in some of the wrinkle lines which had made her look older.

As usual, she had filled her luggage with things for the hospital: a box of bandage scissors, a small case of typing serum (for cross-matching blood for transfusion), a case of plasma, and a batch of the still-new measles vaccine. As ever, she was right on top of what was happening in the medical world outside Africa. She never wanted it to be said that Curran Hospital was behind the times.

Esther, already recognized in Liberia as a foremost expert in obstetrics, now had the freedom to become more involved with country-wide nursing and midwifery. Paul Mertens had taken over the doctor-type cases and the administrative work. Jeanette Isaacson had adapted quickly to bush obstetrics, learning rapidly from Esther practical techniques such as craniotomy and vacuum extraction. Deanna Isaacson, more at home on the pediatric ward and preferring to assist rather than do complicated obstetrics, nevertheless was a very competent midwife and called on Esther less and less as the months went by. Shirley Schneider had arrived to help teach in the School of Nursing. Among the Liberian nurses were such competent people as Irene Morris, Edith Curran, Sarah Jensen and Ellen Murray.

So now every two or three months Esther went down to Monrovia or some other city on official business. She was a founding member of the Liberian Board of Nurse Examiners. She was active in both nursing and midwifery organizations and regularly attended their conventions and working meetings. She much preferred staying right in the hospital in Zorzor but she was also interested in furthering the teaching of national nurses. If speaking in meetings and participating in organizational exercises would promote this, she would do it.

(22)

All of Esther's children were growing up. Ruth, the tiny dehydrated infant who had been abandoned by her mother in 1950, was now 23. She hadn't been able to handle the classes of a registered nurse but had gone through the Curran practical nurses' course and stayed on as an employee for a short time. Then she had followed her man to Firestone but came up to Zorzor in 1959 to show Esther her first baby. In 1964 she moved back to Zorzor to work at Curran, stayed for three years, and then returned to Firestone.

Big Zizzi and Little Zizzi were back with their parents in their villages. Kona had moved into Zorzor and came out to see Esther almost every day; he was making a valiant and successful attempt to learn English. These and all her other children easily integrated themselves back into their villages. Esther had not made the common mistake of dissociating them from their heritage by denigrating that heritage or over-emphasizing Western culture and mores. She had given them a Christian upbringing without destroying their natural love of Liberian ways.

Kirsten Jensen had adopted Esther as her surrogate mother and was a frequent visitor in Esther's house. The bond between them, formed when Esther was stationed at Sanoyea from 1954 to 1956, was stronger than ever. Now, in 1967, Kirsten was a sophomore at the Lutheran Training Institute in Salayea, just fifteen miles down the road. She was already planning to go into nurses' training at the new Phebe when she finished at LTI.

(23)

Curran Hospital with its one doctor, Paul Mertens, was as busy as it had ever been when three doctors were there. During 1967, 840 deliveries were done with a 3% Caesarian section rate and a 3% symphysiotomy rate. In 1968 over 1,200 deliveries were done, an average of almost four a day. The morning clinics, supervised by Paul Mertens and now operating six days a week, were seeing 50,000 patients a year, an average of almost 170 a day. Nurses and medical assistants screened all of them and referred the complicated cases and potential surgical cases to Paul, who then saw them in the afternoon when he finished surgery and ward rounds. Paul was doing an average of two operations a day, one-third of which were considered major. But many of the so-called minor cases would be considered major in a Stateside hospital.

Mertens became acutely aware of the near total lack of supervision of government clinics in the Zorzor District. No physician visited them regularly. Despite his almost impossible work-load at Curran, Paul offered his services and was gratefully accepted. Thus began the very first effort in Liberia to run correlated government-mission well-baby and prenatal clinics, and regular vaccination campaigns.

Maintenance of the facilities was becoming an increasingly complex problem. The hospital itself would have been a full-time job, but there was also the electrical generator, all the missionaries' houses, the nurses' school and dormitory, the primary school, and the vehicles.

In 1966, Dave Urfer, a U.S. Army veteran, came to Zorzor with his wife Ursula (called Margaret on the mission field), whom he had met and married in Germany. His skills in building, auto maintenance and repair, electrical wiring, small appliance repair, and many other fields, were invaluable to the burgeoning hospital. He was a ham radio operator, which was fun for him and often a valuable service to the station. As a sideline he made customized leather shoes for lepers who had lost toes or other parts of their feet. Like most mission "builders" and "maintenance men," he was a jack-of-all-trades, and master of all.

(24)

To the Stateside lay person, life in a bush hospital might seem to be one exotic experience after another. Not so. Days and weeks go by without the intrusion of extraordinary drama.

But drama (translation: Trouble with a capital T) does probably occur with more regularity than in the States.

A tragic incident compounded with humor occurred one day when Esther was watching a lady admitted with a full-term pregnancy and meningitis. Mertens administered high doses of antibiotics but still the patient deteriorated. When he had done all he could, he went home to take a much-needed bath. As he luxuriated in the concrete tub, he heard the front door open and Esther calling, "Where's Dr. Mertens?"

Donna pointed to the bathroom door.

Without stopping to think, Esther burst into the bathroom and said, "Dr. Mertens, the patient with meningitis is dying."

He knew immediately what she wanted. She wanted him to do a Caesarian section in order to at least save the baby. She dashed off and Paul set a new record for getting out of a tub, drying off, and starting off for

the hospital in his truck. He picked up Esther on the way and they took
the patient into the operating room where he quickly opened the abdomen
without anesthesia. They were too late.

"But," Mertens says, "that was rather typical of Esther. If she thought
it necessary to disturb my privacy to save a patient's life, she would do
it." Then he adds, with a chuckle, "although that's the only occasion
when she caught me in the bathtub."

(25)

Another tragic incident occurred about this same time, with no
overtones of humor.

There was a lady in Zorzor-town whose husband felt that they were
married because they already had three children. She, however, felt that
their marriage had never been finalized because the man had not yet for-
malized the marriage with the customary dowery. They began to quarrel
when she began to look around for greener fields. Late one evening he
took a shotgun and shot her.

Fortunately she had been holding the baby in her left arm and the shot
came from the right. The pellets went into her right chest and arm and
the baby was not harmed. Friends brought her to Curran where Esther
began to work on her in the operating room.

Overlooking the operating theater was a small room which had been
used during the early years for morning devotions and staff meetings.
Now it was used by nurses wanting to watch surgery, or by someone
who needed to talk to the doctor or nurse. As Esther and her assistants
were finishing up their work, the husband climbed to the room, shot the
woman again and killed her.

He ran out the back way and ran straight into Beyan Bacon, one of
Esther's children who was confined to a wheelchair but could do a lot
of chores around the hospital. Beyan tried to block the passageway, but
the man pushed him out of the way, ran into the swamp back of the
hospital, and killed himself.

This observation room was sealed off in the new construction taking
place, but it was too late for the lady and her husband.

(26)

There were many, many other times when the teamwork of Paul Mertens and Esther Bacon did save a life. One such incident involved a woman
in labor who began to bleed vigorously one Sunday morning. Esther made
the correct diagnosis immediately: *abruptio placenta*, a condition in which

the placenta suddenly separates from the uterus before the baby is born, causing massive bleeding and usually death of the baby. It was a problem similar to Roslyn Sadler's in 1947, but more catastrophic.

Esther did what she had to do. First she delivered the baby, hoping that the placenta would deliver quickly and allow the uterus to clamp down naturally to stop the bleeding. It did not. She knew that fibrinogen was desperately needed to facilitate clotting. But first she had to stop the bleeding. She rammed a gloved fist up against the cervix vaginally and with the other hand on the abdomen she clamped down firmly on the uterus, slowing if not stopping the hemorrhage.

Fortunately Paul Mertens came by the hospital on his way home from church and was quickly called into the delivery room. In a few words, Esther told him that the patient needed fibrinogen quickly. He found a unit of fibrinogen and pumped that in. Then he corralled several nursing students and without giving them time to object, typed them and drew their blood. They were able to reverse the patient's deep shock and save her life.

The salvage of this patient was a combination of several factors. Esther knew how to execute the maneuver that would temporarily stop the bleeding from the uterus. She knew from long experience and from her constant reading of medical journals that the patient was probably deficient in fibrinogen. Paul Mertens trusted both Esther's diagnosis and her suggested treatment and didn't hesitate a moment in giving both blood and fibrinogen. It was this combination of skill and trust that made the Mertens-Bacon team such a power in Loma-Kpelle-land.

(27)

Esther's effect on the doctors who worked at Zorzor was profound in many ways, not the least of which was her help in surgery and the labor room. That help was not just as a scrub nurse or circulator, though she was certainly invaluable in that capacity. She also passed on to them what she had learned in her long years in the unforgiving College of Rain-forest Medicine.

It was, of course, a two-way street. She learned from the doctors, absorbed their knowledge and techniques like a dry-season swamp soaks up water when the rains return. But that was mostly book-learning. What she taught the doctors usually could not be found in books. She had far more training and experience in obstetrics than any of the doctors coming out to Liberia. Paul Mertens frankly called her the best obstetrician in Liberia, and, he says, ''I don't mean midwife.''

If she could not pass on her mastery, at least she could pass on her methods. If not her genius for improvisation, at least her know-how. If not her adeptness, at least her techniques. If not her competence, at least her confidence.

She taught them all: Earl Reber from 1946 to 1963, Lowell Yund from 1949 to 1952, Franklin Keller from 1952 to 1965, James Stull from 1959 to 1965, Paul Mertens from 1963 to 1972, and the short-termers Bain, Baum, Wright, and the medical students, who were now coming regularly from the U.S. for two to three months of study.

One of the things she taught them was how to do a craniotomy on a dead, unborn baby, the procedure of choice when the mother comes in with the cervix fully dilated but her pelvis too small for the baby to deliver. She taught them how to do evisceration and extraction of a dead baby, a gruesome procedure used when the baby is caught cross-wise with one arm hanging out of the cervix. She taught them to do podalic versions, the turning and extraction of a live baby caught sideways in the uterus.

Mertens tells how Esther got him to do his first podalic version. A lady came in who was delivering twins, both still alive. One twin lay transversely with an arm hanging out of the cervix. Esther showed Mertens the problem and asked him what he was going to do.

He hedged. "Well, Esther, I've been trained that the way to do this is with a Caesarian section. The only other possible way would be a podalic version, but that's hazardous and would be condemned by most obstetricians in the States."

Mertens remembers that her blue eyes seemed more penetrating than usual. "Dr. Mertens, we're not *in* the States."

She gave this a moment to sink in and Paul waited for her to add, "Your training is lacking in the most appropriate techniques for a bush hospital."

Instead, she said quietly, "I really think that with some ether anesthesia to relax the uterus you'd probably do all right with a podalic version."

Before he really knew what was happening, she had cleverly talked him into trying it. She put the patient to sleep with drip ether and instructed him step by step.

"Push the baby's hand back in."

"Done."

"Reach in and grab a foot."

"Got it."

"Pull out the first twin."

He did all this and stood there with a newborn baby, normal except for the previously prolapsed arm which was enlarged with a swelling that would subside spontaneously.

He then looked up at Esther, eyes shining in triumph, ready to do whatever she told him. "Should we wait for the second one or reach in and get it?"

Her blue eyes sparkled. "Go get it!" she ordered. Today she probably would have said, "Go for it!"

He did and they got out two live twins with no damage to the uterus and no abnormal bleeding. The mother did not have a scar on the uterus from a C-section which might rupture during a subsequent labor out in the forest.

Dr. James Stull, who worked with Esther from 1959 to 1965, says, "She was a genius. When I first met her as a young and inexperienced doctor, my training and background in obstetrics were very thin. She taught me practically all the obstetrics I know."

She had the gift of being able to instruct and lead the doctors without coming on too strong — most of the time. She did exert a kind of control over them that might ultimately wear a little thin, as Earl Reber has noted. But knowing that she was usually right, they never shrugged off her suggestions. Besides they knew she was not trying to make herself look important at their expense. She was only trying to help the patient.

Paul Mertens says, "None of us physicians ever really learned to control or regulate her. Esther was mostly a law to herself."

(28)

But Mertens recognized the importance of letting her guide him. He shows how she did this with an incident that happened in 1967.

A student from the Lutheran Training Institute at Salayea came in with headache, nausea, diarrhea. She rapidly became very ill. Mertens started her on choramphenicol, the treatment for typhoid fever.

Esther was not satisfied. "Doctor," she said, "what do you think is wrong with this girl?"

"Well, Esther," Mertens said, "it *could* be typhoid."

"What else?"

"Well, any number of viruses."

"Like what?"

He started to enumerate. "Well, the group B-arboviruses..."

"What are they?"

"Dengue, yellow fever..."

"Ah-hah," she said, and opened a textbook to the chapter on yellow fever and propped it open in front of Mertens.

He had not yet seen a case of yellow fever and had the impression that the patient would be jaundiced. The textbook informed him that this was not always true. It was all there: on the pages Esther showed him was the diagnosis of the girl down at the hospital.

Esther had known all along. She did not say, "Doctor, you're wrong, this girl has yellow fever," which would raise the hairs on the back of any doctor's neck. Rather, she let the doctor make his own diagnosis — with a little help.

Unfortunately there was little to be done for the girl and she died. Mertens learned from Jeanette Isaacson that the girl's roommate at Salayea had also died and had been taken to the morgue at Phebe. Mertens jumped in the car and drove straight to Phebe and knocked on Dr. Franklin Keller's door.

"Franklin," he said, "I've got a girl in the bus dead from yellow fever and you've got another one in your morgue dead from the same cause."

Keller looked at him unbelievingly. "How do you know?"

"Esther Bacon figured it out."

The unbelieving look disappeared from Keller's eyes.

Her control over the doctors was noted by non-physicians. Bishop Payne comments, "She made the doctors work but they didn't think that she was bossing them, that she was showing too much knowledge. She wasn't like that. But she got to the point where they all respected her. When she examined a woman and said, 'Caesarian section,' why, they trusted her judgment."

Irene Morris says, "She knew almost everything about all the diseases and she read so many books. She taught the doctors. She would stand by the doctor and tell the doctor do this, and this is this. She would show the parts of the body to the doctor. She would say to the doctor, 'Don't do that, don't cut here. This will happen if you do that.' "

Carolyn Miller says, "Esther could convince the doctors to try anything. Often she pushed them to go beyond what they thought they could do."

(29)

But never let it be forgotten that Esther Bacon knew she was a nurse, not a doctor. She knew what her role was: when a doctor was available, he was to be called and she never hesitated to do so. Often she had to exceed the nurse role, especially in the early years, but only with good reason. In later years she disliked talking about it, but on at least one occasion she amputated a gangrenous leg. No one knows how many times she incised a tight ring on an incarcerated hernia. And Jim Stull is quite sure that occasionally she did a Caesarian section on women she knew would never make it down the road.

But in all those cases she knew that if she didn't step beyond her nurse-role and do something quickly, the patient would probably die.

Dr. Reber says, "She knew her place as a nurse and she did not try to involve herself in the realm of the physician. She was well read and she did have a lot of ideas. She knew her professional limitations and she fairly well lived within those limitations."

The doctors with whom she worked regularly could always tell when Esther disagreed with their diagnosis or treatment. There was a tilting of her head, or a sudden silence, or perhaps just a frank stare from those blue eyes. Always, when Esther asked, "What else could it be?" or "Is there another way to treat this patient?" the doctor knew he had better take a second hard look at the case.

Sometimes she had to be a little less subtle with short-term doctors who had not yet figured her out. On one occasion a visiting doctor prescribed something for a patient. Esther quite obviously disagreed.

The doctor said, "Oh, what's wrong, Esther?"

"Oh, nothing, you're the doctor, you're the doctor."

As they walked on he turned and saw that she was actually scowling. He said, "What's wrong, don't you think that's the right medicine for this patient?"

With that endearing lop-sided grin she said, "No, I'm just a nurse, I can't tell you what to do. I mean, you're the doctor."

He laughed. "Okay, Esther, what would you have given her?"

"Well, I don't want to tell you what to do but if it had been me, I would have given her . . ."

So, sometimes subtly, sometimes with a jab in the ribs, Esther controlled her doctors.

(30)

It was, during this term, probably in 1968, that Paul Mertens reversed the normal pattern and taught Esther something. He had been reading about a new technique for performing symphysiotomy, a minor obstetrical operation done during labor on a woman with a contracted pelvis or a very large baby. It consists of incising the cartilage that holds together the pelvic bones where they join just above the genitalia. The bones spring apart, enlarging the pelvis and allowing the baby to slip through.

The alternative is usually Caesarian section. The procedure is roundly condemned in Western countries, but it has one clear advantage in developing countries: in her next pregnancy the patient can deliver in her own village without fear of the uterus rupturing through the scar of a previous C-section.

Paul Mertens decided to try it. His first few attempts were traumatic for him but successful for the patient. Esther watched carefully. Mertens became enthused and did eight successful procedures, obviating Caesarian section in all.

Esther remained skeptical.

Then one day Mertens was in Monrovia for the monthly medical meeting and for drug shopping. An OB patient who had had four previous stillbirths came into Curran in advanced labor. Esther examined her, found a markedly contracted pelvis and a thinning lower uterus. The baby was in marked distress, nearly dead. Rupture of the uterus was imminent.

There was no time to send her to Phebe. The baby would die before they got there. The uterus might rupture en route and then both mother and baby would probably die.

Esther smiled grimly and said to herself, "All right, Dr. Mertens, here goes!"

She did the symphysiotomy and delivered a live infant. The patient's uterus did not rupture and there were no complications. Esther was no longer skeptical but for some months continued to call Mertens when she thought the operation should be done.

But then came the day when Mertens was visiting clinics in Konia and Borkeza and Esther had to do another symphysiotomy alone. She did it successfully and from then on Mertens pushed her to do them on her own. She did, and before long the student passed the teacher in competence.

Then, as she so often did, she questioned the conventional wisdom. Even the European texts that had anything good to say about symphysiotomies cautioned against doing it in a breech delivery. "Why wouldn't it work?" Esther asked, and decided there was no reason why. So when the proper case presented itself, she did it, and then did two more.

One day when Esther was gone, Paul Mertens found himself with a desperate situation: a dying baby in a breech presentation. Reluctantly, asking himself who he was to flout the experts, but knowing that Esther had done three such cases successfully, he went ahead and did the symphysiotomy. He delivered a live baby in a case where the alternative was to do a Caesarian section and then probably would have lost the baby.

So the circle had come full around. Esther, who had been taught something, was again the teacher.

(31)

Paul Mertens recalls another instance where Esther's uncanny insight was critical.

A patient came in who previously had had a vesicovaginal fistula (a hole between the bladder and the vagina caused by a prolonged labor) which constantly dribbled urine down her legs. After three attempts (not unusual in these cases), Franklin Keller had successfully closed the defect.

Since another vaginal delivery would tear the repair apart, Keller told her she would need a Caesarian section for her next baby.

Now she was back, at term, not yet in labor. Mertens thought she could go another week or two. Esther disagreed.

"Dr. Mertens," she said, "that infant is large enough to deliver and this lady complains of small pains in her abdomen which I think is beginning labor. I think we should do the C-section now."

With some reservations but from long experience reluctant to go against Esther's judgment, he and medical student Jerry Hirsch opened the abdomen.

Mertens described what he saw. "An extremely baffling sight met my eyes. It appeared as if the uterus was covered with huge blood vessels, running together into a group in the right adnexal (ovarian) area. An indentation extended three-quarters of the way across the uterus from the left toward the right."

He knew he couldn't put the scalpel through such a vascular structure. He extended his abdominal incision for more exposure and lifted up the uterus to look at its back side. There he saw what has been seen by only a very few doctors: a very thin membrane with vernix beneath it.

Mertens was quick, but Esther was quicker. "That's an abdominal pregnancy!" she cried.

Indeed it was. An abdominal pregnancy is one which occurs within the abdomen, but outside the uterus, an extreme rarity. The ultimate ectopic pregnancy. The baby was alive and full-term as Esther had predicted. It was easily extracted by slitting open the membranes.

(32)

Esther was also an accomplished anesthetist. Her methods were not modern, but they were safe, they were sure, and the patient always woke up. She used a pint can of ether with a cork in the neck. She cut a tiny wedge out of one side of the cork and inserted a wick of cotton. With the can upside down, a slow, steady flow of ether dripped from the cotton. With her other hand, Esther held a commercially-made wire screen in the shape of a shallow, oval cup and covered with several layers of gauze. This she held over the pateint's mouth and nose and dripped ether onto it.

She was an expert at recognizing the depth of anesthesia from the pupils and the respirations. She carried the patient deeply enough so that intra-abdominal operations could be done, and then slowly lightened the anesthesia as the surgeon closed the incision. By the time the surgery was over, the patient was nearly awake. Modern anesthetists do this routinely with their rapid-acting and rapidly-absorbed agents, but to do this with ether took exceptional skill and not a little clairvoyance.

Paul Mertens, in talking aout those days, says, "One of my favorite pictures of Esther is of her caring for a patient during surgery, sitting by his head, controlling the anesthesia and making sure that things were going all right." Sometimes she would be so tired that she would begin to nod and nearly fall off the stool. But she never did and always was alert enough to be aware of the depth of anesthesia, the condition of the patient, and the stage of the surgery.

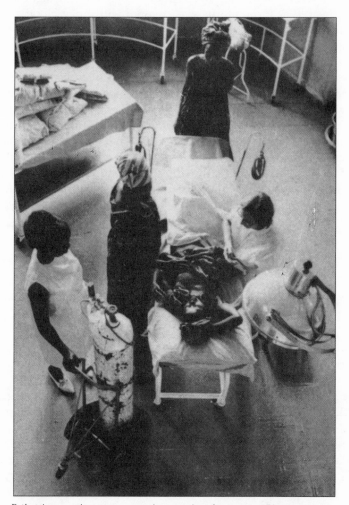

Esther in operating room, preparing a patient for surgery. Picture was taken from the visitors' gallery where the man stood to kill his wife on the operating table.

Chapter Eight

(No angel, she)

(1)

Esther Bacon's working relationship with all the doctors ranged from very good to excellent. They recognized her unique talents and gave her her head. Not that there weren't conflicts. A doctor, especially a missionary doctor, is an independent person. He demands from the hospital staff respect, competence, adherence to rules, yes, even conformity.

Esther had no trouble respecting the doctors at Zorzor; they were uniformly worthy.

Her level of competence was legendary.

Conformity and adherence to rules?

She was an outlaw.

Though Esther Bacon may have been a saint, she was not an angel.

Paul Mertens points this out succinctly: "Lest anyone form the opinion that Esther was a perfect angel, she certainly was not. Esther had her idiosyncrasies, her shortcomings, her faults, and at times definitely an impish streak."

(2)

She was not organized. She could make a mess of a laboratory or medicine shelf, not appreciating that someone else would have to straighten it out. *She* knew where things were!

She rarely recorded what she did for a patient. This irked every doctor she worked with. No one could change her, not even Franklin Keller, who perhaps tried harder than anyone to bring order into the record system. Keller's own records and his neat handwriting were a model of perfection, but it seems that it was *he* who wrote down what Esther had done.

Paul Mertens often scolded Esther for not recording what she had done, what medications she had given, what observations she had made. Many times he left the hospital late at night after writing orders for the nurses to follow on a critically ill patient. The next morning he found that Esther had returned to the hospital after he left, had treated that patient all night in the way she thought right, sometimes changing his orders without calling him, giving medications as they were necessary, almost never writing down what she had done.

Almost every doctor would become livid if a nurse changed his orders. All would demand that progress notes be kept and that treatment — especially medications — be recorded. Paul found that he could not really become angry because the patient was always better. So the disturbing thing to him was not that Esther had ignored or countermanded his orders, but that the chart was blank and he had to question her to find out what she had done.

(3)

Esther's tendency to work long hours was a two-edged sword. She accomplished much — but she became overly tired. Fran Brouse comments on this, "You'd fight with Esther in vain trying to get her to rest. When you took call so she could get some rest, she'd still appear, checking in on the patients."

Deanna Isaacson says, "Bacon couldn't keep any schedule. So if we had her on a schedule, it never worked. She'd come in on our nights, too, so there was no point in putting her on rotation. It was better if Jeanette and I alternated every second night and called her when we needed her."

In her clinics she frequently fell asleep in the few moments it took her aide to bring in the next patient. She sometimes fell asleep in the classroom, usually when the students were writing a test or assignment, but occasionally while a student was reciting or drawing on the blackboard. The students giggled and sometimes let her sleep, but always without rancor because she taught them so much.

She *always* fell asleep when she attended informal Bible studies in missionaries' homes. Because of her fatigue, she tripped easily when walking in the dark, even with her lantern, which she still carried with her. Once after a night delivering babies with Fran Brouse, she knocked over two baby cribs, fortunately baby-less. Another night she fell into a construction ditch between her house and the ward. The classic case was the time she fell asleep leaning against a tree en route to the hospital. It is no wonder that many thought she had fallen asleep when she crashed into the Gbarnga police station.

(4)

One of Esther's less endearing habits was to take the opposite side of almost every question. Margaret Miller calls this her argumentative or ornery side. But Margaret is quick to say that Esther did this just to be sure both sides had a chance to be heard: "You'd make an observation, say on a world issue or a political issue, and she'd say, 'Yes, but...' and then give extenuating circumstances."

But Margaret points out that when Esther took umbrage it was when she could not tolerate what she thought was an unfair attack. Everyone insists that Esther never, ever, said anything derogatory about anyone. "If she didn't have something good to say about a person, she said nothing," says Fran Brouse. "You could be against her but she was never against you."

There are many stories which could be told about Esther's habit of taking the opposite side of any question. One of the most illustrative is the game she played with every doctor. Paul Mertens tells how she did it with him:

A patient in the labor room is having trouble and Esther thinks she needs a Caesarian section. Esther brings Dr. Mertens to see the patient and he agrees with her.

Then Esther starts the game. She points out that the patient comes from forty miles back in the bush and might not come back for a C-section with her next pregnancy, risking therefore a ruptured uterus.

This makes Mertens stop and think. "Well, then, Esther, perhaps we should wait."

Esther pounces again. "But you know, doctor, her membranes ruptured a day and a half ago. If you wait any longer she's certainly going to develop a severe infection."

So Mertens decides to do the surgery right away. Esther keeps up this ping pong game until eventually Mertens puts everything together and makes up his own mind. With Esther's help. Mertens says, "Only Esther really knew — for she'd been following that patient — whether she really wanted a Caesarian section or not, and Esther's ultimate judgment was usually correct."

Esther played this game with all the doctors, literally driving them up the wall. Not all of them saw through her as clearly as Paul Mertens did. He soon learned what to do.

When Esther called him to see a patient in labor, he assumed *a priori* that the patient was at least a candidate for a Caesarian section. So he examined her thoroughy, got a detailed history from both patient and Esther, and had her moved directly to the operating room. He then said to Esther, "She's definitely a candidate for C-section. If you decide she really needs one, call me down in pediatrics."

One of two things would happen. Esther would come to him soon after and say, "Doctor, the baby weighed 7 pounds, 12 ounces."

He'd ask innocently, "What baby?"

"Why, the one that you were going to do a Caesarian section for." This was accompanied, of course, by her impish little lopsided grin.

Or perhaps she'd come a half hour later and say, "Doctor, the patient is on the operating table. Aren't you coming?"

Paul laughs now as he says, "Esther held the cards."

(5)

Esther's tenacity was legendary. Clearly this was one of the traits which made Esther what she was. But it had its flip side. She could be annoying.

Earl Reber remembers the many times he tried to escape to his house for an hour or two of rest, exhausted from long hours at the hospital. Esther followed him up the hill, asking him questions about what to do about this or that. He finally had to say, "Look, Esther, just leave it." But she wouldn't leave it. Earl entered the house and Esther stood outside, still keeping up her conversation through the screen. Earl or Anna Mae would invite her in for tea, or supper if it were late, but she rarely went in.

Jim Stull says, "Esther had a way of pecking away at you to get things done that *she* felt needed to be done. Sometimes it was a little bit stressful because you had your own priority systems of what was most important to do, and then Esther would come along and trammel your priority system with hers... but I listened to her because she taught me so much."

There's no question that in the early years she irritated the zoes. This too was a mixed blessing. She could ill afford to antagonize these powerful people, yet she had to oppose them to achieve her goal. It's apparent that she found the proper blend. But Roland Payne remembers that "she had to fight with the witch doctors here — really fight. I went to some of the villages and the people there confirmed it — they had really struggled. They wouldn't put their hands on *her* but they'd hold the woman and try to take her away from Esther. Just for the first few years..."

Esther was not the least bit shy about imposing her will on others if she knew she was right.

(6)

As a corollary to this, she had a low tolerance for incompetence and slackness. During a yellow fever outbreak near Zorzor, the government sent vaccinators up. They had forgotten the saline diluent. Esther gave them a 500cc bottle, the smallest she had, expecting them to come back the next day for another sterile bottle. Instead, they used the same bottle for an entire week until the people began to develop abscesses at the injection sites. When the vaccinators did finally come back to Curran, Esther literally shook them by the shoulders and scolded them.

This was not an uncommon reaction on her part. Her students knew this, and could be heard saying, "Ay-yah, you do something small wrong, Bayka will get you and she will shake you good."

But Paul Mertens tempers this by saying, "On the other hand, should a student or nurse be criticized by anyone, Esther would be the first one to come to their defense."

The students knew this and loved her for it. Their attitude was that if they had really made a mistake, they deserved a little shaking up and Bayka was the logical one to do it.

(7)

She was persistent to the point of obnoxiousness in obtaining blood. Earl Reber says flatly that Esther could always get a pint of blood somewhere. Sometimes it was Esther herself or one of the doctors who eventually lay down on the table, but most of the time she got it from the men standing around outside the hospital.

Paul Mertens says she cornered the relatives and friends, "then talked and badgered and shamed them into giving blood."

Jim Stull says she simply intimidated them. He remembers one time when he delivered a missionary lady's baby. Esther assisted him and the husband held a lantern because the generator was down. When the baby was safely out, Stull found a deep cervical tear squirting blood. The husband scooted out the door and was sick. Esther helped Stull find and suture the laceration, then went out on the porch and shuffled the men around until she found as many as she needed with the right type. Some turned away or ran away, but once she got hold of someone, he ended up giving blood.

Paul Mertens had many similar experiences but one stands out in his mind. It was nighttime. A woman had miscarried in the forest and was taken to the Konia clinic where the nurse, Mr. Aggrey, immediately put her in a taxi and brought her to Curran. Esther typed the lady, then grabbed the man who had come with the patient and typed him. He had the wrong type, so she typed Nurse Aggrey and found him to be the right type. He pleaded that he had just had malaria and needed to get back to his clinic. Esther had neatly blocked this escape by sending his taxi up to get Paul Mertens. By the time Mertens reached the hospital, Esther had already gotten half a unit of blood from Mr. Aggrey. And before Mertens had finished the D & C, Esther had gotten the lady out of shock with Mr. Aggrey's blood.

Esther had a one-track mind. The only thing that mattered was her patients' welfare. She stepped on toes to obtain her goals. One time Esther found herself in trouble in the delivery room, too much happening at once. She sent a runner up to another midwife's house to ask her to come down and help. She didn't respond. Irritated, Esther went after her but had no better luck in rousing the girl. Finally she climbed in the window and shook her awake. The midwife complained that she had been up all night. "So have I," said Esther. The midwife got up and accompanied Esther down to the hospital.

Early in her work she had started a midwifery course. She enlisted the aid of anyone who could add to the instruction. Many of the nurses and some of the doctors were reluctant to teach. She kept after them. Earl Reber says, "You found yourself teaching the class even when you didn't want to."

During Paul Mertens' time, the other members of the School faculty wanted to reduce the next freshman class from twelve to ten. Esther filibustered at the faculty meeting as only she could. Mertens finally called for a vote and the new limit was imposed. Esther never let them forget that, and made little digs for months afterward, especially when later that year they discovered they were short of personnel due to vacations, furloughs, illness, and rotation to other stations. Nor did she let the Board forget it. On a visit by the Board Secretary, Dr. Ruben Pederson, she cornered him for two hours one night arguing that the school should admit twelve rather than ten. If she knew that it really wasn't his decision, she ignored it. Mertens says, "He didn't agree and finally managed to escape."

She lost that one, but she had grown up and didn't pout. She won the next one.

Many on the Curran staff felt that two months was too long for student nurses to spend at the Catherine Mills Rehabilitation Center, Liberia's hospital for the mentally ill. Esther vehemently opposed a reduction. She knew from long experience that the Loma people did not understand mental illness. They still controlled psychotics by chaining them to a log which had to be dragged along. Esther believed that if the students learned nothing else at Catherine Mills, they would at least gain a degree of sympathy and understanding as to how to respond to mental illness.

The question arose formally in the annual meeting at which such decisions were made. Esther's approach was that of an Arabian camel dealer. She did not simply ask that the two-month rotation be continued, nor did she plead for at least a few weeks. No, she argued vehemently that an *increase* was absolutely necessary. Paul Mertens remembers that "by the time Esther got through arguing, everybody was more than willing to leave Catherine Mills at two months for that year just to get out of the meeting."

(9)

So Esther Bacon was human. But some of the apparently negative aspects of her personality were merely exaggerations of positive aspects. Like a very potent drug, which when given in too high doses becomes toxic, she sometimes came on too strong. Too much tenacity became nagging. Too little sleep became dangerous. Too little organization became annoying. Too scanty records became frustrating.

But no one who knew her would have wanted her to be any different. Esther was Esther.

Chapter Nine

(1968-1972)

(1)

In 1968, Dr. Joseph Wold published *God's Impatience in Liberia*. In it he summarized for the missionaries and national Christians what God had done and what He could do in Liberia. In this story of Esther Bacon's life, justice cannot be done to Wold's great book, but some excerpts can help to re-create the ambience in which Esther worked during the late 60s.

"Liberia is on the brink of a tremendous turning to Christ. Whole villages, even whole clans, are ready to renounce ancestor spirit worship and turn to Christianity."

"Liberians recognize the missionary as a friend."

"Liberians themselves have little race prejudice."

"If uncircumcized, pig-eating Gentiles can receive the Holy Spirit and be baptized (Acts 10:44), then by the grace of God polygamists can become Christians without being forced to thrust a wife into adultery or break a serious and honorable promise to a wife's father and family. . . if a man is lost, let it be because he refused to accept Christ as his risen Lord and Savior, and not because he loved both his wives too much to disgrace and ruin them, or was too upright to lie, or live in deceit."

"The benefits of Western culture and education and medicine...are so obviously superior to the bush schools and the witch doctor that the Church is constantly tempted to use them to found the Kingdom. But if the missionaries continue to spend time, effort, and money on education and medicine without making converts, they freeze forever the relationship between the givers and the receivers. The receiver remains subservient. And if the missionary is forced to leave (as happened in China) there are few leaders left to continue the Church."

It was a landmark book, and it had its impact. Some medical and teaching personnel took umbrage at the last quote, but Dr. Wold had no intention of negating the work of the educators and medical people. He simply wanted to point out that their work was the partner of evangelism, not the end in itself. Esther Bacon was well aware of this. She certainly worked long and hard to restore health and save lives. But it is clear from her letters, her writings, and her actions that she was also supremely interested in the salvation of the souls of those people.

(2)

Curran Memorial Hospital was functioning again as a bush hospital should. The designation "Maternal and Child Health Care Center" was lost to posterity except, ironically, for Esther Bacon. With the imp of perversity sitting on her shoulder, she insisted that the euphemism be used and corrected Paul Mertens every time he said "Curran Hospital." Finally Paul recognized that she was merely playing the game: when he quit, she quit.

Meanwhile the new Phebe Hospital continued its growth. It had become *the* showpiece of African mission hospitals. Now, in addition to Lutheran missionaries, the Board of Directors consisted of a local Liberian Lutheran churchman, an Episcopalian, a Methodist, and representing the government, the Bong County superintendent. Franklin Keller, James Stull, and Alice Dietz were still there as the nucleus of a slowly growing medical staff. Inpatient and clinic censuses showed steady growth but many years would pass before usage even approached that of Curran Memorial in Zorzor.

Changes in personnel at Curran Memorial occurred periodically. Paul Mertens took a short vacation in mid-1968 and for that period Esther was again in charge of the hospital and again doctors came up from Phebe on a weekly basis, usually Dr. Keller or Dr. Chi. Then when Paul Mertens returned, Esther went home for three months in early 1969 and returned to Liberia in mid-May.

Implementing the long-range goal of training nationals to move into more responsible positions, the Church sent Irene Morris and Ellen Murray from Zorzor to London for a six-month midwifery upgrade. Soon after returning from London, Irene went to the States for almost another year of midwifery training. The Church's trust in her abilities, to be put to the test in April of 1972, would be justified.

Esther continued to write to her surrogate mother, Aunt Nora Leander, in Sioux City. She dutifully reported that Kwenyah, her launderer, recovered from a serious illness. Subusu, her cook, took his wife home from the hospital with a baby daughter. Carolyn Miller, the nurse-midwife from Phebe who had come out with the Isaacsons, spent a few days at Zorzor prior to going home to Iowa City for a short furlough. Jeanette and Deanna Isaacson left to begin a three-year master's degree program at the University of Iowa.

Kirsten Jensen graduated from the Lutheran Training Institute at Salayea at the end of 1969 and enrolled in a four-year baccalaureate degree course in the Phebe-Cuttington School of Nursing at Suakoko. She spent many weekends and most of her vacations at Zorzor, usually living with Esther and working at the hospital as an aide.

Paul Mertens doubled the size of both the OB and pediatrics wards, expanding in the way Earl Reber had envisioned twenty years before. In 1968 Esther moved into a ward that was for the first time solely for OB patients. As Esther contemplated the new wards, she wrote, "It is beautiful here — flamboyant (poinciana) tree between my house and hospital has branches wide and spreading with flowers in bloom and ground below covered with red petals. There is bouganvilia (sic) and two other varieties of flowering tree in front of girls' dorm, hibiscus bush in front of the office window where I'm writing this."

By 1970 the hospital was bursting at the seams. Statistics from that year give the picture and demonstrate the problem:

Inpatient		Admissions	Deaths	Mortality
Medical		528	46	8.7
TB		37	6	16.2
Surgical		164	4	2.4
OB and Gyne.		1720	2	0.12
Neonatal		1332	36	2.7
Pediatrics		801	103	12.9
	Total	4582	197	Av. 4.3

Obstetrical	
Deliveries	1308
Maternal deaths	NONE
Stillborns	34

Obstetrical (cont.)

Twins	52
Triplets	3
Caesarian sections	38
Symphysiotomies	36

Surgical

Major ops		169
Minor		291
	Total	460

Outpatient

Adult dispensary		176/day	53,027/year
Pediatric dispensary		68/day	10,887/year
Prenatal clinic		36/day	20,442/year
	Total	280	84,356

(3)

Esther was still after her Aunt Nora to come to Liberia. In April of 1971, she wrote, "I'm told to tell you, folks here want you to come for a visit." In May, when she went to Hawarden for a month-long vacation (which would be her last visit home), she carried with her a large sum of money donated by the people of Liberia for Nora's plane fare. President Tubman himself sent a personal check for $300.

Nora, now 84, still refused to come out to Zorzor, so Esther came back alone. She was considerably embarrassed about the disposition of the money and deposited it in a Monrovia bank in case Nora ever changed her mind.

President Tubman became ill in July of 1971 and went to London for an operation. His postoperative course was stormy and he died on July 23rd. The news came to Zorzor over the radio in the evening. Esther and Irene Morris were in the operating room helping Paul Mertens do a Caesarian section. The announcer detailed the elaborate funeral being planned in Monrovia.

Esther busied herself with her ether can for a moment, then said pensively, "Why should so much money be spent on a funeral? Just think how that money could be used! I don't want to be buried like that. I don't even want a coffin. I just want to be wrapped in woven country mats and be put deep in the ground. And when I die, I want to be buried at night."

Then, in an afterthought, she said, "In Zorzor."

(4)

In August of 1971 Esther made a teaching-lecturing swing through the
northern part of Lofa County, spending a day or two in Bolahun, Kolahun,
Foya Kamara and Voinjama. Then in October she went down to a midwifery meeting in Monrovia. "I was late," she wrote Nora, "but got there
before the meeting was over. First, I overslept till 6 A.M., then had guests
for breakfast, then saw about 25 patients before leaving Zorzor. By then
the early taxis which go all the way were gone, so I had to take three
different taxis."

She was *still* not giving up on getting Nora to Liberia. It almost had
become an obsession. She wrote, "I realize as you say that home is best,
but that is the way I feel about *here!*" An irrefutable argument which Nora
chose to refute.

In that same letter Esther copied out a long chorus which had been sung
at chapel that morning with mandolin accompaniment. Since her letters
were usually just short notes, the fact that she took the time to write out
the entire chorus is clear evidence that it had special meaning for her at
that time of her life.*

> Chorus: All you peoples, clap your hands, and shout for joy.
> The Lord has made all mankind one,
> So raise your voices high!

> 1) All creation shows the glory of the Lord,
> The earth proclaims his handiwork,
> The sky cries out his word.
> Night and day sing out the glories all about,
> So praise the Lord with shouts of joy.

> 2) Let ev'ry man alive remember your command,
> That ev'ry day in ev'ry way we love our fellow man.
> If this command is done, the victory will be won
> And we will all live in peace and joy.

(5)

In October of 1971 Paul Mertens became seriously ill. At first he thought
it was a recurrence of the hepatitis he'd had in June. But a chest X-ray

---

*Author's note: There is no direct evidence, but I have the strong feeling that it was at
this same time that she wrote the poem quoted on page 231.

showed tuberculosis of the left upper lobe of his lung. He started taking isoniazid-thiacetazone and continued work. By November he was so weak that on the 6th he went down to Phebe and consulted with Franklin Keller and later Dr. Robert Patton from JFK Hospital in Monrovia. All agreed that more studies were needed in the States to determine whether he had a recurrence of hepatitis or liver damage from his tuberculosis medications.

At Zorzor, Mertens' place was taken by short-term Dr. Wright. Wright stayed until mid-December and then the hospital was doctor-less until mid-January when Dr. Joseph Baum and his wife Jeanette came out for a four-month term.

Joe Baum took over with great skill, aided by Jeanette, who would prove of invaluable help in the crisis to come in April, and who would be described by Donna Mertens as "cool-headed, another Bacon."

There was at first a clashing of wills between Joe Baum and Esther Bacon. Dr. Baum says, "She could not admit that I knew anything about taking care of her people and I couldn't imagine anyone being so tyrannical without personal gain as a motive."

But it didn't take him long to realize that he wasn't dealing with a petty tyrant. He was dealing with Esther Bacon, a unique individual who set goals impossibly high and then achieved them. She may never have read the Chinese proverb: "Man who says it cannot be done should not interrupt man doing it," but it should have been a watchword for everyone else who came in contact with her.

Joe Baum learned quickly that Esther demanded the same high level of stamina and devotion from others that she expected of herself. Sometimes she scheduled more work for the other nurses and the doctors than they wanted to do.

What Baum didn't realize was that Esther was not working at her *usual* pace. She had actually slowed down. Deanna Isaacson noted this when she came back from her three years of study in February of 1972. She recalls, "She was too tired, too tired," using "too" in the Liberian sense of "very." Baum didn't pick this up because he hadn't known the Esther Bacon that Deanna knew, the one whose schedule was no schedule, the one who walked miles through the high forest just to see an old friend, the one who loved to fight verbal battles in faculty meetings and on the ward, the one who used to play "the game" with anyone who would play. She was, in fact, too tired.

(6)

Meanwhile, Paul Mertens had been sent to Columbia Presbyterian Hospital in New York City and was told he occupied the same room in which Lily Pinneo was treated for Lassa fever 2½ years previously. After three months of testing and treatment he returned to Zorzor in early February of 1972. For a long time after he returned, he was weak and tired easily. He was very happy to let Joe Baum run things while he himself functioned more as a consultant for difficult cases and helped in the dispensary on especially busy days. Fortunately, there was other help: the Isaacsons and Irene Morris had all returned, eager to get back to work.

The Liberian Board of Nursing and Midwifery scheduled a meeting on February 24th of 1972 in Monrovia. Esther decided to go down the afternoon before so she wouldn't miss most of the meeting as she had in October. When she found Paul Mertens to tell him he said that was O.K., and then added, "Oh, by the way, Esther, I've got some good news for you."

She stopped and glanced sideways at him, suspicious. Paul Mertens loved to bait her and she knew it.

"Yes," he said, "Dave Urfer got a radio message this morning that your award presentation has been rescheduled for some time in May."

Esther grimaced and said, "Oh, great."

She had been singled out by President Tubman before his death to receive his personal award, the William V.S. Tubman Award for Achievement in the Medical Field. Originally scheduled for February 14th, it had been postponed and Esther had hoped that they would forget about it entirely.

Already she had been honored twice by the Liberian government. In 1946 she and Earl Reber had been decorated for their outstanding performance in midwifery and medicine. In 1951 she had been honored by being made a Knight Official in the Humane Order of African Redemption. No one would have known about either award if they had had to get the information from Esther Bacon.

Mertens knew how she rebelled against such notoriety. He says, "Esther never talked about such decorations. It really seemed to matter very little to her if she were decorated or not, if people recognized her or not. The important thing with Esther was that her patients got well. Earthly possesions, recognition, or praise, were unimportant. Alleviating suffering and saving human lives were what really counted."

(7)

In mid-afternoon she packed a small bag and walked into town. Down the sloping hill on the shaded path threading through palm trees, flame trees, and luxuriantly green mango trees, past the "Curran Hospital" sign, onto the red dirt road that dipped into the valley of swamp-rice fields between the hospital and Zorzor-town. Women waved to her; some curt-

sied and took her hand. She knew them all, most by name.
A pre-teen girl with artistically corn-rowed hair knelt by
the side of the road, self-effacing, eyes downcast. Esther
knelt with her, took her hand and pulled her to her
feet. Gently she reprimanded the girl, and not for the
first time. The girl, Garmai, always answered, "You my
god, Bayka."

Esther knew what she meant and didn't argue. To most
Loma people, especially the older ones, a "god" was a person who had
done for you a particularly important deed. In that context, Esther met
the criterion: she had raised Garmai from babyhood after her mother died
in childbirth, had often given her money for school fees and clothes.

She squeezed the girl's hand and climbed the hill past the open market
to the intersection of Zorzor's two main streets. Children trailed along
beside her, singing, "Bayka, Bayka, Bayka!"

She had intended to look for a taxi in Zorzor to make the run to Monrovia, but before she found one she spotted a flat-bed ALTCO log truck
gassing up at one of the two stations. On its bed were six giant logs, each
about three feet thick and thirty feet long, so Esther knew it was en route
to Monrovia.

The driver knew Esther. It wouldn't have made any difference to Esther
if he hadn't. She asked him for a ride to Monrovia and he said with a
grin, "Sure, Bayka." It was an honor, though it would never have crossed
Esther's mind that it was. She felt the respect that the tribal Africans ac-
corded her, even the Muslim Mandingoes, and especially the women and
their husbands whose babies she had saved. But never would she have
understood the reverence, the awe, in which many people held her.

Six hours later, about 9 P.M., the truck dropped her off in Monrovia
on Tubman Boulevard at 13th Street, two blocks from the church house
and offices. The driver apologized for not being able to take the giant
truck directly to the door.

She stood for a moment, looking after him, a bemused smile on her
face. She knew he was too young to remember her from the days when
she could walk hours through the jungle, deliver a baby, and then walk
home again. She was fifty-five now, would be fifty-six in three weeks.
Though she really hadn't felt completely well for several months, she
knew this was temporary and she would still be working in the villages
if it were necessary.

She laughed outright as she remembered the night not too long ago
when she had climbed on top of a truck full of produce headed for Zorzor.
A big city policeman came running after the truck and stopped it. He
opened the door on the passenger side and pulled out the two young

men sitting there. "You two, you go sit on top! You let Bayka sit in here! Who you think you are?"

Now she strode down the middle of 13th Street, the roadside being devoid of sidewalks but strewn with trash and garbage. She could hear the skittering of rats' feet over the rusted cans and plastic bottles. It didn't bother her. She had listened to rats in the thatched roof of her own house for over ten years before moving into the duplex.

She could hear the thundering surf now, a peaceful, lulling roar, so unlike the cacophony of sounds that came out of the high forest around Curran Hospital. The church offices and guest house occupied several acres of land almost on the beach. The bigger of the two buildings was a V-shaped, two-story hostel where missionaries and other church people stayed when visiting or passing through Monrovia. The dining room, kitchen, and a tiny office were on the second floor. There was a big lounge on both floors where people gathered to talk and read in the evening.

Esther's assigned room was on the first floor almost at the end of the hall. At the very end was a small apartment where Gloria Swanson, the church secretary, lived. Through the screened window of her own room Esther saw that the light was on. She rapped lightly on the door, called "Bok-bok" to announce her presence, and walked in. Carolyn Miller sat sideways on the bed, her back against the wall, reading her Bible and writing letters home.

"Esther," she said with a broad welcoming smile, "I was so glad when I heard I was rooming with you. We really don't see very much of you, you know."

"Why, I come down the road all the time."

(8)

Carolyn Miller had come to Phebe Hospital from Burlington, Iowa, via Edinburgh, Scotland, in April, 1966. There she had started the Certified Midwifery School and the Nurse-Midwifery School. The nursing students were in a four-year baccalaureate program in cooperation with Cuttington College across the main motor road. Kirsten Jensen was one of her students.

She had first met Esther in Zorzor in 1966 when she went up to visit Deanna and Jeanette Isaacson. Esther invited them over for supper. When they arrived, Esther wasn't there. The table was set and Subusu was bustling around in the kitchen.

Finally Esther rushed in, apologizing for her tardiness. "Sit up, all of you, eat now. I'll just grab a bite and then I've got to go back down. But you take your time."

"Is there anything I can do to help down there?" Carolyn asked.
Esther laughed, her eyes twinkling merrily. "No, no, no, I don't think
so. Everything's under control, actually, or I wouldn't be up here."
Esther didn't even sit down. She walked around the room with her
plate, telling them all about the case she was working on. Halfway
through her meal, she put the plate down and said, "I'm sorry, I've got
to rush." And she disappeared out the door. Carolyn had met the Outlaw
and didn't know whether to feel insulted or honored. But the Isaacsons
laughed and one of them said, "Don't take it personally, Carolyn. This
is the way it always is when you eat at Esther's!"

Now in the church hostel, Esther and Carolyn talked for two hours before putting out the lights. Their talk was entirely about patients. Since
both were primarily midwives, there were many problems to share. As
usual, Carolyn was intrigued by Esther's single-mindedness and awed
by the range of her knowledge.

Only as they were getting ready for bed did Esther stop talking about
patients. She pulled out a small card someone had sent her and handed
it to Carolyn. "Oh, Carolyn, look how beautiful this is, just read it."

Carolyn took the scrap of paper, pushed back against the headboard
of the bed, and read it aloud:

God Is Real

The silent stars in boundless space,
The wonder of a baby's face;
The changing seasons, one by one,
The wind, the rain, the shining sun;
A blooming flower, a flying bird,
A friendly smile, a kindly word.
The things we touch and see and feel
All go to prove that God is real!
And being real, He's present, too,
And always watching over you!
John Gilbert

This was a facet of Esther's personality that Carolyn had heard about
but hadn't witnessed. She recalls now, "The one thing I always heard
was that in her younger days here she used to love beautiful poetry, loved
things that would be sentimental or very touching to her. I never knew
her that way because by the time I knew her she had worked too hard
and she'd forgotten that part of her. . .as far as I knew. I read the verse
on this card and she showed me another verse. I thought, ah, this is the

Esther Bacon as she used to be. I thought, that's interesting, now let me
try to find some other verses that she might like, 'cause I'd picked up
this part of her personality that I'd heard about but didn't know. And
of course before I ever got to do that, Esther Bacon died.''

(10)

Three weeks later, Esther wrote her last letter home to Aunt Nora. Since
it is her last, it is reproduced here with a few minor deletions.

Dear Nora,   3/19/72
I hope you are still managing to live with winter — spring will
soon come. I remember your tulips and all the others last year.
Greetings to Ann Lynn, Ken and Jean, your neighbors, and the
folks you visit with on the phone. I don't think anyone I know
called you — but sometimes folks come visit here and might call
you — even collect!
Two babies arrived this A.M.
The new class is busy with classes. Edith Curran and Jeanette
(Isaacson) were down recently to midwifery meeting. Deanna
Isaacson is going down today with the (Joseph) Wolds who were
here to visit. The Urfers just had 20th wedding anniversary. Dr.
Baum's mother is here visiting. There have been Birthday cake
and dinners — all very nice.
I wish I could send you some of the flowers that are blooming
here — also the fine weather we have — sun is shining.
                                                    With love,
                                                    Esther Bacon

She wrote this on her 56th birthday.

(11)

Two days later, on the morning of March 21st, Esther awoke with a
vague feeling of lassitude. She felt feverish and had a headache, very
unusual for her except when she had malaria, which this didn't feel like.
There was a peculiar aching in her back and some mild joint pains when
she walked. Her throat was sore as if a cold were coming on.
Well, she thought, better take a blood smear, or start on some chloroquin. She didn't take cholorquin regularly for malarial prophylaxis because

it made her skin itch; she preferred an occasional bout with malaria.

Now she chuckled a little as she thought, I guess I'm just getting too old for all this partying! Four nights in a row! When had that ever happened before?

On the 17th she had gone to a birthday party hosted by the Mertenses for herself and Dr. Joe Baum. On the 18th she was one of twenty-four people at the Mertenses' celebrating Dave and Margaret Urfer's 20th wedding anniversary and welcoming back Jeanette and Deanna Isaacson. On the 19th, her 56th birthday, she had gone to the Mertenses' for still another birthday dinner. She remembered now that her appetite had been poor that night and Dr. Mertens had commented on it. Then last night she had had dinner with the Mertenses and the newly arrived medical student and his wife.

She was already late for morning devotions and decided to skip them for once. Subusu gave her a cup of coffee. She accepted it gratefully and wandered around the house with it for a few moments before sitting at the kitchen table to eat an orange. For one of the few times in her life she wasn't in a hurry to get down to the hospital. Finally she roused herself with an annoyed grunt and walked down the hill to the OB ward.

Irene Morris took one look at her and said, "Why, Miss Bacon, you look like you oughta be in bed."

Esther smiled, the twinkle returning as if by magic. That was all she needed, she thought, to go to bed. To Irene she said, half-jokingly, "If I go to bed, you'll have to send a nurse up to sit with me."

"We do that," Irene answered with a wide smile. "Sure we do that."

"And where'll you get her? From the ward! And then the ward'll be short."

That settled, Esther went about her rounds. Among the many patients who troubled her that morning were two obstetrical patients. One had had a Caesarean section a week before. The other had delivered a stillborn after a prolonged labor in the forest and had come to the hospital almost bled out. Both girls had been doing nicely but now were very ill with symptoms curiously similar to those of another patient who had just gone home two days before.

Esther pondered that coincidence. Later, Jeanette Isaacson would also recognize it and from the hospital records demonstrate conclusively that this patient was the index case for the epidemic to follow. Esther's file-cabinet memory recalled the clinical details of that patient. On March 1st, Garbazu, a young girl four months pregnant, had been brought in from

Zigida, 27 miles north of Zorzor in the Wonegizi Mountains.* A week before, she had developed a high fever, nausea, vomiting and severe malaise. Then she began to have symptoms of a threatened spontaneous abortion: lower abdominal cramps and vaginal bleeding.

As sick as she was, she had still tried valiantly to convince Esther that she had done everything she could to prevent aborting. "I did everything right, I'm sure I did."

Esther said, "I'm sure you did." She knew what "everything right" was. The common custom, described so neatly by John Gay in *Red Dust on the Green Leaves*, was for the husband to borrow the blacksmith's tools and lay them in the rice fanner. He kills a red chicken over the tools, spits palm oil on a lighted torch and touches it to the tools. He puts the fanner on his head and shouts, "The town is full of witches. They are found in the air and on the ground, in the night and the day. Whoever tries to bewitch this woman, let this medicine catch him. When he is caught, may he cry my name, saying, 'Flumo, come and save me. I was the one who wanted to eat this woman's child from her stomach.' Let this medicine make his body hot as I am making it hot with this fire. May he not sit down or lie down. May he not sleep or stand up."

But none of this had worked and she was brought to Curran. Nor did Esther's or Dr. Baum's treatment work.

On March 3rd she bled massively from the uterus and spontaneously aborted twins too small to survive. In doing an emergency curettage to stop the bleeding, Esther's surgical gown was soaked through with blood. She had to wash down her legs with soap and water and change the bandages on the small varicose ulcers on her right shin.

When the patient's pulse and blood stabilized, Esther did a more thorough examination. The girl had a high fever, sore throat, weakness, vomiting, and difficulty swallowing. This influenza-like illness was the obvious cause of the miscarriage. Her symptoms improved rapidly with intravenous fluids and antibiotics. In a few days she was sitting up and even walking around a bit. Her family brought in food, but since her appetite was still poor she ate what she could and shared the rest with two other patients in beds next to hers. Two days ago she went home.

---

*When Graham Greene walked through Zigida country years before, he described it as the principal "Buzi" town, where "even the commonest cutlass is beautiful," where the women wore little silver arrows in their hair, twisted silver bracelets, and heavy silver anklets, beaten by the blacksmiths out of old Napoleon coins from French West Africa (Guinea). Men wore primitive signet rings with flattened sides, decorative rings, and twisted rings to match the women's bracelets.

(12)

Now, in the OB ward, examining the two sick girls, Esther realized with a mild shock that these two and the girl from Zigida all had the very symptoms she herself had awakened with that morning.

By late morning she was dragging. Supposing she had malaria, Paul Mertens made her take a therapeutic dose of camoquin. He also ordered her gently (he is a gentle man, and besides, getting tough with Esther would have been futile) to go up to her house on the hill. Not fighting it, which surprised Dr. Mertens a bit, she did so. She lay down and sleep came quickly.

When she awoke, it was mid-afternoon and no one had called her for her outpatient clinic. Her throat pained her even without swallowing. She tried to stand up and found her strength gone. She sat back down on the bed and waited another few moments. Then mumbling to herself that this was silly, she went down to the hospital and worked until late in the evening.

During the next few days all her symptoms intensified. On the 24th, three days after the onset of her illness, she began having chest pains. When Paul Mertens finally got her to take her temperature, it was 103.

When she told him about her difficulty swallowing, Paul looked in her throat and found the cause: small groups of tiny yellowish ulcers, each with a halo of red around it. He found a few more of these strange ulcers on the buccal mucosa, the inside lining of the cheeks.

He drew blood and checked the white blood count, expecting it to be very high. To his surprise it was much lower than normal, only 2500, with a predominance of lymphocytes.

"Not bacterial," he mused to Esther. "Viral. Has to be." He looked back in her throat. "I don't ever remember seeing ulcers like this before."

He felt her neck and found enlarged, tender lymph nodes. Her skin was moist but this was not unusual in that tropical climate. She did look unusually pale, but this was broken occasionally by flushing that would last for ten or fifteen minutes.

Her voice hoarse and strained, Esther said, "Dr. Mertens, remember the girl who aborted twins three weeks ago? That I did the D & C on? She had some funny sores in her mouth. Now two girls on OB have terribly sore throats and high fevers. Ask Jeanette to show them to you."

"I'll go take a look. You go up to the house and get some rest. We can take care of things down here."

Uncharacteristically, she agreed, but with the last word, "I'll be alright. I'm not sick. It's not too bad." She lifted the cotton pledget from the needle stick in her finger and found it still bleeding. She had to hold the cotton in place for the next half hour before it stopped.

On the 25th she was able to work on the wards for only an hour or two at a time. Paul Mertens reported to her that the two OB patients did indeed have sores in their mouths similar to Esther's. He was planning to isolate the girls in one of the TB rooms.

"And I don't want you in contact with any more patients, Esther."

She smiled with the barest hint of the usual twinkle. "Yes, doctor."

The next day, the 26th, she began vomiting, then developed diarrhea. Mertens started IV fluids to counter dehydration. Her mouth was even more painful and her neck visibly swollen. A blotchy rash appeared in several places.

By the 29th she was slightly cloudy mentally. She didn't even try to work in the hospital, a fact noted by Deanna Isaacson: "When she passed one whole day in the house without coming to the hospital, you knew something was wrong with Bacon, because even if she had malaria she drug herself down there."

She was indeed critically ill. Others on the staff and in the student body were also sick. Mertens and Baum thought at first that there was an unusual number of cases of malaria. But with no response to chloroquin they wondered if they had an influenza epidemic. Soon it became evident that it was more serious than that. So, hoping it was typhoid or typhus, they tried chloramphenicol on Esther, Juanita Akoi (an aide), and others.

(13)

That night Paul discussed the four similar cases with Donna. She listened with great concern because Esther was one of her favorite people. He described the throat ulcerations and the bleeding tendency, then said, "This may even be Lassa fever."

Donna agreed and said, "There was a Time magazine article about that."

"Yes," Paul said, "and I got an article from Dr. John Frame of the Centers for Disease Control in Atlanta."

"I'll go look for them."

She found them. Paul read Frame's article and Donna the Time piece. They compared notes and were even more sure that Esther and the others had Lassa fever.

This is the story:

In the tiny village of Lassa in northeast Nigeria, 700 air miles from the coast, a 70-year-old missionary nurse, Laura Wine, became very ill. She was transferred to the Sudan Interior Mission hospital in Jos in northcentral Nigeria. She died on January 26, 1969.

Charlotte Shaw was one of the nurses who took care of her. Two days before Laura died, Charlotte swabbed out the back of Laura's throat with a gauze-covered finger. She felt a stinging where she had stuck herself earlier that day on a rose thorn. Within two weeks she died, on February 13, 1969.

Another nurse, Lily (Penny) Pinneo, who had nursed Laura Wine and helped with the autopsy on Charlotte Shaw, also became ill. She was transferred despite tremendous logistical problems to the Columbia Presbyterian Hospital in New York City. She survived.

Dr. Jeanette Troup, a board-certified pathologist and pediatrician, the only full-time doctor at SIM, survived the first epidemic. Less than a year later she did an autopsy on a victim of the second epidemic, cut her finger, and died ten days later, on February 18, 1970. In that epidemic there were twenty-three cases, of whom thirteen died.

Back in the States, scientists worked frantically to isolate the virus. Dr. Jordi Cassals, a virologist, innoculated mice with the Lassa fever virus isolated by Dr. Sonja Buckley. He had a hangnail which he picked at. A week later he got Lassa fever. He survived.

A laboratory technician, Juan Roman, working with equine encephalitis in the same lab, developed Lassa fever and died. His death prompted the authorities to shut down all Lassa fever research except at the Atlanta Centers for Disease Control.*

(14)

Knowing now that he was probably dealing with Lassa fever, Mertens got in touch with Dr. Robert Patton, Chief of Medicine at JFK Memorial Hospital in Monrovia. Patton made phone contact with the CDC in Atlanta. CDC got in touch with the U.S. State Department's international health office. The State Department asked the Liberian government to summon Dr. Tom Monath, one of their virologists on loan to the University of Nigeria in Ibadan. Since Penny Pinneo was now back in Jos, fully recovered from Lassa fever, Dr. Monath made immediate plans to fly with her to Liberia.

Meanwhile, in Zorzor, others were getting sick: two obstetrical patients, two Liberian nurses, three midwifery students, and Akoi, the aide. With Esther, Garbazu, and another obstetrical patient already discharged, this made a total of eleven. The two nurses, Jetty Ziegler and Phebe Halla-

---

*For the full account, which has the pace and intrigue of a good detective novel, the reader is referred to the book, "Fever!" by John Fuller, published by Reader's Digest Press and distributed by E. P. Dutton. Also available in most libraries.

wanger, were being taken care of in Esther's house. Esther was in her small bedroom in the southwest corner, the other two in the big northwest and northeast corner rooms. Jetty was the least ill of all and her case might have been missed if she had been ill at another time.

Mertens decided to isolate all the rest of the suspected Lassa fever patients in one room at the hospital but there wasn't one big enough. So they carried everything that could be moved out of the laundry room and transferred all the Lassa fever patients in there except Esther, Jetty, and Phebe. There was inadequate space for beds so they slept on the floor. Isolation techniques were followed, as strict as could be done under the circumstances.

Each of the nurses in the Bacon house had her own caretakers. For Esther that was Edith Curran, Grace Moleyeaze, and her adopted daughter, Ruth, now back in Zorzor and working in the hospital as an aide.* Even in this critical illness Esther balked at taking medicine. Grace went to her newly-opened drug store in Zorzor-town, brought back medicines, and told Esther, "Now, Esther, this is not from the hospital, you are *not* stealing from the patients, this is from my drug store, so you *take it*!"

Others came and went, many to stay just long enough to join her in prayer. Others stayed away, too terrified to risk themselves. Deanna Isaacson heard one of the students say, "Oh, I came here to go to school and now my children won't have a mother!"

One of those who came frequently and stayed long was Pastor Paul Swedburg, stationed at Salayea, and at thirty-eight a veteran Liberian missionary. Like Esther, he was a midwesterner, from Minnesota, and he gave Esther much comfort.

Except for the Lassa fever patients and a surprisingly continuous stream of obstetrical patients, the hospital was now officially closed. As fast as he safely could, Mertens discharged the other patients and admitted only the most severely ill. He did no elective surgery.

There was panic in Zorzor-town. Travelers going through town rolled up their windows, preferring to suffer from the airless and humid heat rather than expose themselves to the unknown disease. Those truckers who had to come into town sat in the closed cabs while the townspeople unloaded the trucks. People shunned anyone who looked the least bit sick. A few shopkeepers shut down completely and went home. The roads to the hospital compound were ominously empty.

Washington recalled the two Peace Corps Volunteers based in Zorzor, Bob Dettmer and Henry Walker. Neither left when Paul Mertens reassured them that they were in no danger if they stayed away from the hospital.

---

*Irene Bacon, another adopted daughter, was probably there also.

Esther was dying. Paul Mertens faced a question that all honest doctors face from time to time: am I doing all that's possible? He was *almost* certain he had the right diagnosis. He was *almost* certain that he was giving the right treatment. But that niggling little devil sat on his shoulder asking if there wasn't something else to be done.

He decided to call Franklin Keller on the radio at Phebe Hospital. When he got through, he found that Keller and indeed all of the staff at Phebe were following Esther's illness with hope and prayers.

Mertens' diagnosis of probable Lassa fever alarmed Keller. He knew what that meant. The mortality in previous epidemics had been over 50%, with no clues as to why one patient died and another didn't. Convalescent serum was in very short supply since it could be taken only from people who had recovered from the disease. The Africans were very reluctant to give their blood, so most of the serum available had come from surviving missionaries like Lily Pinneo. The animal host or vector had not yet been identified.*

Keller agreed to come up to see Esther and suggested that perhaps she should be transferred down to Phebe. Mertens had decidedly mixed emotions about that. He was grateful to Keller for the offer because Esther would benefit from additional medical consultation with both Keller and Jim Stull. Also, he hoped Phebe's superior laboratory might prove his suspicion of Lassa fever wrong. But he knew that Curran statistically had as good a salvage rate on the medical wards and lower mortality rates on obstetrics and pediatrics. Yet he was reluctant to authorize the transfer because it meant a hazardous journey, and because it seemed to be an admission of his own failure. He shrugged his shoulders at the latter, but it was there, nevertheless.

Deanna and Jeanette Isaacson's reaction to the transfer was not mixed at all. They were "too relieved." Deanna says, "The tension was so great. Dr. Mertens felt he had to be with Bacon and it wasn't safe for him because he had not fully recovered from his hepatitis. And he was so emotionally involved with her, so snarled up in all this, that it was hard for him to think clearly about what to do."

The Moleyeazes' reaction was not mixed either. They did not want her transferred. They considered her a member of their family. If she was going to die, they wanted her to die in Zorzor. But, Pewu says now, "If she had been left here, I don't think she would have died that time. When

---

*Nor would it be until six months after the Zorzor epidemic when another epidemic hit the Panguma Catholic Hospital in Sierra Leone. There, in the house of one victim, Hawa Foray, researchers caught eight small brownish-gray rats classified as *Mastomys natalensis*. In the Atlanta CDC labs, the Lassa fever virus was isolated from seven of those eight rats.

they came to her with the message (of her transfer) she just gave up. She said, 'I'll be all right.' She didn't want to go."

The transfer was set up for the next day, March 30th, Good Friday.

(15)

The next morning Irene Morris took a steaming bowl of cream of wheat up to the house on the hill. Esther was in bed, sleeping fitfully, her respirations labored, her face flushed, her hair stringy and damp around her face. Grace Moleyeaze and Edith Curran were already there. Ruth Bacon was there, too, wiping Esther's face with a damp cloth; she smiled shyly and moved out of the way when Irene came into the room.

Irene sat down on the bed and spoon-fed the cream of wheat into Esther's swollen mouth. Esther's eyes were dull and lifeless. She swallowed and talked with great difficulty but managed to say, "You shouldn't be taking so much trouble, Irene. Don't they need you at the hospital?"

"Shh," Irene said. "You need me as much."

Esther couldn't finish all the cereal so the other nurses finished it for her. No food was ever wasted in Loma-land.

Paul Mertens came in. "The plane will be here in a few minutes, Esther."

Esther grimaced and whispered, "I don't want to go."

"I know that. But we all think it's for the best."

"What can they do that you can't?"

"Maybe nothing."

"This isn't like what you and I had last July."

"No."

"Do you know what it is?"

"No." He took a deep breath. "We think it's Lassa fever."

Her eyes widened almost imperceptibly, then closed as she nodded just once. She remained silent and Paul took her hand. She opened her eyes and said, "I want you to take what money I have and give it to people who need it."

This was the first time that Paul was really sure that Esther knew just how serious her illness was. She closed her eyes and Paul looked up at Irene Morris. Irene nodded her head as if to say she understood what Esther meant.

Missionary pilot Eugene Le Van* in the Cessna four-seater buzzed the hospital to announce his arrival.

"Time to go, Esther," Paul said.

---

*For a fascinating and detailed look at Le Van and his work in Liberia, see Louise Faust's story in *The Lutheran*, October 12, 1966.

They helped her dress in a slightly faded shirt-waist dress. When they couldn't find the belt, Irene remembered that Esther never wore it. They put on her scuffed, sturdy, tie oxfords and she was ready.

By the time they got her things together, Le Van had landed on the grass strip a hundred yards behind Esther's house and had taxied down the road to the open-sided building which had served as its hangar when the plane was based at Zorzor.

Esther insisted on walking to the plane. Mertens walked on one side, Ruth on the other, supporting most of her weight as they moved out onto the porch. She couldn't make it. They set her down gently on the concrete steps and then eased her onto a stretcher. Four students carried her. The entire staff of the hospital, most in uniform, and seemingly the entire town, followed the stretcher like a funeral procession out to the plane.

People from the hospital and from the village lined the sides of the airstrip. Everyone could see that Esther was sick in a differerent way from what she had ever been before. They could also see that she hated every minute of this special treatment. It went against everything she had ever practiced and preached.

Franklin Keller had come with Gene Le Van. They both had gotten out and were waiting beside the plane. Carefully the students laid the stretcher on the ground in the shade of the wing. Esther opened her eyes, saw the wing, and said over and over, "Bah-oh, bah-oh, bah-oh." "No, no, no."

Keller got into the plane and with the help of several men on the ground lifted Esther bodily into the seat. She collapsed in his lap almost immediately, moaning slightly and breathing heavily. She lay on his lap for the entire trip.

At Phebe Hospital, less than a half hour later, they transferred her into the waiting Land Rover and took her immediately to a semi-private room on the medical-surgical ward all prepared for her.

Four nurses had volunteered to special Esther: Anna Mae Dukuly, a Liberian nurse-midwife who had been trained by Esther; a male nurse, who died a year later of a mysterious illness, probably not Lassa fever; Claire Knaub, a missionary nurse; and Carolyn Miller, who had roomed with Esther in Monrovia just a few weeks before. They had decided to work six-hour shifts, knowing that they had to get enough rest to keep up their own resistance.

Kirsten Jensen wanted to be included in the group specialing Esther. Her wish had been given serious consideration by the staff, but for several reasons she was turned down. They didn't want to jeopardize a nursing student with something they themselves didn't understand. If this were Lassa fever, they didn't want to expose her to it. They thought the responsibilities of nursing Esther might be too heavy for a student, even someone as mature as Kirsten. And, finally, they were aware of the strong emotional ties and weren't sure Kirsten could handle the dual role of nurse and daughter.

Before Esther arrived, and before the doctors and nurses examined her, there had been some talk that the illness was typhoid fever. The special nurses had even gotten booster doses of typhoid prophylaxis. But after Esther arrived, all the talk was of Lassa fever. One nurse was heard to say, "Uh-oh, that means that Dr. Keller and Gene Le Van were exposed, too, all the way from Zorzor."

Everyone was afraid, even the special nurses, because very little was known about the mode of transmission at that time. But they took on the task without hesitation. Carolyn Miller recalls that they all accepted the fact that they might die. Carolyn's biggest worry was her family. She knew she was doing the right thing, but would her family understand? She wrote letters to all of them (which she never sent and still has), so that "if something would happen, they would have a better understanding of why I chose to do it."

Betty Stull remembers that "her sickness was the most terrifying episode in all my years in Liberia because of the specter of death that threatened our lives and especially my fear for Jim's life because he was caring for her."

The nurses followed full isolation technique in Esther's room. A laundry hamper stood outside the door. Everyone going into the room wore a gown, rubber gloves, cloth cap and mask, which they stripped off when they came out and threw into the hamper. Everything was autoclaved before it was used again.

Within 24 hours it was obvious to Jim Stull and Franklin Keller that Esther's condition was deteriorating rapidly. She was, in short, going to die unless something else could be done. They called Dr. Robert Patton of JFK in Monrovia to see her and he agreed that Lassa fever was highly likely.

Dr. Tom Monath and Nurse Penny Pineo arrived from Nigeria with two units of convalescent plasma which were given on successive nights. It was too late in the illness to do any good but they didn't know that then. Consultation by radio with the United States embassy in Monrovia resulted in a promise to transfer Esther to New York on an Air Force jet if her condition would allow. It was hoped that the more sophisticated supportive techniques available in the United States might help.

(16)

Esther was fully conscious the first three days. She insisted on taking care of herself as much as possible. Instead of using the bed pan, she struggled to the bathroom, needing a great deal of help from the nurse on duty. They pleaded with her to let them take care of her in bed, but she refused. She had an IV going in one arm, the bottle hanging from a heavy iron standard, which made it a real struggle to move her across the room. But she didn't want to be a bother, not realizing that she was more of a bother by trying to be independent.

The bleeding tendency that had been noticed a week before, when Mertens checked her white count, was worse. A lumbar puncture, done to rule out meningitis and encephalitis, wouldn't stop bleeding. All of the injection sites bled where she got IVs, antibiotics, and parenteral (injectable) vitamins. The nurses used digital pressure, pressure dressings, and finally a collodion spray, but all were unsuccessful. She was given Vitamin K, which helps control some forms of bleeding tendencies, but nothing stopped the oozing.

It was very hot in the room. Esther lay bathed in perspiration. The nurses tried to cool her down with wet cloths, which did give her some symptomatic relief, but her fever remained very high most of the time. It seemed that she stayed dehydrated, no matter how fast they ran the IV fluids.

The nurses were uncomfortably hot, too, having to wear the heavy gowns and masks. In addition, they were all slightly feverish and headachy from the typhoid prophylaxis they had taken. But they scarcely thought of it as they watched Esther suffer. From time to time, someone came to the door with a pitcher of lemonade, limeade, or water and held it for them to drink through a straw. Sometimes they drank the entire quart down with hardly a breath.

Esther's kidney function and her blood coagulation mechanism continued to deteriorate. She began to develop subcutaneous bleeding (ecchymoses) wherever the slightest trauma occurred to her skin. Never, however, did she bleed from bladder, bowel, nose, or elsewhere.

Drs. Keller and Stull were in and out of the room all day and frequently during the night. There was precious little they could do except speak hopefully. Esther knew she was dying, and the doctors and nurses knew that she knew.

(17)

Back in Zorzor, Dave Urfer got through by ham radio to the United States and talked to Rev. Harvey Currens, who was then Assistant to the Secretary for Africa after long service in Liberia, and whose son Gerald was at that time a missionary in Wozi. Urfer told Rev. Currens of Esther's illness, and Currens immediately phoned Aunt Nora.

Nora organized prayer groups to pray for a miracle healing. Esther's last letter had not come yet, the one written on March 19th in which she said she wished she could send Nora some flowers. But Nora remembered a recent letter in which Esther had said that she would probably die young, and "there's work to be done."

In Zorzor everyone felt hopeless, useless. The Mertenses had planned to go to Monrovia for Easter, but no one felt like going. They didn't even have an Easter dinner and had to force themselves to hide eggs for the children to find.

Paul Mertens went down to see Esther. He took the news that Jetty Ziegler was back to work and Phebe Hallawanger was nearly recovered. But one of the nurses' aides, Juanita Akoi (Ah-kwee), and one of the patients, had died. Both had manifested the same uncontrollable bleeding tendencies that Esther did. From then on, there was never much hope for Esther in the hearts of the people at Phebe. Paul returned to Zorzor, shaken and sad, knowing that only a miracle would save Esther now. He confided to Donna that she had maybe thirty-six hours to live.

The entire Phebe station was subdued. The conversations, thoughts, and prayers of everyone, Liberians, missionaries, and other expatriates alike, turned constantly to Esther. People greeted each other with, "How's Esther?" Morning hospital devotions and private prayers began with, "Lord, we just want to thank you for Esther Bacon's life and ask that you spare her for us . . ."

(18)

Carolyn Miller was with Esther on Easter Sunday morning. She would miss the sunrise service, but that was all right. She was doing the Lord's work.

Daylight came, as it always did, about 6:30. There were the usual noises from the hospital as the day nurses arrived to take over from the night nurses. Bird songs drifted in the open window. The day promised to be especially hot; the rainy season was due, when temperatures climbed and rain sometimes fell for days at a time without ceasing.

Suddenly, Carolyn heard a sweet young voice just outside the window singing, "Christ the Lord is risen today." She sat quietly until the song was over and then went to the window. Sitting cross-legged on the concrete patio was Kirsten Jensen.

Carolyn sat on the bed beside Esther and took her hand. "Do you hear her, Esther? It's Easter."

Now Kirsten sang, "O, for a thousand tongues to sing my great redeemer's praise," and "All hail the power of Jesus' name, let angels prostrate fall," and "Crown him with many crowns, the Lamb upon His throne," song after song, all the hopeful songs of Easter and the resurrection, her way of telling Esther that she was thinking of her.

Then when Kirsten was gone, Carolyn talked to Esther about the hopeful message of Easter. Esther seemed to hear and understand, nodding her head from time to time, though her swollen lips and tongue made it too painful to talk.

Esther Bacon lived for two more days.

Then she died, at 11:15 on the morning of April 4, 1972.

(19)

The nurses who cared for her for five days wrapped her in cloths and then placed her in a plastic bag. They laid her in a simple wooden coffin made by the hospital carpenters and then placed her in the back of a jeep pickup truck. Loving hands pulled palm fronds from the trees and tied them all around the bed of the jeep to shield her coffin from the eyes of the world.

Missionary pharmacist Neal Solvig and Carolyn Miller climbed into the truck and led a small caravan of cars and trucks out through the gates to the main road. They drove slowly down the road toward Gbarnga, made the sharp left turn to follow the dusty, red dirt road to Zorzor. They passed through Wenshu, Belefani, across the new St. Paul River bridge, through Ganglota, Gorlu, Telimu, Salayea, Telemee, Sukolomu, and finally through Zorzor to the Curran Memorial Hospital where Esther had worked for thirty-one years.

While the truck was en route, the Phebe radioman notified Dave Urfer that Esther had died.

Margaret Urfer went down to the hospital and told Paul Mertens. Mertens went looking for Jeanette Isaacson to tell her. Jeanette nodded numbly, not fully comprehending what he had said. But she went looking for Irene Morris, first on the OB ward, then in the OPD. When she said, "Bacon died," Irene had no trouble comprehending what had happened. She started wailing, Loma fashion, and it finally hit home with Jeanette.

The word spread quickly throughout the hospital and into the town. Pewu and Grace Moleyeaze came immediately and sought out Paul and the nurses. At Grace's suggestion they decided to dig the grave on the hillside just outside the OB ward so that the people working there could look out and be inspired by Esther Bacon even after death.

Pewu organized the digging but it was no problem finding willing hands. He had never seen such crowds pouring out of the town. Jeanette remembers, too, that "no man turned more than one shovel of dirt that day. All the Mandingo men — Muslims who wouldn't normally be there for a Christian burial — came and dug that grave. They passed the shovel around."

They wouldn't be able to wrap Esther in woven country mats as she had wanted, but to fulfill her wishes as closely as possible they lined the grave with mats.

Then they waited. It was very quiet. Some were crying softly. Hospital people came and went. Deanna remembers that "if you had to go do something, you did it and then came back to the porch to be with each other."

Margaret Miller made a very insightful observation. She said softly, "Nobody is saying, 'No min yah.' Why is nobody saying, 'No min yah.'?" (Translated literally, means "never mind," but in a Liberian setting means, "I'm sorry," an expression of sympathy, or apology.) When she asked this, Jeanette realized it was true, nobody said it. Why? "Because *who* do you say it *to*? When *everybody is hurting*."

One of the patients who had been ill with Lassa fever, and who was recovering from it, sat on the sidewalk outside the ward and watched the gravediggers work. When they were through she got up without a word and went back into the hospital.

(20)

Bishop Payne was in Monrovia at an Executive Council meeting. The morning session had just ended and he was in his room waiting for lunchtime. The phone rang.

"Bishop Payne?"

"Yeah."

"I'm sorry."

"For what?"

"Esther is dead."

Unbelieving, he exclaimed, "What?!!"

He had known she was very ill at Phebe, but the news that she was dead struck him so hard that he had to sit down. He finally said to the caller, "Get the plane. I must go up."

He landed on the grass strip at Zorzor just as the pickup truck arrived at the grave site. His handsome face twisted in grief, he climbed out quickly and walked down the sloping lawn to join Reverend Paul Swedberg at the grave. They conferred in hushed tones for just a few moments and then were ready.

The coffin was carefully pulled out of the truck by Phebe hospital workers wearing rubber gloves and masks. They lowered the coffin gently into the grave with ropes, but there came a point where they had to let it drop. It was too much. Choked-back tears, smothered emotions, and swallowed wails, all let loose in a torrent. Jeanette remembers, "Everyone just started crying and wailing. We had been crying and then we got it together again, but we all fell apart at that point. *Too* heavy. And then they had scripture and prayers but I don't remember what people said."

Deanna recalls a similar blankness. "There was a prayer — but I don't remember it — I was right there but I don't remember what was said or what was done."

The workers tossed their gloves and masks on top of the coffin and stepped back.

About fifty Liberian and missionary staff from Zorzor and Phebe had gathered with other expatriates who had heard the radio transmission between Phebe and Zorzor, and who were close enough to get there in time. It was imperative that Esther be buried right away because of the nature of the disease and the tropical heat.

The sun was going down as Rev. Swedberg and Bishop Payne led the prayers for the dead. The violent emotions of a few moments before had subsided. The medical personnel of both hospitals were drained physically and spiritually. Tears came easily. Irene Morris, who with Jeanette Isaacson had taken over Esther's duties, recalls that "everybody, everybody — there was no one got in this area who didn't cry." Even fourteen years later Carolyn Miller stumbled as she tried to describe the scene: "We just took, took the, took the truck, backed the truck up near where the grave site was dug..."

As darkness fell, the chug-chug-chug of the hospital generator rumbled from the rice paddies down the hill on the road to the mission houses in the forest. Lights winked on in the hospital. The usual night sounds of insects, frogs and night birds filled the air. The wind died and the humid air lay heavy on the earth.

Everybody at that graveside had memories of Esther Bacon.

Roland Payne remembered the attractive young woman who had arrived from the cornbelt of Iowa and had challenged the power of the zoes, the diviners, and the magicians who were at the zenith of their power in Loma-Kpelle-land. He remembered how she had turned the Church upside down for the good of everyone. He had called her "an Outlaw for God."

Pewu Moleyeaze remembered how, in her very first term, she had broken down the barriers of mistrust with values his people could appreciate and understand. He remembered with a wrench those early years when in the simmering dawn of a new day she rode off fresh and clean, only to return days later, tired and soiled, leading the horse with a patient clinging to its back. He remembered the times he had lighted her way through the jungle with a blazing bamboo torch, leading the horse, or perhaps carrying a newborn baby.

Grace Moleyeaze remembered Esther as a sister, as a member of the family. She remembered the times she had called Esther across town with a fake illness just to get Esther to relax and rest for ten minutes. She remembered how Esther would sleep with her shoes on so she wouldn't waste time getting to the hospital.

Jeanette Isaacson pondered that all the missionaries, including herself, had hurt Esther by not understanding her. She had loved Esther, had fought with her, had envied her, had first resented and then accepted that she could not emulate her, but she had never understood her.

Edith Curran remembered how Esther had once told her that she could do anything a two-legged person could do. Now she felt that Esther had left somebody with her: God. She knew that until this world is ended, no one would forget Esther Bacon.

Deanna Isaacson did not doubt for a moment that Esther was a saint. Through her tears she tried to smile because she knew as well as anyone that it's not always easy to live with saints. Esther was less concerned for self, was more for others, than anyone Deanna had ever known.

Paul Mertens remembered with an aching heart all the times he and Esther had played the game and she had won. He would, perhaps, miss her most of all when in the dark of the night he battled for the life of a new mother or a newborn babe and could no longer turn and see Esther standing beside him with her skill, her compassion, and her love. (Later that night, as he came back from the hospital, he would see the Southern Cross at the meridian, and would always remember it as the symbol of God's love on the night that Esther died.)

Lilliana Bartolomei, who had been teaching in the high school at Salayea all these years, had two conflicting thoughts. First she wondered why a nurse so talented and so loving should die so young. Then immediately came a second thought: perhaps Esther had done what God had wanted her to do. Now it was time for others to remember what Esther had taught them, to take hold of her work and make it go forward.

Donna Mertens remembered how Esther had always been the happy one among them, never complaining, always looking at the silver lining around the dark clouds.

Dave Urfer had no doubt that they were cleaning out a special room in Heaven that day.

Bob Dettmer, one of the Peace Corps Volunteers, remembered Esther as one of the people who made Curran Memorial a ''pure hospital,'' a hospital that did its job undiverted from its purpose by extraneous influences. He remembered the many times he had given blood when Esther sent for him, and how once she had made a special trip into town the next day to thank him for coming, even though the patient had died.

Margaret Miller remembered the times she had seen Esther fight for the life of a patient, never giving up, always going on. Many times she had seen the clear flame — not a flickering flame — of commitment and devotion, a care that was *real*. She remembered the many times Esther had walked the twelve miles from Zorzor to Wozi and then fell asleep at the dinner table. She remembered most of all the compassion with which Esther accepted the motherless babies and the deformed children as if they were her own.

Ruth Bacon remembered the love Esther had lavished on her when what she needed most was love.

Irene Morris remembered with awe-ful clarity the night, nine months before, when she had been in the Operating Room with Esther and Paul Mertens doing a Cesarean section. Word had come of President Tubman's funeral. Esther had said, "I don't want to be buried like that. I don't even want a coffin. I want to be wrapped in woven country mats. And when I die, I want to be buried at night." Then, "In Zorzor."

So three of her four wishes were granted. Her coffin was wrapped in woven country mats. She was buried at night. In Zorzor.

And a lady passing by was heard to say, "Oh, Esther, Esther, Esther."

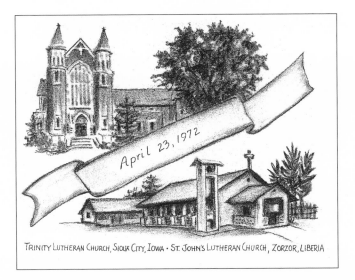

Chapter Ten

Tributes and Epilogue

TRIBUTES

The death of Esther Bacon was mourned throughout Liberia. Never before, and never since, has that country given an expatriate such a show of love, reverence and the clear indication that it would feel her loss.

The Lutheran Church responded quickly with two memorial services. The first was held on April 16th in St. Peter's Lutheran Church in Monrovia, led by Bishop Roland Payne. The second was held on April 23rd in St. John's Lutheran Church in Zorzor, jointly led by Pastors James Vankpana, Peter Giddings, Ronald Diggs, Henry Dugulu, and Joseph Diggs, with Bishop Payne delivering the eulogy.

Also on April 23rd, a thanksgiving and memorial service was held in Trinity Lutheran Church in Sioux City, Iowa.

At the second service, in Zorzor, tributes were given personally by many people, representing government, missionaries, staff, and friends. Others sent their tributes by letter.

Excerpts from these show clearly the thoughts that went through the minds of her friends as they began to absorb the fact that Esther Bacon was dead.

The Right Reverend Roland Payne, Bishop of the Lutheran Church in Liberia: One of the great truths Esther discovered in her life, which made her the great saint she was, was the statement of Jesus when He said, "The Kingdom of God is within you." Esther took that literally and believed in it with her whole personality. And right she was! By her discovery of this great truth, she discovered the meaning of her life. Esther felt the indwelling Christ in her personality; that is why she was never afraid of death.

They came and went; but she remained. Many people live long, useless lives. They never contriute anything to life. The Bible said Methuselah lived 969 years and died. The only thing he ever did was to beget sons and daughters. He simply added years to his life. Esther lived 56 years and added more life to her years. To me, she lived longer than Methuselah.

Is Esther Bacon really dead? Physically, yes. Spiritually and personality-wise, no! I tell you the supreme truth: personality never dies.

No, Esther is not dead as long as Loma and Kpelle women have their babies in the hospital. No, Esther is not dead as long as her revolutionary attitudes in prenatal care remain with us and we are putting them to use.

No, Esther is not dead. For the Bible tells us: "They that wait upon the Lord shall renew their strength; they shall mount up with wings as eagles; they shall run and not be weary; they shall walk and not faint." (Isaiah 40:31.)

Looking back over the many years of Esther's sacrificial work in the name of Christ, and the countless lives she saved, I, too, can say with conviction, "Truly she was a daughter of God."

Farewell, dear Esther! The rest is silence. May the flight of angels guide you to your eternal rest to meet your Pilot face to face.

The Honorable Henry B. Fahnbulleh, Assistant Minister of State for Presidential Affairs: For us in Liberia, Miss Bacon was "our lady of the lamp," the Florence Nightingale of Zorzor. The lamp she carried has come to mean care for the sick, regard for the welfare of the ordinary men and women. She did not forget her purpose — service to God and those she loved, the men and women of Liberia. In the midst of unpleasant and disreputable conditions, she carried on her life's mission without criticism, without grumble and without blaming others. Whenever saintly nurses are commemorated in Liberia, we shall remember Miss Esther Bacon as our Florence Nightingale.

David L. Gamon, Counselor, American Embassy, Monrovia, Liberia: I think Esther's success was due to three important factors, among others. She was a pioneer. She was a serious-minded professional. She was a woman who was guided by a deep sense of the spiritual aspects of her mission.

In thinking of her I have mixed emotions of pride, humility and thankfulness that she was a fellow American. I trust that you Liberians have the same sentiments when you consider that your country became her adopted one.

In addition, Esther was a member of a wider, deeper kingdom, citizenship which is based on the brotherhood of man.

Pastor Al Swingle, President, Association of Lutheran Missionaries in Liberia: Esther poured out all that she has and all that she is, and having emptied herself, she now hears the words of her Father: ''Come, receive the heavenly kingdom prepared for you.''

Dr. James Stull: I will remember Bacon in four way: She was a genius. She was tenacious. She was always there. She was simple — simply Bacon.

Dr. Earl Reber: She is irreplacable. The people in the Zorzor area have lost their most loving, most devoted and sincerest friend. I have seen about Liberia those who have given much to its people, but there has never been one who gave as much as did Esther Bacon.

Rev. Ben L. Byepu, Sr.: Esther was truly a universal medical mother. This death she has faced will affect Liberia and Guinea. It is going to affect our wives and children. It is going to affect the fatherless and motherless children. It will affect both the young and the aged.

Edith Curran: The people from Guinea, the people from Kpaiye, the people from *all over*, they came to Curran Hospital. They came because of Esther Bacon. Her treatments became like you know how if you break a bottle of perfume it just spreads all over the world, that's how this hospital was.

Rev. Joseph C. Wold: Esther Bacon has laid down her life for others, night and day she laid down her life for others. We who knew Esther Bacon had a rare and great privilege — we have seen with our own eyes a person who actually followed the example of Christ — a person who thought of others more than she thought of herself. It was easier for me to believe in the mercy and goodness of God, having seen his mercy at work in the life of Esther Bacon. She never considered a person's station — whether the person was a poor illiterate girl with no husband, having her first baby, or a fellow missionary and co-worker, or an important official of government, Esther Bacon always laid down her life for anyone who needed her care. A person could believe that God never sleeps if he saw his servant Esther Bacon going days without sleep to care for a serious patient around the clock. We who knew Esther Bacon have seen a person lay down her life. We know it is possible to be selfless. Her death can only cause us to examine our own life. If we ever think we are serving others, let us remember her service. If we ever think we are giving up something, making sacrifices for others, let us remember Esther Bacon.

Dr. Ellen Moore Hopkins (on behalf of the Officers and Members of the Liberian Midwives Council): As Sisters of the Royal Blue, we are honored to accept Esther's lantern. Esther lives!

She lives in the arms of hundreds of women to whom she has bravely said, "Take this child and nurse it."

She lives in the hearts of boys and girls for whom she spent hours to nurse, money to educate, and love to share.

She lives through the hills, mountains, bushes and streets of Loma country. She lives through the smokey huts of Zorzor, the village streets of her towns.

Fellow Sisters, she lives. She lives. Esther lives on in our hearts. She lives! Since her lantern is now ours to use and pass on to posterity, we hereby do bravely accept the challenge and let her live on! She lives.

Dr. Joseph Baum: When asked to describe Esther Bacon I feel like Thomas Aquinas trying to pour the ocean into a hole in the sand. Courage certainly was Esther's strongest attribute. She faced angry natives, dying babies, and critical missionary peers with such fervent dedication as to rattle the most rational.

Bonded to this great courage was a coolness of attitude which made great frustrations nothing more than another job that must be done. And to be done meant at the earliest opportunity, not at the next appointed time. To this end, days ran into nights and days of the week lost their meaning.

Blessed with unusually strong stamina, Esther was able to display her dedication seemingly without end.

When I think of what Esther has taught me I think not of tropical medicine but of personal sacrifice and humility. And when the need rises up in me to give back some of what I have learned I think not of buildings and numbers but of returning to nature's pool some of the same courage and compassion she gave to me.

Dr. Paul Mertens: Sometimes with brilliance, more often with faith and stubbornness, Esther Bacon worked among us until 4 April, 1972, always on hand, always making sure that things with the patient were going all right.

Rev. Henry Dugulu (first Loma pastor): The best thing about Bacon? There was nothing wrong. She helped everyone.

Norma Bloomquist Brookhart: The legend of Esther Bacon — true, incredible, prodigious — will not end with her death. It will not end, for she taught patiently, persistently, carefully, simply the people she left behind. The town of Zorzor was her home for more than thirty years. It is the place where her body rests and her spirit lives.

John Gay (author of *Red Dust on the Green Leaves*, in a letter to Nora Leander): Esther has joined the saints with God in heaven, of that I am sure. This is a triumphant and glorious time for her, and for those of us who knew her. She did not die slowly and painfully, or live out the last years of her life in retirement. She died quickly and easily at the height of a beautiful life. We can only give thanks for her life, and for her death, and pray that we too may be found worthy and willing to give our lives for others.

Rev. Louis and Virginia Bowers: We know the whole Loma country will miss her. But what she did, especially for expectant mothers, cannot be easily lost. She will be personally missed, but her work will live on and on to the comfort and health of hundreds and thousands. And may they give the final praise to our Lord Jesus. That is how Esther lived, that the Lord might be praised. Kpirai eee?

Loma elder: Bayka loved us more than we loved each other.

The penultimate tribute: a monument.

There was no question that Esther should be memorialized in some appropriate manner. Discussions went on at various levels for months. Some Loma and Kpelle people wanted to erect a statue of her somewhere on the Curran Hospital grounds. The idea was given some consideration, but eventually voted down. Knowing that animism and ancestor worship were still very much a part of the culture, and knowing the awe and reverence in which many people held Esther, church leaders were afraid that a statue might become a shrine to which people would come and worship.

The fact that Esther had been slated for the William V. S. Tubman Achievement Award offered a solution: a small monument over her grave with the citation on it. Stones from every county were lovingly brought and formed into a cairn on a concrete slab covering Esther's grave. A bronze placque was cast and placed on the cairn. It reads:

TO THE LOVING MEMORY OF
ESTHER ELEANOR BACON

R.N., B.Sc., M.P.H., MIDWIFE, NURSE, TRUE SERVANT OF MERCY

For more than thirty years of outstanding health service rendered to the people of the Republic of Liberia,
For the love and devotion that have changed fear and suspicion of the tribal people to confidence and trust,
For countless nights spent watching at the bedside of patients,
For spending her own money to buy medicine and equipment for the sick poor,
For feeding and clothing and housing patients,
For riding out on horseback to far flung villages to help women in childbirth,
For helping to train outstanding nurses and midwives,
For doing everything that has made the name "Bacon" a synonym for service in Lofa and Bong Counties,
This plaque is dedicated to her loving memory by her Liberian friends for whom she gave everything, even her very life.

This citation was also cast in bronze on a small plaque which today hangs in the office of the director of the School of Nursing. The school itself was renamed the Esther Bacon School of Midwifery and Practical Nursing. Trinity Lutheran Church in Sioux City established a Birthday and Memorial Fund. A church in Monrovia was named after her. A school in Monrovia, originally started as a night school by Loma teachers and now part of the Consolidated School System, was named The Esther Bacon School. Countless articles, stories, essays, sermons, and other references to the life of Esther Bacon have appeared from the time of her death even to now.

The last tribute, but confidently not the least, is this story of Esther's life, the author's tribute to Esther Bacon.

EPILOGUE

Donna Mertens took on the responsibility of cleaning out Esther's rooms. There was very little of monetary value. There was much of sentimental value. Except for her watch, Donna felt that it was appropriate to let people just take things as mementos. Jeanette Isaacson, for example, took a blue serving bowl.

Esther's watch, given her by Trinity Lutheran just a few years before, was entrusted to the Urfers to take to Nora Leander. They left it off in Hawarden on their way to Montana.

Nora Leander was now 85 years old. Her two brothers and their wives, her three sisters and their husbands, were all dead. Her health was failing slowly, though she would not die for another four years. She wanted Ruth Schuldt, long-time secretary at Trinity, to have the watch. Ruth thought Ken Carlson should have it, but Ken insisted that she keep it.

Ruth still has the watch. She says, "I've felt so privileged receiving this watch, but do feel it should go back to Trinity." She treasures it as one of the few items left on this earth that once belonged to Esther Bacon.

But Ruth knows, as do thousands and thousands of others, that Esther Bacon left a much more precious legacy that cannot be calculated in dollars, weighed in pounds, measured in inches, placed in a safe box, hung in a closet, or parked in a garage.

In the kitchen cupboard, stuck loosely in Esther's Bible, Donna Mertens found a poem written by Esther in the fairly recent past. Many people have read it now.

Irene Morris: "It's about her life, about her *life!*" Then she adds, almost apologetically, "She didn't seem to be herself when she wrote that poem." Irene thinks she wrote it very shortly before she got sick.

Jeanette Isaacson Kpissay: "It refers to people not understanding her and the pain. Sort of a paraphrase of scripture."

Grace Monson: "It's a very African sort of poem — paranoid, gloomy...an African would understand it."

DEAR GOD, RESPOND TO YOUR SERVANT
IN DISTRESS MAKE SOON IN YOUR LOVING
GRACE FOR A DISCIPLE IN DESPAIR
HASTEN TO THE PAINFUL AGONIES OF A
CHILD WHO IS DEPRESSED AND UNHAPPY.

O YE PEOPLE AROUND ME
YOU WHOM I THOUGHT WERE MY FRIENDS,
WHY DO YOU KEEP HACKING AT ME?
GLOATING OVER MY ERRORS
REJOICING AT MY FAILURE
ALWAYS LOOKING FOR THE VERY WORST IN ME
I MUST REMEMBER THAT I TRULY DO BELONG TO GOD
THAT HE DOES FEEL FOR ME WHEN I HURT.

Chapter Eleven

(Brief history of the country of Liberia, the Lutheran Church in Liberia, and Lutheran medical work in Liberia, up to 1941 when Esther Bacon arrived.)

(1)

According to the Encyclopedia Britannica, awareness of West Africa began with the reports of Necho II, the Egyptian pharaoh who sent a Phoenician fleet around the coast of Africa in 600 B.C. But it would be almost two thousand years before Europeans became interested in the "Grain Coast" — short for "grains of paradise" coast — so-called because it was the source of Melegueta, or Guinea, pepper, *Xylopia aethiopica*, then as valuable as gold. The French established settlements between 1364 and 1413 where Buchanan and Greenville now stand, that is, the middle third of the coast of present-day Liberia.

In 1461 the Portuguese named Cape Mesurado where Monrovia is situated, as well as Cape Mount and Cape Palmas. In 1663 the British built two trading posts at Mesurado and Grand Sesters, only to have them destroyed a year later by the Dutch.

The origin of the sixteen major indigenous tribes of Liberia is not well known. But what is known is of great importance: the central and coastal tribes were already well established in the early 19th century when inbound immigration of former slaves began. The northern-most tribes probably spread south 100-150 years ago across the mountains of what is now Sierra Leone and Guinea. Linguistically they form three groups: the Mande, Kru, and Atlantic. Both the Kpelle and Loma tribes are from the Mande-fu branch of the Mande, the Mandingoes (a Muslim tribe) from the Mande-tan branch.

The modern history of Liberia really began in 1816 when local African chiefs granted the American Colonization Society possession of Cape Mesurado. The first freed slaves from the Americas landed there in 1822, but before they found a place to settle, twenty-two of the blacks and all of the accompanying whites were dead of disease. The survivors paid $300 for a strip of land measuring 140 by 40 miles.

They were followed shortly by Jehudi Ashmun, a white American, who became the real founder of Liberia. In 1824 he was joined by Ralph Randolph Gurley, who suggested the names Liberia (for "freedom"), and Monrovia (for James Monroe). When Ashmun left in 1828, the territory had the beginnings of a government and an economy.

Thousands of New World blacks followed these pioneers until the end of the Civil War in 1865. Of the 4,456 blacks who immigrated between 1822 and 1840, 2,198 died of malaria, dysentery and yellow fever.

One of those who came and survived was a free-born octoroon from Virginia by the name of Joseph Jenkins Roberts. He rose quickly to leadership of the colony, proclaimed it an independent republic in 1847 and drew up a constitution based on that of the United States. Liberia
therefore became the first republic in black Africa — by about a hundred years — and the only black African state never subjected to white colonial rule. Roberts was named the first president.

The immigrants remained on the coast and were known as the "Congo People," or Americo-Liberians, in contra-distinction to the "Native-born People." In about 1856 they formed the True Whig party, which according to the Encyclopedia Britannica distrusted Europeans and sought development on national lines. Frontier disputes with the French and English went on until treaties with those countries were drawn up in the last decade of the century. In 1919 another treaty gave France 2,000 square miles of hinterland that Liberia could not control.

Political power remained chiefly in the hands of the descendants of the "Congo People." (This "Establishment" would continue until April 12, 1980, when President William R. Tolbert was executed after a coup by the People's Redemption Council under the leadership of Master Sergeant

CHRISTIAN GLOBAL CONCERNS 1994

OUTLAW FOR GOD

Margie Williams   94
Margaret Eaton   94
Edie Maley   94

Emma Saeger - 3-26-95
Dorothy Reed   12-26-95

Samuel K. Doe. The 133-year-old constitution was suspended. Mr. Doe would remain in charge until the civil war of 1990-91 when he would be deposed and killed.)

Firestone Tire and Rubber Company received a concession of a million acres of land in 1926 and began a business which to this day remains one of the keystones of Liberian economy. At the same time, a private U.S. loan of $5,000,000 stabilized the government.

Sizable reserves of rich iron ore — ranging up to 70% iron in the far-north Nimba range — were found. At least half the land was suitable for cultivation of rubber, hardwood timber, rice, cassava, coffee, kola nuts, palm oil, palm kernels, sugarcane, peanuts, and cotton.

Roads were virtually non-existent except along the coast so political authority extended inland for only about twenty miles. Though there had been some attempts to integrate the native-born tribes into the system, those peoples remained aloof. The wedge between the Congo People and the Native-born People was driven deeper by the scandal of 1931: a claim that native-born tribesmen were being shanghaied to Spanish plantations in Fernando Po proved true and resulted in the resignation of President King and Vice-President Yancy, and the election of Edwin Barclay.

So this was Liberia as Esther Bacon saw it in 1941. But in just a few years Esther would see dramatic changes. At the onset of World War II, Liberia's rubber plantations would be the only source of natural rubber except for the plantations in Ceylon (now Sri Lanka). Robertsfield, named for Liberia's first president, would be converted to an international airport. Strategic road building would begin. Within twenty years the economy would expand fifty-fold. Many factors would be at work, not the least of which would be the leadership of President Tubman (see Chapter Five, Part 1).

(2)

The Lutheran Church had its beginnings in Liberia in 1860 when Rev. Morris Officer founded Muhlenburg Station at Harrisburg. His first major project was to build a school. The tribal elders ordered a boycott and no students came. Officer's cause was not aided when word got out that he had said of the local Golah language: "A hoarse gutteral lingo which can never be acquired by white men and which is totally inadequate for the conveyance of moral or religious truth."

He finally got twenty boys and twenty girls, all orphans, from a slave ship captured in the Congo River by an American man-of-war and brought to Liberia for release.

Dr. Joseph Wold, writing in *God's Impatience in Liberia*, describes three problems faced by the early Lutheran missionaries. First, for many years the Muhlenburg School continued to produce only a small number of young Christians. Even when the tribal elders later relented, graduating students — almost without exception — went down river and dispersed in the Americo-Liberian coastal settlements among mostly non-Christian people. Some joined already established Methodist, Baptist and Presbyterian community churches. No local Lutheran churches were started.

Secondly, few missionaries went out in the early years. For one five year period there were none at all. Of the first twenty-two who went out, nine died and the others left after one or two years. Dr. David Day was an exception; his story has been sketched in Chapter 1, Part 1. After sixty-two years, up to 1922, there were only 192 baptized Lutherans in Liberia.

Thirdly, mission work was limited to the coastal settlements, partly because there was indeed a need there and partly because there were no roads into the interior. But the fields inland were even more ripe for the harvest. And no one went.

It is generally recognized now that one of the reasons the early missionaries failed to establish a significant beachhead was that they equated Christianity with Western culture. Strong, godly, fearless, and ready for martyrdom, their failure to understand or appreciate the inherent value of the indigenous cultures made them rigid and often pharisaical. Their vision alternated between myopia and tunnel-vision. Bishop Roland Payne describes a Church disarticulated into many segments, none of whom could worship with each other. The disciplines of the Sunday service and Wednesday prayer meeting, and the emphasis on the church building, often overshadowed the preaching of the gospel.

And to tell Esther Bacon's story, it is not necessary to dwell on that, neither flagellate the early missionaries, nor apologize for them. They did what they thought right, and against great odds they *did* plant the church. Indeed, Bishop Payne says, "Long before employers or governments were concerned with the Africans as anything more than servants, missionaries were concerned with the minds and souls of Africans, building schools and establishing churches, and helping the Africans to discover themselves as persons."

Lutheran work began to expand in 1908 when the central government established effective control over the interior, making it safe for missionaries to travel. Four more stations were developed in the St. Paul River Valley, all in Kpelle and Loma tribal lands, spanning the country from the coast to the mountainous border with French West Africa: Kpolopele (Po'-lo-pel'-eh) in 1908, Sanoyea (Sahn'-uh-yay) in 1917, Zorzor (Zaw-zaw') in 1923, and Belefani (Bell-uh-fun-ai') in 1932.

The pattern, as at Muhlenburg, was to build a school and develop the church from a nucleus of graduated students and English-speaking employees of the mission. Missionaries rarely visited the villagers to give them the chance to become Christian. Not much had changed since Morris Officer filled his school with slave-ship orphans.*

These student converts quickly dissociated themselves from their village origins by virtue of their new religion and their new culture. Most refused to go back to the tribal life and tried to find jobs in the towns. Some went on to higher education, sponsored privately by missionaries and mission scholarship funds.

For Lutherans in Liberia, the change began in 1927. In the village of Sanoyea, half way between Muhlenburg and Zorzor, Rev. David Dagel baptized Somo Yakbors, the first convert to Christianity who hadn't been a schoolboy or a mission employee. Rev. Dagel continued to make the rounds of the villages, teaching and preaching the gospel of Jesus Christ. Pastor Dagel's iconoclastic work was continued by Rev. Louis Bowers at Sanoyea; in 1939 he reported baptizing thirty people in Kpolopele and fourteen in Parakwele on one trip.

Dr. Wold tells one benchmark story that illustrates what was beginning to happen in Kpelle-land. ''When (Rev. Louis) Bowers went across the St. Paul River to Parakwele in answer to the call of the evangelist there, he found fourteen men ready for baptism. The whole town turned out to see the service. When the time came for the baptisms, the zo stood up and declared, 'I forbid these men to be baptized.' Then, turning to the men, he announced, 'If you let this man baptize you, you will be dead by this time tomorrow.' The men were surprised, and Bowers told them it was up to them. 'You know Christ,' he said. They went outside and had a meeting to decide. After five minutes they came back and said, 'Baptize us. If we die, we will be with Jesus.' When the service was over the zo came to Bowers secretly and said, 'Tell me about this Jesus. His power is greater than mine.' ''

This story illustrates graphically that unschooled villagers could grasp the strength of the Gospel and stand up against the zoes. It showed also the value of native evangelists: they could speak the language, live in the native houses, eat the food, drink the water; most importantly they could answer the questions of the villagers in terms of their own culture.

Louise Faust, a registered nurse married to Rev. Harold Faust, missionaries to the Barabaig Tribe in the Rift Valley of Tanzania, calls this the

---

*Author's note: this was not a *Lutheran* phenomenon. For example, my father, a Methodist missionary in India in the '20s, had as his primary responsibility a boys' school. He preached in Tamil once a month in a city church a mile from his compound.

beginning of "a whole new theory of going and getting the headman, getting the natural leaders in the community and teaching them about the Christian faith."

This pattern was to continue as the Lutheran Church expanded in the interior. In 1947 the Evangelical Lutheran Church in Liberia would be organized under the leadership of Dr. Luther Slifer, sent specifically to perform this task. Increasing literacy spurred by Welmers' Kpelle grammar and Sadler's Loma grammar would help. In 1949 the parishioners at Toteta would begin to sing hymns in their own language to their own native tunes. Gradually the other churches followed suit.

It was into this awakening church that Esther Bacon brought her dedication and her own ideas as to what Christianity was all about. She would not always agree with her church's policies. Bishop Payne says, "From the time of her arrival in Liberia to the time of her death, life was never the same for the Lutheran Church in Liberia. She turned the church upside down for the good of us all." In fact, he often called her, lovingly, an "outlaw."

(3)

The development of Lutheran medical work in Liberia was very slow. In 1888 Rev. E.M. Hubler, who had had six months of medical training, arrived at Muhlenburg, but he died within a year. Dr. Augustus Pohlman arrived in 1896 and worked for six years. From 1902 to 1919, the Lutheran Mission had no doctor, but medical work was carried on by three nurses: Sister Gertrude Temps (1912-14), Sister Laura Gilliland (1915-40), and Sister Jennie Larmouth (1918-27).

When Dr. Charles Nielsen arrived in 1919, Phebe Hospital was under construction. Meanwhile Nielson turned the old one-room chapel on the boy's school compound into a temporary hospital, which he called Day Hospital, presumably after Rev. David Alexander Day.

Phebe Hospital opened in 1921 with the first nurses' training school in Liberia, under the direction of Sister Ruth Robeson. A Medical Assistants Training Course was soon added.

Also in 1921 dispensaries at Kpolopele and Sanoyea were begun. Phebe Hospital's second story was completed in 1926, giving it 34 beds.

A small medical clinic was opened in Zorzor in 1924. This was expanded in 1926 when Dr. Worrall from Phebe went up to Zorzor to open a hospital. He named it the John B. Franke Hospital in honor of Mr. Franke of Ft. Wayne, Indiana, who had endowed it. His head builder was Oldman Kpadeba Pewu of Zolowo. (Oldman was still alive in 1974 and on the 50th anniversary of medical work in Zorzor shared his memories of those days.) This was the hospital near the cemetery that burned down in 1934. But Worrall did not live in Zorzor and made infrequent visits for two years until Dr. Erwing Lape arrived there in 1928.

John B Franke Hospital Zorzor 1926

Dr. Lape arrived in 1928 to set up the first clinic with a permanent physician. He had been an army aviator during World War I and hoped to bring a plane to Zorzor. He had been promised one by Mr. Franke. Soon he realized that there were too few patients to make a plane practical.

Following Dr. Lape came Drs. Jacob Jensen and George Guelk, about which very little is known.

Dr. Norman Sloan arrived in 1934 and made the first important breakthrough in treatment. On the shelves in the drug room he found a cache of bismuth subgallate which someone had ordered but no one had ever used. He knew what it was for — yaws — but didn't know how to put the almost insoluble substance into injectable form. An assistant told him that an old German doctor in Bolahun knew the secret. Sloan made the two hundred mile return trip by footpath and found that the old man did indeed know. Sloan returned to Zorzor and persuaded a few mission workers to take the injections. Magically their lesions melted away. The news spread rapidly.

Dr. "Skipper" Moore's work from 1937 through 1941 broke through the barriers of resistance of some of the *men*, especially of the neighboring Belle people, when he successfully operated on their Paramount Chief's huge inguino-scrotal hernia. The goodwill Moore developed opened the door a crack for a *woman*, Esther Bacon, when he had to leave.

It was to this hospital, awakening yet still so far from realizing its potential, that Esther came in 1941 with her skills, her energy, her tenacity — and her love.

SOME OF THE PEOPLE IN ESTHER'S LIFE

Anderson, Lucille. Member of Mabel Dysinger's Circle, Trinity Lutheran Church, Sioux City, Iowa.
Bacon, Alva. Esther's father.
Bacon, Anna (Leander). Esther's mother.
Bacon, Ruth. Esther's "adopted" Liberian daughter.
Bartolomei, Lilliana ("Lana"). Missionary teacher, Zorzor, Salayea.
Baum, Dr. Joseph. Short-term missionary doctor, at Zorzor at the time of Esther's final illness.
Biederbeck, Hazel, RN. Missionary nurse, Zorzor, Phebe.
Bowers, Rev. Louis. Missionary pastor at Toteta during most of Esther's time at Zorzor.

Bloomquist, Norma. See Brookhart.

Brookhart, Norma (Bloomquist). Missionary teacher, Muhlenburg, later Director of Literacy Campaign.

Brouse, Fran, RN. Missionary nurse, Zorzor, Phebe.

Bunger, Marianna, RN. Missionary nurse, Zorzor.

Buschman, Gertrude. Missionary Bible woman, Zorzor.

Carlson, Charles. Esther's uncle, husband of Lizzie Leander.

Carlson, Eleanor. Esther's cousin, daughter of Charles Carlson.

Carlson, Ken. Esther's cousin, son of Charles Carlson.

Carlson, Jean. Ken's wife.

Carlson, Lizzie (Leander). Esther's aunt, wife of Charles.

Carlson, Ruth. Esther's cousin, daughter of Charles Carlson.

Curran, Edith, RN. Liberian nurse, close friend of Esther's.

Currens, Rev. Gerry. Missionary pastor, son of Harvey Currens.

Currens, Rev. Harvey. Missionary pastor, then Assistant to Secretary for Africa in Board of Missions in New York.

Dettmer, Robert. Peace Corps Volunteer, Zorzor.

Dietz, Alice, RN. Missionary nurse, Zorzor, Phebe.

Dukuly, Anna Mae, RN. Liberian nurse-midwife, who specialized Esther during her final illness.

Emerick, Ethel. Missionary teacher, Muhlenburg, Zorzor.

Faust, Alberta (Holtzinger), RN. Missionary nurse.

Faust, Louise, RN. Missionary nurse, writer, from Tanzania.

Flexman, Dr. Doctor at Muhlenburg when Esther arrived from States in 1941.

Flora, Rev. George. Missionary at Zorzor, Monrovia.

Greiner, Dorothea, RN. Missionary nurse.

Heilman, Bessie. Missionary at Sanoyea. Aunt of Dr. Earl Rober.

Heilman, Rev. Harry. Missionary at Sanoyea, president of Lutheran Church in Liberia during Esther's first term. Uncle of Dr. Earl Reber.

Holm, Gladys, RN. Operating room supervisor in Sioux City, Iowa, under whom Esther studied during 1947 furlough.

Hosterman, Maebelle, RN. Missionary nurse.

Howard, Nora, RN. Liberian nurse.

Howard, Pewu. See Moleyeaze, Pewu.

Howard, Grace. See Moleyeaze, Grace.

Isaacson, Deanna, RN. Missionary nurse-midwife.

Isaacson, Jeanette (Kpissay), RN. Missionary nurse-midwife.

Jensen, Kirsten Marie (Ma), RN. Missionary nurse-teacher from Denmark, at Sanoyea during most of Esther's time.

Jensen, Kirsten. Namesake of "Ma" Jensen. Protege of Esther's.

Keller, Dr. Franklin. Missionary doctor at Zorzor, 1952-1965, then transferred to Phebe Hospital. Treated Esther there during her final illness.

Knaub, Clare, RN. Missionary nurse who specialized Esther during her final illness.

Koenig, Bertha. Missionary teacher, at Kpaiye during most of Esther's time.

Kpissay, Jeanette. See Isaacson, Jeanette.

Leander, Alfred. Brother of Leander sisters.

Leander, Eleanor (Nora). Esther's aunt, surrogate mother, to whom Esther wrote regularly for thirty years.

Leander, Frank. Brother of Leander sisters.

Leonard, Frances. See Morris, Frances Leonard.

Leafstedt, Elsie (Lundberg). Esther's cousin, daughter of Amanda Lundberg.

Lewis, Paul. Missionary builder, Zorzor.

Lundberg, Amanda (Leander). Esther's aunt, mother of Elsie Leafstedt.

Lundberg, Ernest. Esther's uncle, husband of Amanda.

Marquardt, Dian. Missionary, wife of William.

Marquardt, Rev. William. Missionary pastor, at Toteta during most of Esther's time.

Mathies, Della (Leander). Esther's cousin, daughter of Alfred Leander.

Miller, Carolyn, RN. Missionary nuse-midwife who specialed Esther during her final illness.

Miller, Margaret. Missionary literacy worker, Wozi.

Miller, Miriam. Missionary, mother of Margaret Miller.

Mertens, Donna. Missionary, wife of Paul Mertens.

Mertens, Dr. Paul. Missionary doctor, at Zorzor 1963-1965, 1966-1975. Esther's physician at Zorzor during her final illness.

Moleyeaze, Grace (Howard), RN. Liberian nurse who worked with Esther, and who organized her graveside services.

Moleyeaze, Pewu (Howard). Now District Commissioner in Zorzor, who as a young schoolboy carried a torch for Esther on her early medical trips into the forest. Took the name of ''Howard'' as schoolboy, later dropped it and took back his family name ''Moleyeaze.'' Husband of Grace.

Monson, Grace. Missionary in Zorzor, 1980-present. Wife of Mark Monson.

Monson, Dr. Mark. Missionary doctor in Zorzor, 1980-present. Challenged author to write the story of Esther Bacon.

Moore, Dr. George. Missionary doctor, Zorzor, 1936-1941. Came down from Zorzor just days before Esther first went up there.

Morris, Frances (Leonard), RN. Liberian nurse from Kpelle country who walked with Esther on her first trek to Zorzor in 1941.

Morris, Irene, RN. Liberian nurse-midwife who became co-chief of obstetrics at Zorzor when Esther became ill.

Otto, Elsie. Missionary teacher, Monrovia, Sanoyea.

Payne, Priscilla, RN. Liberian nurse, wife of Roland Payne.

Payne, Rev. Roland. Liberian laboratory technician who rose to become the first Liberian bishop of the Liberian Lutheran Church.

Raynie, Eleanor (Carlson). See Carlson, Eleanor.

Reber, Anna Mae. Missionary, wife of Dr. Earl Reber.

Reber, Dr. Earl. Missionary doctor, first doctor to come to Zorzor after the war, and first doctor to work with Esther, 1946-1963.

Sadler, Roslyn. Close friend of Esther's, wife of Wesley Sadler. Zorzor, Fassama, Wozi.

Sadler, Rev. Dr. Wesley. Missionary pastor, linguist, who first reduced Loma to a written language, and produced the first Loma grammar. Zorzor, Fassama, Wozi.

Swedburg, Rev. Paul. Missionary Pastor in Salayea who joined with Bishop Payne for Esther's graveside service.

Schwertz, Rev. Albert. Esther's pastor at Trinity Lutheran Church in Sioux City, Iowa.

Stull, Betty. Missionary, wife of Dr. James Stull.

Stull, Dr. James. Missionary doctor at Zorzor, 1959-1965, instrumental in developing the new Phebe Hospital at Suakoko, and transferred there in 1965. Treated Esther during her final illness.

Tubman, Wm. V. S. President of Liberia during most of Esther's time there.

Urfer, Dave. Missionary maintenance man, ham radio operator in Zorzor.

Urfer, Margaret (Ursula). Missionary, wife of Dave Urfer.

Veatch, Dr. Everett. Presbyterian missionary, at Bolahun during Esther's first term.

Weiss, Karl. Missionary builder, maintenance man, Zorzor.

Wiley, Elizabeth, RN. Missionary nurse, Zorzor.

Wold, Rev. Joseph C. Missionary pastor who wrote *God's Impatience in Liberia*.

Yund, Dr. Lowell. Missionary doctor, Zorzor, 1949-1952.

Yund, Ruth, RN. Missionary nurse, wife of Dr. Lowell Yund.

Ziegler, Pauline, RN. Missionary nurse, "old" Phebe at Muhlenburg.

SOURCES

Annual Report, 1988, Curran Lutheran Hospital, Zorzor.

Anderson, Lucille. Interview, Sioux City, Iowa, 6/25/88.

Appelt, Martin. Interview, Sioux City, Iowa, 6/25/88.

Archives, Evangelical Lutheran Church in America, 8765 W. Higgins Road, Chicago, IL 60631.

Bacon, Esther E. Tribute, printed by the Lutheran Church in Liberia, 4/73.
Bacon, Esther. Letter to Mrs. Carl Ruhrer and Geraldine, 4/30/42.
Bacon, Esther. Letters to Eleanor (Nora) Leander, 9/30/41 to 3/19/72.
Bacon, Esther. *Lutheran Woman's Work*, 1/57, "The 'Good News' in Liberia."
Bacon, Esther. *Lutheran Woman's Work*, 5/54, "Women's Work at Zorzor."
Bacon, Esther. *Lutheran Woman's Work*, 12/51, "Another Village Road."
Bacon, Esther. Talk for United Lutheran Church Women, Sioux City, Iowa, 9/9/61, "What — Then, Today, Tomorrow."
Bacon, Esther. Unpublished writings, all undated:
"Children in Liberia"
"Back of a Boy"
"Oxygen and Our Babies"
"Dedi"
"Little Pewu and his brother Zizzi get acquainted with our nurses"
"Zawu"
"On The Way to School"
"What a hospital can do in interior Liberia to help children grow up healthy and strong"
" 'No-Ground-Left' "
Bacon, Ruth. Interview, Zorzor, 3/27/86.
Bartolomei, Lilliana ("Lana"). Telephone interview, 1/89.
Baum, Joseph, M.D. *The Lutheran*, 6/21/72, Letter to Editor.
Brookhart, Norma (Bloomquist). *Lutheran Women*, 7/8/72, "Remembering Esther Bacon."
Brouse, Fran, RN. Telephone interview, 11/88.
Bourse, Fran, RN. Letters to author, 11/19/88, 12/18/88.
Brush, CO, newspaper. Article (obituary, Alva Bacon).
Bulletin, Lutheran Church in America, "Esther Bacon," 1960.
Carlson, Ken. Letter to author, 2/89.
Carlson, Ken and Jean. Letters to author, 7/88, 4/89.
Carlson, Ken and Jean. Interview, Sioux Falls, SD, 6/23/88.
Curran, Edith, RN. Interview, Zorzor, 3/3/89.
Curran, Lutheran Hospital program bulletin, Golden Jubilee, 1974.
Currens, Rev. Gerald. Letter to author, 3/13/86.
Currens, Rev. Gerald. Letter to Ruth Schuldt, 9/6/77.
Currens, Dr. Harvey. Letter to Pastor Olson of Trinity Lutheran Church, Sioux City, Iowa, 4/14/72.
Dettmer, Robert. Letter to author, 11/88.
Dopoe, Samuel T., M.D. Interview, Zorzor, 3/86.
Dorbor, John. Interview, Little Ganta, 3/8/89.
Encyclopedia Britannica, 1986.

Executive Newsletter, *Lutheran Woman's Work*, 7/41.

Faust, Louise, RN. Interview, Spread Eagle, WI, 3/29-30/88.

Faust, Louise, RN. *The Lutheran*, 10/12/66, "Eugene LeVan: Flying Missionary."

Faust, Louise, RN. *Viewpoint*, 2/12/1967, "Those Witch Doctors Never Had A Chance."

Faust, Louise, RN. *World Encounter*, 2/67, "White Medicine Woman of Zorzor."

Flora, Rev. George. Letter to Board of Foreign Missions, 7/6/48.

Fuller, John. *Fever!*, Readers Digest Press, Pleasantville, NY, 1974.

Gay, John. *Red Dust on the Green Leaves*, Intercultural Press, Yarmouth, Maine, 1973.

Gay, John. Letter to Nora Leander, 5/8/72.

Greene, Graham. *Journey Without Maps*, Uniform Edition, Viking, 1983.

Greene, Barbara. *Too Late to Turn Back*, Settle Bendall, London, 1981.

Harley, Winifred J. *A Third of a Century With George Way Harley in Liberia*, Dept. of Anthropology, University of Delaware, Newark, NJ.

Health Habit, Golden Jubilee issue, 12/74.

Holm, Gladys, RN. Interview, Sioux City, Iowa, 6/25/88.

Hometown, The High Forest, 1/85, Loma Literacy Center, Wozi, Liberia, compiled by Margaret D. Miller.

Iowa Synod Lutheran, The, 12/72, posthumous articles on Esther Bacon.

Isaacson, Deanna, RN. Interview, Monrovia, 3/9/89.

Kpissay, Jeanette (Isaacson), RN. Interview, Monrovia, 3/1/89.

Leafstedt, Elsie. Interview, Sioux Falls, SD, 6/23/88.

Leafstedt, Elsie. Letters to author, 7/88, 4/89, 5/89.

Leander, Nora. Letter to Pastor Olson of Trinity Lutheran Church in Sioux City, Iowa, undated (probably April, 1972).

Leander, Nora. Letter to Ruth Schuldt, 5/10/72.

Lutheran Hospital of Sioux City, Iowa, booklet commemorating Fifty Years of Progress, 1952.

Marquardt, Rev. William. Interview, Liberian-American Mining Company (LAMCO), 3/19/86.

Marquardt, Dian. Interview, Liberian-American Mining Company (LAMCO), 3/19/86.

Mathies, Della. Letter to author, 5/89.

Memorial Service Program, St. Peter's Lutheran Church, Monrovia, Liberia, 4/16/72.

Mertens, Donna. Letter to Ruben and Helen Pedersen and Erville and Harvey Currens, 4/72.

Mertens, Dr. Paul and Donna. Letter to Editor of *Lutheran Women*, 5/30/72.

Mertens, Dr. Paul and Donna. Letter to friends of the church, 5/30/72.

Mertens, Paul, M.D. *Morbidity and Mortality*, 7/21/72 (*Atlanta Centers for Disease Control*), "International Notes, Lassa Fever — Liberia."

Mertens, Paul, M.D. Taped monologue, 1972.

Mertens, Paul, M.D. Monograph, "The Development of Health Care in Zorzor, Liberia," 1974.

Mertens, Paul, M.D. Letter to Drs. Ruben Pedersen and Harvey Currens, 4/13/72.

Miller, Carolyn. Interview, Phebe Hospital, Suakoko, Liberia, 3/9/86.

Miller, Carolyn. Letter to author, 12/4/88.

Miller, Margaret. Interview, Liberian-American Mining Company (LAMCO), 3/19/86.

Miller, Margaret. Letters to author, 6,7,8/88.

Miller, Margaret. Interview, Wozi, 3/7-9/86.

Moleyeaze, Pewu. Interview, Zorzor, 3/8/89.

Moleyeaze, Grace, RN. Interview, Zorzor, 3/8/89.

Monograph, "Hospital History," author unknown, circa 1971.

Monograph, "Our 'Bush Hospital' in Zorzor — Curran Lutheran Hospital," author unknown, circa 1971.

Monograph, "The Meaning of *Sale* or Medicines," author unknown, undated.

Monograph, *Partners in Mission* series, "Bacon of Liberia," Lutheran Church in America, 1966.

Monson, Mark, M.D. Monographs, "Liberian Medicine at a Glance," 1985, 1989.

Monson, Mark, M.D. Letter to author, 3/11/89.

Morris, Irene, RN. Interview, Zorzor, 3/27/86.

Payne, Bishop Roland. Interview, Zorzor, 4/7/86.

Payne, Bishop Roland. Unpublished *History of the Liberian Lutheran Church*.

Payne, Bishop Roland. *World Encounter*, 6/14/74, "Missionaries Through an African's Eyes."

Payne, Bishop Roland. Letter to Rev. Harvey Currens, 4/6/72.

Payne, Bishop Roland. Letter to Dr. Ruben Pedersen, 6/27/72.

Payne, Bishop Roland. Speech to Convention of the Lutheran Church in America, 1948.

Raynie, Eleanor (Carlson). Letter to author, 5/89.

Reber, Earl, M.D. "Your Liberia Doctor Speaking," narrative accompanying slide show, 1950.

Reber, Earl, M.D. Taped monologue, Harbel, Liberia. 3/86.

Sadler, Roslyn. Letter to author, 12/17/88.

Sadler, Roslyn. *The Lutheran*, 6/21/72, "If It Hadn't Been For Esther."

Sadler, Roslyn. Taped monologue, Corvallis, OR, 8/11-16/88.

Sadler, Roslyn. Phone interview, 5/10/89.

Sadler, Dr. Wesley. Monograph, ''Bayka,'' circa 1950.

Schmid, Delores. Telephone interview, 1/21/89.

Schuldt, Ruth. Letter to author, 2/15/89.

Schuldt, Ruth. Interview, Sioux City, Iowa, 6/25/88.

Sioux City, Iowa, Journal. Article (obituary of Esther Bacon), 4/9/72.

St. John Lutheran Church, Zorzor, Liberia. Church Bulletin, Memorial Service for Esther Bacon.

Stull, Betty. Letter to author, 3/27/89.

Stull, James, M.D. Interview, Manchester, Iowa, 11/27/88.

Stull, James, M.D. Letter to author, 2/5/89.

Stull, James, M.D. Letters to Dr. Herman Gilbert, 5/22/58, 12/15/59, 2/25/60, 7/16/60, 12/2/60.

Stull, Dr. James and Betty. Letters to church friends, 9/59, 10/59.

Trager, James. *The People's Chronology*, Holt Rinehart Winston, New York, 1979.

Trinity Lutheran Church, Sioux City, Iowa. Church bulletin. Service of Thanksgiving and Memorial for Esther Bacon, 4/23/72.

Wold, Dr. Joseph C. *God's Impatience in Liberia*, Eerdman's Publishing Co., Grand Rapids, Michigan, 1968.

Wold, Dr. Joseph C. *World Encounter*, 10/72. ''I Stopped Acting Like an American.''

Youngstown, Ohio, Vindicator, article, 6/6/59.

Zorzor Lutheran Hospital, booklet commemorating the Fiftieth Anniversary of Medical Work in the Zorzor District, 1974.

Esther Bacon, age 3 in Colorado

Alva Bacon, Esther's father.

Esther with her mother's 3 sisters. Nora Leander, Lizzie Carlson, Amanda Lundberg and Esther Bacon.

Some Candid Photographs of General Interest

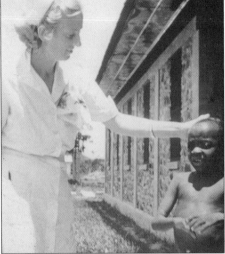

Gertrude Buschman and
Mama Yama. Circa 1943.

Esther Bacon with a young patient. Circa 1948.

Dr. Franklin Keller, Esther Bacon, and Dr. Paul Mertens. Circa 1964.

Some Candid Photographs of Esther's Life

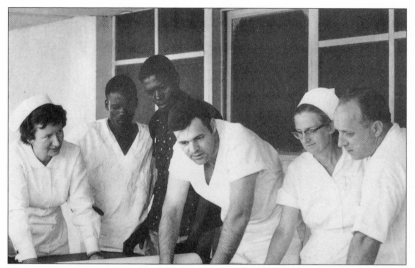

Studying blueprints for Phebe Hospital: Alice Dietz, R.N., two African hospital workers, Dr. James Stull, Esther Bacon and Dr. Earl Reber. Circa 1961.

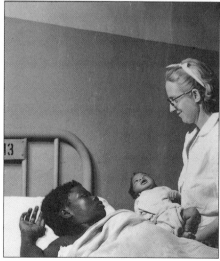

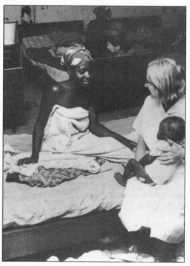

Esther Bacon bringing a newborn to mother.

Esther Bacon on the pediatric ward counseling a new mother.

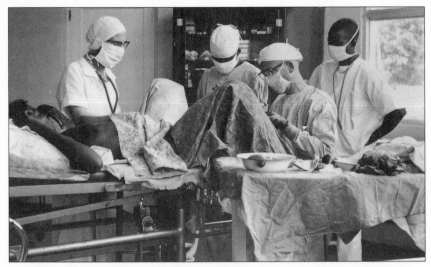

Esther Bacon and Dr. Franklin Keller delivering a baby.

*Esther Bacon assisting
at delivery of baby.*

Esther Bacon with a patient.

*Dr. James Stull and
Dr.Earl Reber*